Nation Under God

Nation

Under God

A Religious-Patriotic Anthology

Edited by Frances Brentano

 CHANNEL PRESS · GREAT NECK · NEW YORK

Printed in the United States of America
by The Colonial Press Inc., Clinton, Massachusetts

Designers: Ernst Reichl Associates

Copyright Acknowledgments

The editor and Channel Press, Inc., extend their sincere gratitude to the authors, agents and publishers who have granted permission to reprint in this anthology material from their publications. Every effort has been made to give full and correct acknowledgment in the following pages for such use. If any errors or omissions have nevertheless occurred, they will be corrected with full apology in subsequent editions, and to this end it is requested that notification be sent to Channel Press, Inc., Great Neck, New York. The acknowledgments which follow are indexed by author.

Charles Francis Adams, "A Disputed Question," and "An Understanding Heart," from *Familiar Letters of John Adams and His Wife, Abigail Adams.* Copyright 1875 by Charles Francis Adams. Published by Hurd and Houghton.

Courtney Anderson, "America's First Foreign Missionary," from *To The Golden Shore.* Copyright 1956 by Little, Brown and Company. Used by special permission.

Nathan Ausubel, "Thomas Kennedy and 'The Jew Bill,'" from *A Pictorial History of the Jewish People.* Copyright 1953 by Nathan Ausubel. Used by permission of Crown Publishers, Inc.

Catherine Drinker Bowen, "Adams and Jefferson—Not Alone in Their Faith," from *John Adams and the American Revolution.* Copyright 1949, 1950, by Catherine Drinker Bowen. By permission of the publishers, Little, Brown and Company.

Chester Bowles, "The Friendly America," from *Ambassador's Report.* Copyright 1954 by Chester Bowles. By permission of Harper & Brothers.

William Bradford, "The Landing of the Pilgrims," from *A History of Plymouth Plantation.* Copyright 1908 by Charles Scribner's Sons; reprinted by permission.

Harriet Connor Brown, "Grandma Foster's School," from *Grandmother Brown's Hundred Years, 1827-1927.* Copyright 1929 by Harriet Connor Brown. By permission of the publishers, Little, Brown and Company.

Paul H. Buck, "The Pacificator," from *The Road to Reunion.* Copyright by Paul H. Buck. By permission of the publishers, Little, Brown and Company.

Struthers Burt, "The Liberty Bell," from *Philadelphia: Holy Experiment.* Copyright 1945 by Struthers Burt. By permission of Doubleday & Company, Inc.

Carl Carmer, "The Trial of John Peter Zenger," from *American Scriptures.* Copyright 1943, 1944, 1945 by U. S. Rubber Co.; 1946 by Boni & Gaer. Courtesy United States Rubber Company.

Peter Cartwright, "Messengers of Salvation," from *Autobiography of Peter Cartwright, the Backwoods Preacher,* edited by W. P. Strickland. New York: Nelson & Phillips, 1856.

Joseph B. Clark, "The Northwest Territory," from *Leavening the Nation*. Copyright 1913 by Fleming H. Revell Co.; reprinted by permission.

Calvin Coolidge, "Taking the Oath of Office," from *The Autobiography of Calvin Coolidge*. Copyright 1929 by Calvin Coolidge. Reprinted by permission of Rinehart & Company, Inc., New York, publishers.

Josephus Daniels, "The Woman-Suffragists Bombard Wilson," from *The Wilson Era; Years of Peace, 1910-1917*. Copyright 1944 by The University of North Carolina Press; reprinted by permission.

William O. Douglas, "The Martyrdom of Elijah P. Lovejoy," from *An Almanac of Liberty*. Copyright 1954 by William O. Douglas. Reprinted by permission of Doubleday & Company, Inc.

Alice Morse Earle, "The New England Primer," from *Child Life in Colonial Days*. Copyright 1899 by The Macmillan Company; reprinted by permission.

Dwight D. Eisenhower, "Atomic Power for Peace," an address made before the General Assembly of the United Nations, December 8, 1953. Through the courtesy of the Department of State and the United States Mission to the United Nations.

Edward L. N. Elson, "Dwight D. Eisenhower and the New Awakening," from *America's Spiritual Recovery*. Copyright 1954 by Fleming H. Revell Co.; reprinted by permission.

Dorothy Canfield Fisher, "Public Libraries in a Democracy," from *The Library of Tomorrow*. Used by permission of the American Library Association.

"The Founding of Harvard College," from *New England's First Fruits*. New York: G. Sabin, 1865; reprinted from London edition, 1643.

Paul Leicester Ford (Editor), "Three Letters to Patsy Jefferson," from *The Writings of Thomas Jefferson*. Copyright G. P. Putnam's Sons; reprinted by permission.

Benjamin Franklin, "Field Preacher," from *The Autobiography of Benjamin Franklin*. Copyright 1801, 1829, by The Macmillan Company; reprinted by permission.

Frances D. Gage, "Sojourner Truth 'Speaks in Meeting,'" from *History of Woman's Suffrage*, by Elizabeth Cady Stanton, Susan B. Anthony, and Matilda Joselyn Gage. New York: Fowler & Wells, 1881.

Mrs. Colquhoun Grant, "Penn's 'Holy Experiment,'" from *Quaker and Courtier*. Published by John Murray, Ltd., London; reprinted by permission.

Hermann Hagedorn, "The Great Adventure," from *The Roosevelt Family of Sagamore Hill*. Copyright 1954 by Hermann Hagedorn. By permission of The Macmillan Company.

Learned Hand, "The Spirit of Liberty"—an address made at the "I Am an American Day" ceremony in Central Park, New York City, May 21, 1944. Used by permission.

Gertrude Hartmann, "The United Nations," from *America, Land of Freedom*. Reprinted by special permission of D. C. Heath and Company, Boston.

Alden Hatch, "The Great Charter," from *The Life of Franklin Delano Roosevelt*. Copyright 1947 by Henry Holt and Company, Inc. Reprinted by permission of the publishers.

Walter Havighurst, "Saint of the Busy West," from *Land of Promise*. Copyright 1946 by The Macmillan Company; reprinted by permission.

"He Lost a War and Won Immortality," an advertisement of the John Hancock Mutual Life Insurance Company, which appeared in the "Saturday Review of Literature" for July 31, 1954.

Stanley High, "Billy Graham's Crusades," from *Billy Graham.* Copyright 1956 by Stanley High. Reprinted permission of McGraw-Hill Company, Inc., and the author.

Stewart Holbrook, "Webster's Great Dictionary," from *Lost Men of American History.* Copyright 1946 by The Macmillan Company; reprinted by permission.

Herbert Clark Hoover, "Good Neighbors," from *The Memoirs of Herbert Hoover: Volume II: The Cabinet and the Presidency.* Copyright 1951, 1952 by Herbert Hoover. By permission of the Macmillan Company.

H. E. Jacob, "I Lift My Lamp," from *The World of Emma Lazarus.* Copyright 1949 by Schocken Books, Inc.; reprinted by permission.

Mary Jenness, "The Man Who Asked God Questions," from *The Man Who Asked God Questions* (containing a conversation quoted from the Indianola Tribune, June 4, 1941, lent by the President of Simpson College). Copyright by the Indianola Tribune. Reprinted by permission of Friendship Press, publisher.

J. William Jones, "The Christianity of Robert E. Lee," from *Personal Reminiscences, Anecdotes, and Letters of Robert E. Lee.* By permission of D. Appleton-Century-Crofts, Inc., publishers.

Howard Atwood Kelly, "Dr. Walter B. Reed's Work in Yellow Fever," from *Walter Reed and Yellow Fever.* Copyright by Remington Putnam Book Co., reprinted by permission.

George C. Kenney, "Pledging Help to Korea," from *The MacArthur I Know.* Copyright 1951 by George C. Kenney. By permission of Duell, Sloan & Pearce.

E. P. Linn, "Faithful to Duty," from *Golden Gleams of Thought.* Copyright 1881 by Jansen, McClurg & Company.

Henry Cabot Lodge, "The Right of Petition," from *Hero Tales from American History.* By permission.

Halford E. Luccock, "Wrap It Up in a Person," "The Big Parade," and "Frances Willard Minds Her Own Business," from *Endless Line of Splendor.* Copyright 1950 by Bishop William C. Martin and Bishop G. Bromley Oxnam; published by The Advance for Christ and His Church; reprinted by permission.

Janet Mabie, "Round Top and Auditorium," from *Heaven on Earth.* Copyright 1951 by Janet Mabie. By permission of Harper & Brothers.

David Macrae, "Stonewall Jackson's Character Illustrated," from *The Americans at Home.*

James Madison, "Franklin Proposes Prayer," from *Journal of the Convention of 1787;* edited by Laillard Hunt. Copyright 1908 by G. P. Putnam's Sons. Reprinted by permission.

Mary Peabody Mann, "The Life of Horace Mann," from *The Life of Horace Mann.* Boston, Walker, Fuller and Company, 1865.

Robert McElroy, "Cleveland Selects a Cabinet," from *Grover Cleveland, The Man and the Statesman.* Copyright 1923 by Harper & Brothers; used by special permission.

Phyllis McGinley, "Lessons for Today: From McGuffey's Readers." Copyright © 1951 by The Reader's Digest Association, Inc.; condensed from The New York Times Magazine (May 20 '51) copyright 1951 by The New York Times Co., Times Square, New York 18, N. Y.; reprinted by permission.

Frank S. Mead, "Sheldon Jackson," from *On Our Own Doorstep,* reprinted by permission of the publishers, Friendship Press, Inc.; "The Battle of Boston," reprinted from The Christian Herald, October, 1936, copyright 1936 by the Christian Herald Association, Inc.; used by special permission.

Blair Niles, "Union," from *The James.* Copyright 1939 by Blair Niles. Reprinted by permission of Rinehart & Company, Inc., New York, publishers.

Saul K. Padover, "Champion of Religious and Intellectual Freedom," from *The Complete Madison*. Copyright 1953 by Saul K. Padover. By permission of Harper & Brothers.

"Momentous Reversal in the Court," reprinted from Life Magazine, September 10, 1956, published and copyright by Time, Inc.; used by special permission.

Norman V. Pope, "Educator, Minister, Patriot," reprinted from *Presbyterian Life;* used by special permission.

Herbert Quick, "The Children Taught One Another," from *One Man's Life*. Copyright © 1925, 1953; used by special permission of the publishers, The Bobbs-Merrill Company, Inc.

Ruth Painter Randall, "Lincoln's Faith Was Born of Anguish," from The New York Times Magazine, February 7, 1954. Reprinted by special permission.

Adolph C. Regli, "Defender of Religion in Medicine," from *The Mayos, Pioneers in Medicine*. Copyright 1942 by Julian Messner, Inc.; reprinted by permission.

Jacob Riis, "A Consecrated Pen," from *The Making of an American*. Copyright 1901 by The Macmillan Company; copyright 1929 by Mary Riis.

Betty Rogers, "A Deeply Religious Man," from *Will Rogers—His Wife's Story*. Copyright © 1941; used by special permission of the publishers, The Bobbs-Merrill Company, Inc.

Theodore Roosevelt, "Pioneer Preachers and Settlers," from Volume II, *From the Alleghanies to the Mississippi,* of the four-volume *The Winning of the West*. Copyright 1899 by G. P. Putnam's Sons; reprinted by permission.

Carl Sandburg, "Lincoln Speaks at Gettysburg," from *Storm Over the Land*. Copyright 1939, 1942, by Harcourt, Brace and Company, Inc.

Reprinted by permission of the publishers.

Margaret Bayard Smith, "Why Are These Libels Allowed?" from *The First Forty Years of Washington Society*. Edited by Gaillard Hunt, New York 1906. Charles Scribner's Sons.

Elizabeth Cady Stanton, "The Napoleon of Woman's Rights," from *Eighty Years And More*. Copyright 1897 by Elizabeth Cady Stanton. Published by New York European Publishing Company.

Anson Phelps Stokes, "Cardinal Gibbons," from *Church and State in the United States*, by special permission. Copyright 1950 by Harper & Brothers.

Charles Edward Stowe, "The Rushing of a Mighty Wind," from *The Life of Harriet Beecher Stowe*. Copyright 1889 by Charles E. Stowe. By permission of the Houghton Mifflin Company.

Ida Tarbell, "The Chautauqua Movement," from *All in the Day's Work*. Copyright 1939 by The Macmillan Company; reprinted by permission.

Edwin Way Teale, "The Wilderness World of John Muir," from *The Wilderness World of John Muir*. Copyright 1954 by Edwin W. Teale. By permission of the Houghton Mifflin Company.

Louise Hall Tharp, "Until Victory," from *Until Victory*. Copyright 1953 by Louise Hall Tharp. By permission of Little, Brown and Company.

Dana Thomas, "Frank Laubach," from *Crusaders for God*. Copyright 1952 by A. A. Wyn, Inc. All rights reserved. Reprinted by permission.

Harry S. Truman, "The Marshall Plan," from *Years of Trial and Hope:* Volume II of Mr. Truman's *Memoirs*. Copyright 1956 by Time, Inc.; published by Doubleday & Company, Inc. Used by special permission.

Carl Van Doren, "Jefferson's Inaugural Address," "Narcissa Whitman," and "The Transcontinental Railway," from *American Scriptures*. Copyright 1943, 1944, 1945 by U. S. Rubber Co.; 1946 by Boni & Gaer. Courtesy United States Rubber Company.

Alan Villiers, "God Works a 'Mirakle,'" from *The Wild Ocean*. Copyright © 1957 by Alan J. Villiers. Reprinted by permission of McGraw-Hill Company.

Booker T. Washington, "Black Race and Red Race," from *Up From Slavery*. Copyright 1901 by Booker T. Washington. Reprinted by permission of Doubleday & Company, Inc.

Thomas Jefferson Wertenbaker, "A Covenant of Grace," from *The Puritan Oligarchy*. Copyright 1947 by Charles Scribner's Sons. Reprinted by permission of the publishers.

William L. White, "Bernard Baruch," from *Bernard Baruch: Portrait of a Citizen*. Copyright 1950 by W. L. White. Reprinted by permission of Harcourt, Brace and Company, Inc.

Walt Whitman, "Lincoln, the Conservator," from *Autobiographia, or The Story of a Life*. Copyright 1875, 1882, 1888, and 1891, Walt Whitman. Copyright 1892 by Charles L. Webster & Co.

Harry Emerson Wildes, "Sturdy Friends of Freedom," from *The Delaware*. Copyright 1940 by Harry Emerson Wildes. Reprinted by permission of Rinehart & Company, Inc., New York, publishers.

Roger Williams, "God Makes a Path," from *The American Spirit: A Basis for World Democracy;* edited by Paul Monroe and Irving E. Miller. Copyright 1918 by World Book Company.

Wendell L. Willkie. "One World," from *One World*. Copyright 1943 by Wendell L. Willkie. By permission of Simon & Schuster, Inc.

Woodrow Wilson, "The Centennial Year," from *Division and Reunion*. Copyright 1893 by Longmans, Green & Co.; reprinted by permission.

Francis Winwar, "Walt Whitman's Family Stood With Elias Hicks," from *American Giant*. Copyright 1941 by Frances Winwar Grebanier. By permission of Harper & Brothers.

A Note of Thanks

I_N gathering "other men's flowers" for an anthology such as NATION UNDER GOD, an editor owes cordial appreciation to many helpful friends and associates, as well as to the authors, publishers, and literary representatives named in the list of copyright acknowledgments. Here I wish to thank all these co-workers, and to mention only a few whose interest, counsel, and untiring aid have been of vital importance:

Miss Ruth M. Elmquist, editor of Christian Herald's Family Bookshelf, my guide and close collaborator for more than five years. Without her enthusiasm, patience, and utmost cooperation, this book would not have been undertaken or completed.

The entire staff of the Mercantile Library Association of New York. They rendered constant assistance in painstaking research, with suggestions about material, and they gave lavishly of their time, services, and rich resources.

TABLE OF CONTENTS

Nation
Under God

WHEREVER freedom's holy light shines forth it imparts and impels liberty of soul and mind and body, lifting men to all their God-given rights as His free children. Justice, human dignity, freedom, brotherhood, the right to truth—these are shafts of the Eternal Light, lit by God Himself for mankind . . . in the beginning.

ONE

Freedom's

Holy Light

THE rights and privileges we accept so easily today were not brought here "in full plant and flower" by the first settlers. What they carried with them was a potent but fragile seed: a burning desire for religious freedom. Guarded by men of granite with Bible in hand, nourished by liberty's light, and strengthened by human trial and suffering, the seed yielded precious fruit: freedom of choice in the welding of government and the worship of God.

To an Unknown Shore . . .

What motivation was in the hearts and minds of the men and women who boarded the Mayflower that September day in 1620? What made them willing to face the perilous westward voyage, and endure the hardships of the crowded, rocking vessel with its sea-washed decks? It was because in their homeland the light of freedom had been flickering feebly or not at all, while in their hearts there glowed a yearning for liberty for themselves and their children. They wanted to live where they could worship God according to their own beliefs and conscience. They would carry this light of freedom to a solitary shore in the New World, but they would never themselves know the far-reaching influence of their venture.

Following the course of the original Mayflower, the now historic Mayflower II set sail from England early in 1957. Alan Villiers, the captain of this ship, has written a remarkable book, The Wild Ocean, in which he depicts the first voyage. Two ships, the Speedwell and the Mayflower, were chartered. Twice the ships left port and returned; and finally the captain of the Speedwell had to abandon the idea of sailing. Many families from this ship could not crowd onto the Mayflower, and so were left ashore. To one of these men, a passenger despairingly sent a message saying, "If ever we make a plantation, God works a 'mirakle' . . ."

God Works a "Mirakle"

BY ALAN VILLIERS

THERE had been settlers in plenty who sailed westbound across the North Atlantic before, but the Pilgrim Fathers may be regarded as the first of the true pioneers. They set out from Eu-

3

rope not with an eye over their shoulders at the land which they had left and intending to return at the first opportunity, nor misled by promoters seeking to make a quick profit out of them, careless of what then might be their fate. They were the first cohesive and united body of men, women, and children who sailed for the new land seeking neither a way around it to a richer East nor quick wealth from the easy exploitation of its precious metals. They sailed for the new land to make a new life in and of that new land, to bring up their children and their children's children there, with a new freedom, a freedom of body, of spirit, and of mind.

These were great ideals; but not one of their contemporaries would have looked twice at the Pilgrim Fathers, nor—if they could help it—once at their famous *Mayflower*. The thing they did grew after them. The fame of the ship came long after her undistinguished timbers had dissolved to dust or had been transferred ashore to a multitude of allegedly historic barns. The Pilgrims did not call themselves the *"Pilgrim Fathers";* that title came afterward too. They thought so little of the ship which carried them upon their now most famous voyage that, as far as the records have come down to us, not a single one of them ever mentioned her by name, and the only contemporary account of the voyage makes no mention of her name at all.

The English exiles who were later to achieve so much undying fame did not regard themselves as heroic. What they sought was peace, not immortality. The *Mayflower* voyage, grim and profoundly uncomfortable as it must have been, was just another incident in the long story of trials and persecution and hardship which had formed their lives. The immense moral courage and infinite fortitude with which they took that voyage in their stride, and then proceeded in the harshest months of winter to carve out a colony upon the hard shores of New England, were already well established in their lives long before they sailed for America. . . .

The Pilgrims were poor folk, who neither had nor sought money. It is reasonable to expect that the ship which took them to America was the cheapest that could be found. There were no passenger ships for long voyages in those days. Any ship had to do. In a sense (in that she carried whole families, and many of them) the *Mayflower* may be regarded as the first transatlantic passenger vessel, but she had no amenities for passengers.

She was just any old ship which was unemployed at the time and available for cheap charter. Not that the Pilgrims themselves chartered the *Mayflower:* that was done for them. They were a group of plain English folk from a diversity of places as far apart as Scrooby in Nottinghamshire, Chelmsford and Billericay in Essex, Cambridge, Colchester, and Duxbury, and their common bond was exile—exile for their religious principles. Refusing to conform to the strict dogmas of the established Church of England, they were Separatists who had been forced to leave England and live at Leyden, in Holland. Here they made a hard living among the Protestant Dutch, but they feared that their children would grow up neither good religionists nor good Englishmen, for the Hollanders took life as they found it and made merry while they could. So the Pilgrims looked abroad for a new homeland, where they could go their own ways in peace and worship God as they wished. . . .

Putting their trust in God, of Whom they were asking a great deal, the Pilgrims sailed at last in their two ships, intending to make the westward crossing directly from Southampton to somewhere in North Virginia—the farther north the better. . . .

Sixty-seven days out from England, on the eleventh of November, 1620, the bark *Mayflower* anchored off Provincetown, in what is now the Commonwealth of Massachusetts, and, to all intents and purposes, the great crossing was made. The anchorage was sheltered and there was sea food and firing in abundance, but there was precious little else, not even a sufficiency of fresh water.

The Pilgrims did not appreciate a diet of clams and Cape Cod oysters, though both are sea delicacies supreme; as a main food supply they palled, and were otherwise inadequate. The *Mayflower* dallied a month while the shallop—its planks and thwarts much strained by the people who had been forced to sleep on them for so many weeks—was put together and used for discovery. Poor Mrs. Bradford fell or jumped into the sea, so discouraged did she become at last with the appalling cold and the bleak prospect of the sand dunes about Cape Cod. . . .

The cold was savage, ceaseless, and beyond all bearing, even after a decade and more of winter's east winds in Holland. Some of the poor people, deluding themselves that New England was in the same latitudes as Spain, had thought the climate might be as warm. It was not. They had to build their homes, to plant their crops, to do all things for themselves. They were weak from the long crossing in such crowded conditions and from the great turbulence of the ocean. If they had not had the hearts of lions they might all have jumped into the bay. . . . Instead they signed their famous compact, by which they bound themselves to each and all for the furtherance of their great project, and having found at length the better site of Plymouth, shifted the ship to an anchorage near there, and went ashore. Half of them died the first winter, but when the time came in the spring for the *Mayflower* to return to England, not a single survivor sailed with her, nor wanted to. That is the measure of their spirit.

God had indeed worked a "mirakle"—and at that a greater even than the Pilgrims knew. For harsh as was the combination of natural circumstances against them, they were spared the worst. This was the armed and determined hostility of the aborigines, the unfortunate Indians whose land, after all, they had invaded and appropriated. It so chanced that all that area had been denuded of Indians by an epidemic which was most probably some minor ailment introduced by previous Europeans. The few Indians who had returned, and met them, were friendly. One of these was a brave named Squanto who spoke passable English, having been carried off as a captured slave some years before and taught English in England and Newfoundland. Squanto and the friendliness of the Indians were worth a battalion of armed soldiery to the decimated Pilgrims, which was just as well, for they had no such battalion. Their resources in arms were small, and their soldiery but a fraction of a company under the hotheaded Miles Standish. If there had been serious fighting to be done, the chances are that they would have been lost.

Yet this factor was entirely fortuitous and could not have been known to any of them. Rather should they have expected implacable hostility and treacherous murder. They were prepared for such things. Night after night, as their decimated menfolk died, the survivors carried them silently and without lights to a secret graveyard, where they buried them and leveled off the new graves in order that the Indians would not know how dreadfully their numbers were reduced. They need not have worried. With Squanto's help and the friendliness of the chief Massasoit (whose statue stands nobly over the Plymouth of today), the Pilgrims were suffered to establish themselves, and before long their own nobility and steadfastness of purpose, their indefatigable determination, abiding and inexhaustible courage, and strong faith in God had "planted" the firm foundations of such a settlement that flourished and grew, prospered, spread, and in due course, became a nation.

The Mayflower Compact

The Mayflower Compact represents a landmark on the long road from feudalism to freedom and equality. Yet it lay neglected for almost two centuries, until John Quincy Adams acclaimed it in 1802 as "the first example in modern times of a social compact or system of government instituted by voluntary agreement, conformably to the laws of nature, by men of equal rights, and about to establish community in a new country."

Here we read in the vivid words of William Bradford, historian as well as fatherly governor of the settlement, how the Pilgrims drew up a solemn contract that has been called "the birth certificate of American democracy."

The Landing of the Pilgrims

BY WILLIAM BRADFORD

BEING thus arrived in a good harbor and brought safe to land, they fell upon their knees and blessed the God of Heaven, who had brought them over the vast and furious ocean, and delivered them from all the perils and miseries thereof, again to set their feet on the firm and stable earth, their proper element.

. . . Being thus passed the vast ocean, and a sea of troubles before in their preparation, they had now no friends to welcome them, nor inns to entertain or refresh their weather-beaten bodies, no houses or much less towns to repair to, to seek for succour. It is recorded in scripture as a mercy to the apostle and his shipwrecked company, that the barbarians showed them no small kindness in refreshing them, but these savage barbarians when they met with them . . . were readier to fill their sides full of arrows than otherwise. And for the season it was winter, and they that know the winters of that country know them to be

8

sharp and violent and subject to cruel and fierce storms, dangerous to travel to known places, much more to search an unknown
coast. Besides, what could they see but a hideous and desolate
wilderness, full of wild beasts and wild men? and what multitudes there might be of them they knew not. . . .

What could now sustain them but the spirit of God and his
grace? May not and ought not the children of these fathers
rightly say: Our fathers were Englishmen which came over this
great ocean, and were ready to perish in this wilderness; but
they cried unto the Lord, and he heard their voice, and looked
on their adversity. Let them therefore praise the Lord, because
he is good and his mercies endure forever. Yea, let them which
have been redeemed of the Lord, show how he hath delivered
them from the hand of the oppressor. When they wandered in
the desert wilderness out of the way, and found no city to dwell
in, both hungry and thirsty, their soul was overwhelmed in them.
Let them confess before the Lord his loving kindness, and his
wonderful works before the sons of men. . . .

I shall a little return back and begin with a combination made
by them before they came ashore, being the first foundation of
their government in this place; occasioned partly by the discontented and mutinous speeches that some of the strangers amongst
them had let fall from them in the ship—That when they came
ashore they would use their own liberty; for none had power to
command them, the patent they had being for Virginia, and not
for New England, which belonged to another government, with
which the Virginia Company had nothing to do. And partly that
such an act by them done (this their condition considered)
might be as firm as any patent, and in some respects more sure.

The form was as followeth:

> In the name of God, Amen. We whose names are underwrit-
> ten, the loyal subjects of our dread sovereign Lord, King James,
> by the grace of God, of Great Britain, France, and Ireland king,
> defender of the faith, etc., having undertaken, for the glorie of
> God, and advancement of the Christian faith, and honor of our
> king and country, a voyage to plant the first colony in the north-
> ern parts of Virginia, do by these presents solemnly and mutu-
> ally in the presence of God, and of one another, covenant and
> combine ourselves together into a civil body politic, for our better
> ordering and preservation and furtherance of the ends aforesaid;
> and by virtue hereof to enact, constitute, and frame such just and
> equal laws, ordinances, acts, constitutions, and offices, from time

to time, as shall be thought most meet and convenient for the general good of the Colony, unto which we promise all due submission and obedience. In witness whereof we have hereunder subscribed our names at Cape Cod the 11 of November, in the year of the reign of our sovereign Lord, King James of England, France and Ireland the eighteenth, and of Scotland the fifty fourth. Anno Dom. 1620.

After this they chose, or rather confirmed, Mr. John Carver (a man godly and well approved amongst them) their governor for that year. And after they had provided a place for their goods or common store (which were long in unlading for want of boats, foulness of winter weather, and sickness of diverse) and begun some small cottages for their habitation, as time would admit, they met and consulted of laws and order, both for their civil and military government, as the necessity of their condition did require, still adding thereunto as urgent occasion in several times, and as cases did require.

Roger Williams

Roger Williams—Anglican, Puritan, Separatist, Baptist, and finally Seeker—was the most eloquent, inquiring and liberal of the early Colonial leaders. He taught and preached that all human beings are God's children, and therefore equals and brothers; that a royal charter cannot convey rights to lands already owned by Indians; that Church and State must be separate; that heads of families, and not only church members, should be given the right to vote; that "a Magistrate is not only the Minister of God but the Minister or servant of the People"; and that the persecution of anyone for "reason of conscience" violates the teachings of Christ. In the fervor of his own writings, as in the poem which follows, he revealed the depth of his faith. In the charter of his own colony, Roger Williams set down clear guarantees of civil and religious freedom.

The Reverend Frank S. Mead dramatically presents the trials and sufferings of this valiant lover of freedom whose precepts, so bold in seventeenth-century America, are now the very essence of religious liberty as we know it.

God Makes a Path

BY ROGER WILLIAMS

GOD makes a path, provides a guide,
   And feeds in wilderness.
His glorious name while breath remains,
   O that I may confess!

Lost many a time, I have had no guide,
   No house, but hollow tree

11

In stormy winter night no fire,
No food, no company.

In Him I found a house, a bed.
A table, company:
No cup's so bitter, but's made sweet.
When God shall sweet'ning be.

The Battle of Boston

BY FRANK S. MEAD

On a cold morning in 1631 the good ship *Lyon* dropped her anchor in Massachusetts Bay off Nantasket: a barren, frozen, perilous coast ruled by men of blood-and-iron. A hardy bark, this *Lyon;* she had fought her way for two bitter winter months through icy seas, through storm and death-laden gale. On her decks shivered twenty passengers, chilled to the bone and thanking God for sight o' land. Down in his cabin a young minister awaited the reception committee; he was the most notable man aboard, a gallant rebel on the run before the wrath of His Majesty King James and therefore loved in advance by all in The Bay. He came recommended by friend and enemy alike as "a good friend, a good man and a godly young minister, passionate and precipitate and divinely mad." With him came Mary, his young bride, who thought him divine but hardly mad.

The folk of The Bay cheered him ashore, and they made much of him at the great public feast of thanksgiving on February 22nd. All eyes were on him, as all eyes in that day and place were always on the minister; Napoleonesque, wherever he sat at that table was the head of the table. A rebel fit to live with rebels, and lead them: this they saw in him, and this they loved. But: A man with a troubled spirit who never once had said, "Be still, my soul." A man, as Cotton Mather came later to describe him, "with a windmill in his mind." A man as far ahead of these colonists in his quest for peace and the truth of God as the Wright brothers were ahead of the rider of the horse-and-buggy, as Edison was ahead of the kerosene lamp. Boston did not see this man in Roger

Williams. They were shocked when they discovered how short-sighted they had been.

It was a matter of days when a delegation from the Church in Boston came knocking on Mr. Williams' door. Their teacher in religion, the Reverend John Wilson, was about to return to England, and, in council assembled, they had settled upon the good and godly Roger as his successor. They extended their invitation, and sat back, knowing of course that the young man would jump at it; this was the ecclesiastical prize of the new world, offered to a raw youth hardly out of the frigid cabin of the *Lyon*. They blinked as the amazing young man told them quietly that he was not interested, that he could not accept such a position until they changed their ways in Boston, until they became clearly "a separated people" from the despised Church of England, and until they separated Church from State in their colony. If they'd do that, he might think about it.

But . . . Mr. Williams . . . this is Boston! This is the First Church of America, with all the First Families and all the best people in her pews. This is the opportunity of a lifetime. Think of the prestige . . . Yes, yes, Mr. Williams had thought of all that. But he thought more of peace than of prestige, more of first principles than of First Families. He'd crossed 3,000 miles of icy brine for these principles of his, searching for a land and a State where men were honestly free and able to worship the Almighty as they saw fit. He'd broken forever with State Churches; he'd come this far to find "soul-liberty," or room for his soul to grow, and he didn't intend to compromise. That was first, to him. That was insanity, to the delegation: they left his house, and they never entered it again.

There was an opening for a minister in Salem, and to Salem Roger Williams took his way, throwing over his shoulder a few parting vitriolic remarks about the manner in which the civil authorities in The Bay were allowed to punish spiritual offenses, and about how wrong it was that a man was forced to be a church member before he could be a citizen. Salem had her tongue in her cheek when she called him; this was a chance to show her disdain of Boston, on whom she lavished no love. The General Court of Boston sent a letter warning Salem against the windmill-man, but Salem laughed, put Roger Williams in charge at once and rejoiced that now they had a leader who would lead them against the overbearing General Court and in the general direction of the mercy-seat.

That was in the spring of 1631; by the end of the summer,
Roger Williams was in trouble in Salem. He had gone the limit
in his preaching; he was a bit *too* outspoken about Boston; he
stood for such a radical separation of Church and State that even
Salem became alarmed. They weren't ready for this, yet; better
go slow with such ideas, counseled their elders. Better move on,
Roger Williams. He moved on. He moved to the only place left
to move to. To Plymouth.

Now Plymouth, suspect as it was of being "Separatist," was not
that at all. As a matter of fact, there was no Separatist Church,
in the rigid sense, anywhere in New England. And there was as
much persecution for non-conformity in Plymouth as elsewhere,
and as little real religious liberty, and as solid a union of civil and
ecclesiastical powers. But there was also a more pronounced dislike for the Church of England and all her episcopal works; there
were many in Plymouth who hated even the name of that Church,
and who would no more think of going back to her than they
would have thought of going back to England. They were *more*
separated here than anywhere else in New England and Roger
Williams went to them gladly.

He divided his time between the Indians and the whites. He
went to take the gospel to the red man a full fourteen years before John Eliot appeared upon the scene; God, he said was
'pleased to give me a painful patient spirit to lodge with them
in their filthy smoke holes . . .", and he came to thank God for
it, soon afterward. For things did not go so well in Plymouth as
he expected. The Pilgrims gasped at some of the things he said
to them. He went so far, one Sabbath, to say that the whole of
New England was founded on a lie . . . the lie that the colonists
really had a right to the land they were living on. The Indians
owned the land, said Roger Williams; the colonists had stolen it.
But didn't they have a patent, a charter from the King? Not worth
the parchment it was written on, said the preacher: had the King
paid the Indians for the land? He had not! Therefore the King
had never owned it, either. Shame on you, Plymouth, for your dis-
honesty. And shame on you for this miserable union of Church
and State. Ere long the good Governor Bradford was writing in
his diary that Mr. Williams was "a man godly and zealous, having many precious parts, but very unsettled in judgments . . . I
hope he belongs to the Lord!" The difficulty was, of course, that
Bradford and Williams represented two vastly different schools
of thought; the Governor was a conservative, clinging to the old;

the preacher was a radical, thinking of the new. One wanted to hold fast to what he had, in government and polity of Church; the other wanted to seize on something new. Bradford was a child of his hour; the chief sin of Roger Williams was that he was too far ahead of his hour. It was a dilemma, solved only when Salem, mercifully and unaccountably, asked him to come back and preach there a second time!

He went joyfully. Salem knew him, and Salem wanted him! General Court, in Boston, advised Salem that no good would come of this, but only "ill consequence"; General Court may have sensed the fact that this second call to Salem was the beginning of the end, the prelude of the most violent controversy ever to shake the colony. Williams preached furiously against the theft of land from the Indians; he went the limit in demanding the separation of civil and religious powers, the end of civil interference in ecclesiastical and church affairs; he refused to take the oath of submission to the authority of the General Court and he demanded that Salem, Plymouth and Boston alike become immediately a clearly "separated people." He was an agitator, a disturber without a peer; wherever he went, there was trouble and turmoil. No need for a beadle to keep folks awake when he preached; those who sat in his pews sat up straight, wondering what was coming next. He raged against the "idolatry" of the presence of a cross in the English flag, which flew from the blockhouses; shortly after the sermon, John Endicott drew his sword in the street and hacked out the cross. And shortly after that, General Court went into action. This was the last straw; the colony needed the aid of England, depended on the help in Parliament of such men as Warwick, Pym and Hampden, and this was flagrant insult to the English. The Court stepped in, put Roger Williams "on probation" for a year. Williams never paid the slightest heed to his "probation." He resigned from his pulpit, rather than embarrass the church; he was a preacher without a pulpit, a clergyman without a congregation. He was the first rebel against the New England church; he was the symbol of dissent. No one, not even Mary, dared guess what the end might be. Mary went each Sunday to sit in her pew at the church, where she maintained her membership. Roger Williams never interfered with her in that; he believed in religious liberty, and that liberty began at home. She went to church; he stayed at home, preaching and teaching impromptu to whoever came to hear him. So many came that General Court, its patience at last exhausted,

summoned him to appear in Newtown, for "trial." This was 1634.
Roger Williams had been in the colony just four years; in that
time he had fomented a revolution, had forced into the open a
consideration of the most important problem in the history of
the American people.

What was on trial that day in Newtown was not a man but a
principle. Not what was going to happen to the rebel, but what
was going to happen to a religion in America, was the issue.
This day was the cause of liberty haled to the bar; this day it
was to be decided whether conformity or free conscience were
to rule the land; whether you and I were to worship, pray, and
believe as we chose, or as the magistrates and governors and
mayors dictated. Roger Williams, in rebellion against dictation,
was only the hapless individual in whom the issue came to a
head; he was but an instrument, the human instrument, in the
hand of God.

Court met in Thomas Hooker's Church in Newtown (we call it
Cambridge today), a bare, bleak, Puritan church, coldly Calvinistic. There was a dirt floor and there were wooden benches
for pews, stiff and hard. There was no heat in Thomas Hooker's
Church, and this was October. On the benches sat fifty fathers
of the Commonwealth, fifty hardened, seasoned, storm-tried men
who had torn their living from the rocky soil and staked their
lives and destinies in a cold and hostile land. At their head sat
Governor Haynes, patrician, pompous, responsible to the King
for peace and progress overseas. Nearest him sat the magistrates,
Thomas Dudley, William Coddington, John Winthrop and his
son John, and five others not so well known. There were twenty-
five deputies. There were all the other ministers of the colony,
come to see justice done and the plague ended. Watching the
ministers, among the spectators, was a bearded little man in a
skull-cap: this was John Endicott, demoted and in disgrace for
hacking at the flag, close friend of the man on trial and utterly
unable to speak a word in his defense. Among the preachers sat
John Cotton who had known Williams in England, and Thomas
Hooker, shortly to leave for the Connecticut Valley in protest
against the very men who were about to punish Roger Williams.
Hooker and Cotton were also friends of the rebel. Cotton was
the only man to disapprove of what the Court did that day;
Hooker tried his best to make his friend recant, and "see the error
of his ways!"

There was no trial; Roger Williams was no more on trial here than Jesus had been before Pilate, or Luther before Charles the Fifth at Worms. Every man in the church had long since made up his mind about the culprit. All they did was to read out the list of errors Williams had committed, to ask him if he had committed them, and to pass sentence. Confronted with the list, Roger Williams said yes, he had been guilty of all of it; asked if he would recant and bow to the authority of the Court (is this Newtown, or Worms?) he said plainly, "No!" Hooker reasoned with him, argued with him; he might as well have tried to reason with the North Star or the north wind. There was no recanting in him, no regret, no turning back. Hooker threw up his hands. A hush fell. This was the climax. The Governor rose, looked long at Roger Williams, began reading from a legal document. Williams looked away from him, out of the window, at scarlet leaves falling from the trees outside through the crisp October air. Luther had his cheering Europe at his back; even Jesus had his James and John and his Simon of Cyrene. But of all the rebel-pioneers of history, Roger Williams was the most deserted and alone. He had no one, save Mary, and Mary could not come . . .

The Governor droned on, recounting again the sins of the accused, coming at last to this: ". . . Mr. Williams shall depart out of this jurisdiction within six weeks next ensuing . . . not to return any more without license from the Court." Banished! Mr. Williams rose without a word and walked out of the Church. No man looked at him.

He went home. He was a sick man, worn of body and weary of mind. He told Mary. That was difficult, for Mary was soon to become a mother. Mary took it calmly, but her eyes asked, "Where now?" Salem took it not so calmly as Mary; Salem, now that the harm had been done, was so mad that the Court grew suddenly merciful: Mr. Williams need not go until the baby had arrived, until the snows of winter had melted, and he had recovered from his illness. But Mr. Williams, through the winter, was not to preach, not to hold any meetings in his house, not to teach his heresy to anyone nor "go about to draw others to his opinion." (So he had been banished not for any crime, but for an opinion!) He'd behave himself, keep the peace, and with the warm winds of spring, get out.

The baby came; they named her Freeborn, in further defiance of the Court. Mary kept one foot on the cradle, one eye on her husband. Visitors were coming, regularly, to her house; at first they came singly, then by twos and threes. They lingered, they talked far into the night. The town knew all about it, immediately; Boston heard of it. This was treason. Roger Williams was drawing members away from the Church, and the Church was the State. He had broken his parole, and the Court struck swiftly. Up the street marched Captain Underhill, from Boston, with fourteen good men and strong at his back; they knocked on Roger Williams' door. Mary opened the door, and stood there with Freeborn in her arms. Mr. Williams . . . they had a warrant for the arrest of Mr. Williams. Mary smiled and shook her head. Mr. Williams was not at home. Where was he? Really, she did not know. Well, then, how long had he been gone? Three days, said Mrs. Williams. She closed the door. Valiant Captain Underhill and his fourteen men marched down the street again. The rascal had slipped through their fingers.

He was gone beyond their reach, gone floundering through the forest snow to the wigwam of Massasoit, to the only haven he had left this side of heaven, to the "filthy smoke holes" of the Indians. Gone to found Providence, a city of refuge for all dissenters, a city with gates wide open to all who searched for God and truth and who found Puritanism too small a house for their souls to live in. It was the first city of its kind in the New World. It was a city set on a hill, wherein no ears were cropped in the interests of conformity nor Quakers whipped at carttails in their quest of Inner Light. (Williams never liked the Quaker, but he never persecuted him.) A city on a hill in whose bright light was born the epochal and revolutionary statute which flowered at last in these words, in the Constitution of the United States:

"No religious test shall ever be required as a qualification to any office or public trust under the United States."

"Congress shall make no law respecting an establishment of religion, or prohibiting the free exercise thereof." We got that from Roger Williams. Rebel and outcast to his Puritan contemporaries, he has become to us a Galahad of God who fought single-handed and alone, that day in Thomas Hooker's church in Newtown.

Martin Luther gave us the right to be Protestant; Roger Williams gave us the right to be any kind of Protestant. When he won this battle of Boston by allowing himself to be banished, he established himself as the true father of the American dream of a really free commonwealth in which all of us were on equal footing before God and the law.

Anne Hutchinson

*Gallant Anne Hutchinson was the daughter of a Puritan clergy-
man, the wife of a wealthy merchant, and the mother of fourteen
children. With her family she came to Massachusetts in 1634,
following the Reverend John Cotton, because Mrs. Hutchinson—
"dear saint and servant of God," as her husband described her—
so enjoyed his preaching.*

*Not content with listening only, she began a series of Monday
evening meetings in her Boston home at which the previous day's
sermons were discussed. Here she also presented her own mystic
and, for that day, startling views. This inevitably led to friction
with the local clergy, and there began a long persecution which
ended in her excommunication and banishment. But Anne Hutchinson's courage never failed. Leaving the court, she declared,
"The Lord judgeth not as man judgeth. Better to be cast out of
the church than to deny Christ."*

*Anne Hutchinson met death heroically, fighting vainly to save
her children from vengeful Indians whom she had earlier be-
friended. With sympathy and scholarly knowledge Thomas Jefferson Wertenbaker portrays the struggles of America's first feminist
in an early, meaningful testing of civil and religious freedom.
Like Roger Williams, Anne Hutchinson proved to be ahead of
her times; yet she moved her new homeland one more step forward toward democracy.*

A Covenant of Grace

BY THOMAS JEFFERSON
WERTENBAKER

It was perhaps inevitable that the Massachusetts Bay colony in
its infancy should be shaken by theological disputes, since the
colonists brought division with them from England itself. In

some cases, when "dissenters" reached New England, they fell under the influence of the prevailing group and in good time "saw the light." But when they persisted in their views and tried to win converts to them, they became an element of danger. Such had been the origin of the Roger Williams controversy and such was the origin of the still more serious Anne Hutchinson heresy which followed close behind it.

Mrs. Hutchinson and her husband arrived in the colony in 1634, and established themselves in a house opposite that of Governor Winthrop, almost in the shadow of the meeting-house. Mistress Anne is described as a woman "of a nimble wit and active spirit and a very voluble tongue, more bold than a man." She was also possessed of ambition, magnetism and determination. Consciously or unconsciously she craved leadership, and leadership in the infant colony meant influence over the minds of men and women in theological matters. Had fate placed her in a later age she would have been an active suffragette or a member of Congress. As it was she tried to unhorse the New England clergy from their seat of power so that she herself could occupy it.

She began by holding a series of gatherings in which she recapitulated and explained the sermons of John Cotton and other clergymen. The ministers beamed their approval, for at first it looked like a revival, an awakening. But when the good woman began delivering sermons of her own, in which she often expressed views at variance with those of the established order, some began to have serious misgivings. When Adam and Eve violated the terms upon which the Creator had given the earth to them and their seed, it put an end to the Covenant of Works, Mrs. Hutchinson contended. But God, in His mercy, had made a new agreement, the Covenant of Grace, under which not all mankind, but only such as He elected, should be saved.

With this the clergy would probably not have quarrelled had not Mrs. Hutchinson taken it upon herself to decide who was under the Covenant of Works and thus destined to damnation and who under a Covenant of Grace and so among God's elect. This vital decision they had reserved for themselves as the very foundation of their power. And when Anne actually pronounced some of the clergy themselves, men who were revered as models of piety, among the unelect, resentment was deep.

The anger of the clergy increased when it was rumored that she taught that those living in a Covenant of Grace were set aside from the unelect by the dwelling within them of the spirit of the Lord, or an Inner Light which sanctified and guided them. In this she came very near the position of the New Lights of a century later, when Theodorus Jacobus Frelinghuysen, George Whitefield and others preached that a religious experience or inner manifestation of God's spirit was necessary to salvation. But Mrs. Hutchinson went much further than Frelinghuysen and Whitefield when she claimed direct messages from God in the same manner as Abraham and other Biblical prophets. This it was which finally brought her downfall.

But for a time, in her own town, Anne seemed to be carrying all before her. "It was a wonder," wrote Governor Winthrop, "upon what a sudden the whole church of Boston (some few excepted) were become her new converts, and many also out of the church, and of other churches also; yea! many profane persons became of her opinion."

This great success is explained in part by the support which the influential John Cotton gave her. Strength was added also with the arrival of Sir Harry Vane in October, 1635, and of the Reverend John Wheelwright in April, 1636, both of whom became her warm advocates. Vane was a deeply religious, winning young patrician, the son of a member of the Privy Council and thus possessed of influence at Court which might be used to the great benefit of the infant colony. Wheelwright was an ardent Puritan who had been deprived of his living in England for nonconformity. By nature a controversialist, he would probably have sided with Mrs. Hutchinson under any circumstances, but the fact that he had married her sister-in-law made the bond doubly close.

On the other hand Anne incurred the hostility of Governor Winthrop and the undying hatred of the minister of the Boston church—John Wilson. Though she failed to unseat Wilson, she humiliated him by having him censured by his own congregation in his own meeting-house. It must have been with deep resentment that this stern, bigoted man listened to the reproachful words of those to whom he had ministered. "It was strange to see how the common people were led by example to condemn him," stated Winthrop, "and that such as had known him for so long and what good he had done for the Church should fall upon him with such bitterness."

It was inevitable that in a Bible Commonwealth a religious controversy of such import as that brewed by Mistress Hutchinson should become involved with political affairs. The side which won the support of the government could brand their opponents as factious or as heretics and subject them to the full weight of the law. Thus the election of 1637 assumed unusual significance. Vane, who had been chosen Governor in 1636, was seeking re-election, with the support of Wheelwright, Cotton and the free-men of Boston; Winthrop was the choice of most of the ministers and freemen of the other towns. Amid scenes of great excitement in which angry words and even blows were exchanged, the vote was taken. The result showed that the conservative party had won an overwhelming victory, not only electing Winthrop but a ma-jority of the magistrates.

This sealed the doom of the Hutchinson faction. Vane left the country; Cotton saved himself by renouncing his "heresies." When Wheelwright persisted in his opinions he was brought before the court on a trumped-up charge of sedition and sentenced to banishment. Shortly afterwards he preached a farewell sermon to his congregation and, turning his face northward, made his way through the snowdrifts to New Hampshire. One member of the General Court was expelled, disfranchised and threatened with banishment; another was expelled and driven out of the colony. Other ardent followers of Mrs. Hutchinson were forced to recant on pain of having their arms and ammunition confiscated.

The last act of the drama came with the trial of Mistress Anne herself. Though there could have been no doubt as to the out-come, the court weighed the evidence carefully. Their task was made easier by Anne's inability to bridle her tongue. The most damning charge laid at her door was that she claimed to be above the clergy, a prophetess to whom God spoke directly, and this she admitted readily.

"It was revealed to me that they should plot against me," she declared to the Court. "The Lord bade me not to fear, for that he delivered Daniel and the three children, his hand was not shortened. And, behold! this scripture is fulfilled this day in my eyes. Therefore take heed what ye go about to do unto me. You have power over my body, but the Lord Jesus hath power over my soul. . . . I fear none but the great Jehovah, which hath fore-told me of these things, and I do verily believe that he will deliver me out of your hands. . . . For this you go about to do to me, God will ruin you and your posterity and this whole State."

At this point one of the court enquired: "How do you know that it is God that did reveal these things to you, and not Satan?"

"How did Abraham know that it was God that bid him offer

his son, being a breach of the sixth commandment?" was the rejoinder.

"By an immediate voice," replied Dudley.

"So to me by an immediate revelation."

This was enough. The court found her guilty and sentenced her to banishment "as being a woman not fit for our society." When she said, "I desire to know wherefore I am banished," the Governor answered, "Say no more; the Court knows wherefore and is satisfied."

The Massachusetts leaders have been severely criticized for their ruthless suppression of freedom of thought. With the banishment of Mrs. Hutchinson the voices which pleaded for toleration, civil liberty, the religion of love were silenced. But the colony had not been founded on the principles of toleration, liberty and civil rights, but upon those of the Puritan State, with its emphasis upon conformity and suppression of error. When Anne Hutchinson made an open assault upon the very foundations of this structure, it was to be expected that the men who had sacrificed so much for the ideal of a Wilderness Zion should fight back with every weapon at their command.

George Whitefield

A hostile clergy banished Anne Hutchinson, and silenced her; but their disapproval of a famed traveling preacher from England, George Whitefield, merely forced him out of the pulpit and into pastures and fields, where vast throngs could hear him speak. One evening in 1739, more than thirty thousand persons massed in Boston Commons to listen to him preach.

England, Ireland, Wales, Scotland, and then America—this was Whitefield's parish. Seven times in his zeal to spread the Christian gospel in the New World he made the hazardous voyage across the Atlantic. Here he lived a third of his public life, beginning his journeys in Savannah and Charleston, moving north to New England, leaving few historic old towns unvisited. Writing in his Autobiography, Benjamin Franklin describes Whitefield's spectacular visit to Boston, when "it seemed as if all the world were growing religious."

Field Preacher

BY BENJAMIN FRANKLIN

In 1739 arrived among us from Ireland the Reverend Mr. Whitefield, who had made himself remarkable there as an itinerant preacher. He was at first permitted to preach in some of our churches; but the clergy, taking a dislike to him, soon refus'd him their pulpits, and he was oblig'd to preach in the fields. The multitudes of all sects and denominations that attended his sermons were enormous, and it was a matter of speculation to me, who was one of the number, to observe the extraordinary influence of his oratory on his hearers and how much they admir'd and respected him, notwithstanding his common abuse of them by assuring them they were naturally *half beasts and half devils.*

24

It was wonderful to see the change soon made in the manners of our inhabitants. From being thoughtless or indifferent about religion, it seem'd as if all the world were growing religious, so that one could not walk thro' the town in an evening without hearing psalms sung in different families of every street. . . .

Mr. Whitefield had a loud and clear voice and articulated his words and sentences so perfectly that he might be heard and understood at a great distance, especially as his auditories, however numerous, observ'd the most exact silence. He preach'd one evening from the top of the Court-house steps, which are in the middle of Market-street and on the west side of Second-street which crosses it at right angles. Both streets were fill'd with his hearers to a considerable distance. Being among the hindmost in Market-street, I had the curiosity to learn how far he could be heard, by retiring backwards down the street towards the river; and I found his voice distinct till I came near Front-street when some noise in that street obscur'd it. Imagining then a semicircle, of which my distance should be the radius and that it were fill'd with auditors, to each of whom I allow'd two square feet, I computed that he might well be heard by more than thirty thousand. This reconcil'd me to the newspaper accounts of his having preach'd to twenty-five thousand people in the fields.

The Muhlenbergs

"There is a time to preach and a time to pray; but there is also a time to fight, and that time has come." Thus militantly did Lutheran Peter Muhlenberg conclude his farewell sermon to a spellbound congregation in January, 1766. And then, doffing the clerical garb under which he wore his soldier's uniform, he marched out to take up freedom's cause. Together with his brother, Frederick, also a minister, he was to render distinguished military service during the Revolution.

Their father had blazed the trail of adventure some thirty years earlier. Arriving in Philadelphia from Germany in 1742, Henry Melchior Muhlenberg gave forty-five years of devoted service to the building of American Lutheranism on a firm foundation. With Ecclesia Plantanda—"The church must be planted"—as his motto, he became an itinerant bishop, almost constantly on horseback in travels from New York to Georgia, ministering to the needs of his scattered parishioners, speaking German, English or Dutch as needed.

The contribution of the Muhlenbergs, father and sons, adds an exciting chapter to American history. In the pithy dialogue of some well-informed Continental soldiers, Harry Emerson Wildes captures and brings home the spirit of that contribution.

Sturdy Friends of Freedom

BY HARRY EMERSON WILDES

THESE German settlers were sturdy friends of freedom. Mennonites and Schwenkfelders, Moravians and Lutherans, were to a man devoted to the cause of liberty, and so widespread was their reputation in this regard that even in pre-Revolutionary days men moved down to Pennsylvania from the Dutch settlement of New

York to find freedom that was not elsewhere to be so easily secured.

Graduates of the best Swiss and German universities, the pastors of these backwoods regions promoted culture unsurpassed in other portions of the colonies. Franklin knew of them and catered to their tastes; more than half the books that issued from his press were German volumes for the upstate homes. The two Christopher Sowers, Pennsylvania publishers who fought for social reform and abolition of the slave trade, found ready markets for new books. The elder Sower printed the Bible in German for these people forty years before any printer in America brought out an English version. John and Andrew Krauss, before they reached their twentieth year, planned, designed, and built the first pipe organs ever made in the Americas.

Such were the people to whose protection the Americans were hurrying. Once across the Schuylkill, the Continental Army could rely upon ample stores of food and clothing. Each hausfrau, said the Pennsylvania officers, would bake the troops an ovenful of rich, dark rye bread, the kind that screeched as the knife cut through the crust. Shoes and blankets would be instantly available.

One young lieutenant was unimpressed. "I was here," said Jim McMichael, "two months ago. I know the country. I went from Bethlehem to Reading and met only one person who could talk English. They thought me a barbarian because I couldn't speak their German, but they appeared to me like so many dumb brutes. I did talk Latin to them till I found that they knew less of that than they did of English. So, I concluded, to my own satisfaction, that they were devoid of all the qualities that make for happiness —unless, of course, they are content to mix only with others as ignorant as themselves."

"You don't know the Muhlenbergs," protested Anderson. "They are an amazing clan. I've known them now for thirty years. The old man, Henry Melchior Muhlenberg, came out to Trappe when I was twenty-three. He seemed a little fellow then, too thin and scraggly to endure the kind of life he had to live, but he was stronger than we thought. The folks across the river didn't know that he was coming; they hadn't sent for him. He walked alone to Trappe, over those thirty miles of almost unbroken country, swimming the creeks because he did not know the fords, and when he got there people laughed at him. But not for long. He settled down to preach, and those sermons of his were the finest things that had been heard in Pennsylvania. He's the pride of the community right now. Talks to them in four different languages, especially in Latin."

"German, isn't he? One of those Dutch fellows that you have up here."

"Came over when he was thirty. Told me once that he picked Pennsylvania because he could not find a place to preach in the East Indies. Took up an eight-year-old call for a preacher that the Pennsylvania folks had forgotten that they ever sent. That's why he had so hard a time to get accepted here."

"He's the father of the general, I suppose, but," interrupted Jim McMichael, "I don't see how that makes him so remarkable. You said it was an amazing clan. Why so? They're just preachers, aren't they?"

"Oh, yes, they're preachers. All the men. Six boys, all strapping big and every one of them's a preacher. Big John the general is the oldest. He's the chap who went to Germany to go to school and who ran away when his German guardian tried to bind him out to be a grocer. The Muhlenbergs don't like to trade."

"They don't?" asked Caleb North. "That's curious. Their grandfather, old Conrad Weiser from up Reading way, was the biggest Indian trader in the province. That Weiser family, father, mother, and all fifteen of the youngsters talked Indian oftener than they talked German. Those Weisers liked to trade. It's mighty odd that these Muhlenbergs don't like to dicker."

"Father, maybe, taught them to be scholars. Folks who wear spectacles don't seem to do so well at business."

"The Weisers did," continued North. "Old Conrad was the finest scholar that you ever saw. Had a complete law library in his backwoods cabin up there at Womelsdorf. Sent down to Philadelphia for an organ. Old Conrad said he had to have a music room. Music in a frontier cabin! Do you have that sort of thing up your way, Jim?"

"We fight Indians up in Paxtang, we don't give concerts for them. But Pat here said the Muhlenbergs were something special and all I see is that they're preachers who don't trade. What's so remarkable about the Muhlenbergs? Except this funny shaped church of theirs—"

"That funny church, as you are pleased to call it, my Paxtang friend," interrupted the silent Charles Willson Peale, "is the only one of its kind in all these states. That gambrel roof, the triangular apse, the strange windows in the gallery, the ax-hewn timbers

framed with tenons and dowels, is an architectural masterpiece.
You don't know it, but this is a German-rural style of architectural
design, and one of the very few works of art outside Philadelphia
in all this commonwealth of yours. People will be coming here
for generations after you are dead to look at this little jewel."

The soldiers were silent. The outburst was unprecedented from
Peale and, if all the truth is to be told, the soldiers probably had
no notion of what the artist was talking about. Pat Anderson was
the first to regain his tongue.

"Yes, they're all preachers, but the Muhlenbergs are more than
that. The old man is a doctor and a lawyer, and if he put his
mind to it he could be the biggest businessman in Pennsylvania.
He can handle men. That soft, dignified, tenor voice of his can
make you do anything he asks. Fred, the man, you know, who
sent the letter to Big John rebuking him for mixing revolutionary
ideas in his sermons, just came back here from New York. He was
pastor of the Old Swamp Church over there. He's the writer and
the politician in the family; he'll go far if we succeed. You and I
fight the wars and then fat Fred comes in and runs the government. You watch Fred Muhlenberg. Gotthilf, who has a temper
like a fiery furnace, knows more about the plants and trees near
here than anyone else I ever met. He goes walking all over the
country, walked once to Lancaster, they tell me, and he knows
every blade of grass between Lancaster and the ocean. That boy
talks five different languages, including Greek. I'll bet you fellows
never even heard of Greek. Oh yes, indeed, those Muhlenbergs
are brilliant."

"Well, if you went to church more, you'd know about this
Augustus Church you're seeing," added one of the Pennsylvania
Germans. "We call this place the shrine of Lutheranism. If you
could read that dedicatory stone over the main entrance, you'd
see why. It says, if I can still read my Latin: 'Under the auspices
of Christ, Henry Melchior Muhlenberg with his Council,' and it
gives the names of six, as you see, 'erected from the very foundation this building dedicated by the Society of the Augsburg Confession. A.D. 1743.' This church is famous, too, because it has
one of the first pipe-organs ever built in any country church, because it had a long schoolhouse where Muhlenberg used to teach,
and because this little stone annex is the place where the first
charity school in the province was located. Ben Franklin and
Conrad Weiser, Provost Smith of the university, and Governor
James Hamilton all came up here to supervise the school. This

Trappe church is an extremely important place for us Lutherans."

"It will be important for us too, maybe," said Jim. "A place like this makes a good hospital. If the redcoats cross the river, this Trappe church, with all these fancy trimmings Peale talks about, will be crowded with the wounded. We'll burn those old carved doors for campfires."

Anderson, during the later moments of the conversations, had been called aside by one of the general's green-ribboned aides. He nodded vigorously as he listened to the instructions that the aide was evidently giving. Then, turning to his friends, he told them to go off to find their quarters. He, it seems, had orders to report to Washington at once.

"Does that mean the British are near here?" McMichael asked the aide. It was a question that strict military discipline should not have permitted, but the aide was young and none too strict. "It means," said he, "that if you go over to that hilltop and look west you'll see the redcoats at Valley Forge. Our couriers report that they are moving up the river in the direction of Reading."

"Conrad Weiser's country," said North. "Muhlenberg will wish to hear of this. I'll go over to the parsonage to tell him what is happening."

William Penn

"A place where the people are secure from the abuse of power"
*—to find such a place, or if need be to create such a place, was
the steadfast dream of William Penn. His own life was vivid evidence of the need for a free community: his father had been arrested when Penn was but a youth; he himself was jailed in the
Tower of London for his Quaker beliefs.*

*In 1670, Penn's father died, leaving him an annuity of fifteen
hundred pounds and a claim against the crown of sixteen thousand pounds. Then but twenty-six years old, Penn persuaded the
King to settle the royal debt with a grant of territory in the New
World. In his father's honor, Penn named the new community
"Pennsylvania"; and the freedom and justice on which he insisted attracted a wide variety of religious groups. William Penn
wanted a place of sanctuary not merely for Quakers, but for all
who were oppressed and persecuted.*

*Mrs. Colquhon Grant, a descendant of the founder, shows how
Penn set about organizing the colony, and how he drew up the
remarkable Indian Treaty of Shackamaxon—"the only treaty,"
according to Voltaire, "never sworn to and never broken."*

Penn's "Holy Experiment"

BY MRS. COLQUHOUN GRANT

On September 1, 1692, William Penn sailed from the Downs
in the ship *Welcome* with a party of about one hundred Friends,
full of courage and high resolve, but leaving all he loved best
behind him. The weather must have been propitious, for the
voyage was a short one; but they had only just got out to sea
when a virulent outbreak of small-pox occurred, which swept
off one-third of the passengers who had embarked at Deal. Penn

31

worked indefatigably among his stricken brethren, and putting aside all fears of infection for himself, ministered to the bodily and spiritual welfare of the sick and dying. On October 24, the vessel reached the "Capes," and on the 28th arrived at New-castle, and there Penn first stepped on the soil of the new world. He was hailed with acclamations by the Swedes and Dutch, who had a court-house there, and two gentlemen, John Moll and Ephraim Hannan, performed *livery of seisin* by handing him turf, twig, water, and soil, with due formality.

Out of respect for the Duke of York, before going further, he travelled to New York to visit the colony which was nominally held by His Royal Highness. From there he journeyed to Mary-land to see Lord Baltimore, at whose house the two governors met with much friendliness on both sides, and they endeavoured to fix the boundaries of their respective provinces.

Owing to the lateness of the season they decided to postpone further business until the spring. Lord Baltimore was a most courteous gentleman, and, although he was a Roman Catholic, and had peopled his colony with those of his own persuasion, he had the same liberality of spirit as William Penn, and showed no ill-feeling towards the Quaker governor, but was ready to allow liberty of conscience to all who cared to settle in his province.

From there Penn returned to Uplands, afterwards called Chester; he also held an assembly there. When an Act of Union was passed, annexing the "Territories" to the province, the Dutch, Swedes, and foreigners of all descriptions were natural-ised, and the code known as the "Great Law" was passed. This was for the purpose of establishing absolute religious liberty for all those who believed in one God, but required all officeholders to profess belief in the divinity of Christ. After arranging for the welfare of the Friends, he proceeded to the spot where in after years the capital city of his great province was to rise as a memorial of him for all time. He left his retainers and posses-sions on this occasion, and with a party of his friends simply rowed up in an open boat between the wooded banks of the Delaware River, beautiful in all their primitive luxuriance of vegetation.

He landed at a low and sandy beach called Dock Creek. Al-ready there was a little settlement of European colonists, and near the Creek were the wigwams of the Indians. A low wooden house was in process of erection, afterwards the Blue Anchor Tavern, which may have been his first shelter.

Governor Penn's first care was to meet the Indian subjects of his little kingdom. These consisted of tribes who had migrated from mountainous regions in the west to the country of the Delaware.

This great array of strange men in their war paint and feathers, and fully armed, must have struck terror to the hearts of the little band of devoted Englishmen. But faith in their leader, now their ruler, restored some courage to their faint hearts, and they found strength in the righteousness of their cause.

A meeting was now arranged at a spot called Shackamaxon, higher up the river. . . . and was held under the widespread branches of a great elm tree, that grew near the banks of the Delaware. . . . Hither the leaders on both sides repaired . . . William Penn was only distinguished from the rest of his followers by wearing a sash of sky-blue netting around his waist. At his right stood Colonel Markham, and he was followed by a train of Quakers. In his hand he held a roll of parchment containing the terms of the treaty. . . .

A chief advanced from the rest and placed upon his own head a small horn; this was a token that the spot was sacred, and it also served as a signal to the tribes. In an instant the Indians threw down their bows and arrows, and seated themselves in the form of a half moon on the ground, and the Sachem who acted as interpreter announced to Governor Penn that the nations were ready to hear him.

It is to Benjamin West, the painter, that we owe the picture of the treaty, but he has given us a very false idea of the real occurrence. It is too modern in tone, with houses in the background which did not then exist. . . . besides the unpardonable misconception in representing the graceful athletic Penn of thirty-eight as a fat, common-looking old man, West has put him and his companions in dress, which if ever worn at all, was certainly not until thirty or more years later.

William Penn now addressed his people. He told them of the Great Spirit who ruled over heaven and earth, of his desire to live in hearty fellowship with them, and that all was to be openness, brotherhood, and love between them. Then, having unrolled his parchment, article by article was read out of the conditions of the purchase, and the terms of his government.

He afterwards solemnly laid the roll of parchment on the ground, in token that the soil was common to both peoples. . . . The Indians pledged themselves according to the manner of their country, to live in love with William Penn and his children as long as the sun and moon should endure. . . .

Governor Penn now turned his attention to the founding of his capital. He pitched upon a spot, called in the vernacular "Coaquannoc," as the most commodious place for the new city. It was situated between the rivers of Schuylkill and Delaware just at their confluence. The junction of two such rivers, both of them navigable, and the great width and depth of the latter was admirably calculated for commerce. There were also immense stone quarries in the neighborhood.

Having once decided on the site, Penn, with his usual energy, at once ordered plans to be drawn, and Thomas Holme was entrusted with the work. . . .

The city having been thus planned in 1683, Penn gave it the name he had long reserved for it, "Philadelphia," in token of the principles of brotherly love, in which he had come to that country. The early settlers now lost no time in building houses, and Penn proceeded to divide the Province and Territories into counties. He then laid out townships and lots, and as a testimony of respect for the venerable George Fox, he reserved him an allotment of 1000 acres.

In his letters home, William Penn expressed his general satisfaction: "I bless the Lord I am very well," he writes, "and much pleased with my place and portion. The land is good, the air clear and sweet, the springs plentiful, and provisions good and easy to come at. An innumerable quantity of wild fowl and fish. In fine, here is what Abraham, Isaac, and Jacob would have been well content with, a land of promise, and service enough for God, as the fields are here white for harvest.

"Oh how sweet is the quiet of these parts, freed from the anxieties and troublesome solicitations, and hurries and perplexities of woeful Europe!"

Penn was feudal lord of Pennsylvania, with right to advise his Government. He drew up what he called "Frames"; the first one contained twenty drafts, and was full of alterations, showing the care he took in its composition. He had the power to appoint judges and establish courts, his charter having conferred on him and his representatives full authority, and as the first emigration party was entirely composed of Quakers, they formed almost the whole of the council.

When the news reached England of William Penn's safe arrival and settlement in North America, numbers of persons longing for peace and liberty of conscience, and others in search of ease and plenty, prepared to follow him. Vessels were chartered, and they set off from home, arriving in due time, sailing up the river Delaware to their destination. Nearly two thousand souls, mostly Quakers, had come to try their fortunes in the new world, in search of an Elysian shore. Many had brought out property in the shape of frame-houses, tools, implements, and furniture. Others were not so well provided, and had to find places of shelter as best they could. The Indians were very kind to them, and hunted for them, considering them all as the children of the Great Onas.

Emigration was extensive from England, Ireland, Wales, besides Holland and Germany. William Penn, writing to Lord North at the end of 1682, says: "22 more sail have arrived, and 300 farms settled," and to the Marquis of Halifax he writes: "I must without vanity say I have led the greatest colony into America that ever man did upon a prosperous beginning." . . .

In a very short time three hundred houses were erected, and the city of Philadelphia began to take shape. Sheriffs were appointed; a general assembly was formed; and a post-office was established, with runners carrying letters between Philadelphia, Newcastle, Chester, and the Falls. . . .

. . . From 1682 to 1684, he devoted his whole time and thoughts to its welfare, in the manner he thought most pleasing to his Creator. Difficulties and unpleasantnesses were often his lot, in spite of the general success of his undertaking—"The Holy Experiment," he called it. Above all else, he craved to return to his home. So far, all had been well with his wife and children, but now Gulielma wrote in great sorrow, over the death of her mother, Maria Pennington, a sad loss to them all. This made William Penn more than ever anxious to return for a time. A ship, the *Endeavour*, having come in, he thought it advisable to take this opportunity to return in this vessel, on a short visit home, and he began to consider the necessary arrangements for carrying on the government of the provinces and territories during his absence.

He signed a commission empowering the Provincial Council to act in his stead, and named Thomas Lloyd, a Quaker preacher, as President and Keeper of the Great Seal. His cousin, Colonel Markham, he made Chief Secretary, and to others he gave power to act as Justices of the Peace and Provincial Judges. He did not expect to be more than two years away, and thought there would be no difficulty in these men carrying out his laws and regulations. Much sorrow was felt at his departure by the whole colony, the foreigners as well as his own people, and by the Indians, who had now become very dependent on his love and care for their welfare.

As he was leaving the fair city which owed its being to him, he apostrophised it in the following words:— "And thou, Philadelphia, the virgin settlement named before thou wert born, what love, what care, what travail there has been to bring thee forth. I hope to be with thee next fall."

He sailed in the *Endeavour* on August 12, 1684, and arrived in England on October 3, and landed "within seven miles from home," as he mentions in a letter, and found his wife and children well and overjoyed at his return. In peaceful Worminghurst, the distant land must have seemed almost a forgotten dream; but William Penn was no visionary, but a man of action, and there was as much to be done for the province in England, as when he was reigning in the midst of it. His one desire was to advance the cause, and that would best be affected by raising up an interest in it and protection for it at home, and not depend entirely on his personal efforts.

"I purpose to leave to myself and successors no power of doing mischief, so that the will of one man may not hinder the good of the whole country." Such were his noble sentiments, expressed in his own words.

Thomas Jefferson

About a year before his death in 1826, Thomas Jefferson wrote his own epitaph, and set forth on the same sheet of paper his plans for the location of his grave, and the size and material of his tombstone.

He had served his country long and well. He had made distinctive contributions in a number of fields. But he singled out three achievements for which he hoped posterity would remember him. "Here," he wrote, "was buried Thomas Jefferson, Author of the Declaration of American Independence, of the Statute of Virginia for Religious Freedom, and Father of the University of Virginia."

Jefferson's autobiography contains these few short and meaningful paragraphs about an accomplishment which posterity has indeed found unforgettable—"The Bill for Establishing Religious Freedom in Virginia."

The Bill for Establishing Religious Freedom in Virginia

BY THOMAS JEFFERSON

Wʜᴇɴ I left Congress, in '76, it was in the persuasion that our whole code must be reviewed, adapted to our republican form of government; and, now that we had no negatives of Councils, Governors, and Kings to restrain us from doing right, it should be corrected, in all its parts, with a single eye to reason, and the good of those for whose government it was framed. Early, therefore, in the session of '76, to which I returned, I moved and presented a bill for revision of the laws, which was passed on the

24th of October; and on the 5th of November, Mr. Pendleton, Mr. Wythe, George Mason, Thomas L. Lee, and myself, were appointed a committee to execute the work. We agreed to meet at Fredericksburg to settle the plan of operation. . . . We met there accordingly, on the 13th of January, 1777. . . .

When we proceeded to the distribution of the work, Mr. Mason excused himself, as, being no lawyer, he felt himself unqualified for the work, and he resigned soon after. Mr. Lee excused himself on the same ground, and died, indeed, in a short time. The other two gentlemen, therefore, and myself, divided the work among us.

We were employed in this work from that time to February, 1779, when we met at Williamsburg, that is to say, Mr. Pendleton, Mr. Wythe and myself; and meeting day by day, we examined critically our several parts, sentence by sentence, scrutinizing and amending, until we had agreed on the whole. We then returned home, had fair copies made of our several parts, which were reported to the General Assembly, June 18, 1779, by Mr. Wythe and myself, Mr. Pendleton's residence being distant, and he having authorized us by letter to declare his approbation . . . but the main body of the work was not entered on by the general legislature until after the general peace, in 1785, when, by the unwearied exertions of Mr. Madison, in opposition to the endless quibbles, chicaneries, perversions, vexations and delays of lawyers and demi-lawyers, most of the bills were passed by the legislature, with little alteration.

The bill for establishing religious freedom, the principles of which had, to a certain degree, been enacted before, I had drawn in all the latitude of reason and right. It still met with opposition; but, with some mutilations in the preamble, it was finally passed; and a singular proposition proved that its protection of opinion was meant to be universal. Where the preamble declares, that coercion is a departure from the plan of the holy author of our religion, an amendment was proposed, by inserting the words "Jesus Christ," so that it should read, "a departure from the plan of Jesus Christ, the holy author of our religion"; the insertion was rejected by a great majority, in proof that they meant to comprehend, within the mantle of its protection, the Jew and the Gentile, the Christian and Mahometan, the Hindoo, and Infidel of every denomination.

John Witherspoon

John Witherspoon once said proudly that he had "become an American" the moment he set foot on these shores in 1768. To his newly-adopted land, the Scottish-born minister made immediate and enduring contributions in the realms of education, religion and government.

At the age of forty-five, after holding leading pastorates in Scotland, Witherspoon voyaged to America on urgent invitation to take office as president of the College of New Jersey, at Princeton. In his academic work as in his political activities, he preached complete religious freedom. Toleration was not enough, since it implies superiority or condescension. The only principle worthy of adoption in a republic, he said, is the liberty to worship as one wishes, or not at all.

Witherspoon was the only clergyman to sign the Declaration of Independence. It was a document he could wholly believe in; only a few weeks earlier, he had said in a sermon: "There is not a single instance in history in which civil liberty was lost, and religious liberty preserved entire. If, therefore, we yield up our temporal property, we at the same time deliver conscience into bondage. Whoever is an avowed enemy of God, I scruple not to call him an enemy to his country."

Dr. Norman V. Pope, a native Scotsman who largely shares John Witherspoon's educational background, now teaches theology at Princeton University. For the magazine Presbyterian Life, he prepared a striking and comprehensive portrait of Witherspoon, portions of which appear in the following condensation.

Educator, Minister, Patriot*

BY NORMAN V. POPE

In July, 1776, at the height of the debate which decided the destiny of thirteen British Colonies in North America, one timid member of the Continental Congress protested that the colonies were not "ripe" for independence. This gave John Witherspoon, president of Princeton College and delegate from New Jersey, just the opening he wanted. "Sir," he thundered in reply, "they are not only ripe, but rotting for the want of it!"

The speaker was no ordinary man. Born near Edinburgh, Scotland, in 1722, and educated at the university there, he had served two Scottish parishes, at Beith and Paisley, before coming to America in 1768. As a minister of the Church of Scotland, Witherspoon won fame as a supporter of liberty in ecclesiastical matters. . . .

Despite—or perhaps because of—his rigid attitudes in religion and morals, Witherspoon's fame as a church leader spread even beyond the borders of his native Scotland. He was called to be minister of the Scottish church in Rotterdam, Holland, and also to a church in Dublin, Ireland; but he turned down both invitations. In 1766, however, the College of New Jersey—now Princeton University, an institution which had been founded by Presbyterians twenty years before as a school "where religion and sound learning should receive equal attention"—elected Witherspoon as its sixth president. . . .

Witherspoon's administration was a memorable episode in the history of Princeton College. When he took over, the school was deeply in debt. In fact, the trustees were at first unable to pay Witherspoon the hundred guineas they had promised him for moving expenses. But Witherspoon promptly bent his energies to that perennial problem of college presidents, money-raising, and so successful was he that, until the Revolutionary War, his college had no difficulty in balancing its budget.

Witherspoon made no radical change in the actual content of

* Excerpted and condensed

the curriculum though he added a few extra subjects of instruction and enlarged the teaching faculty. But he started new methods of teaching. Most noteworthy, he substituted the lecture system for the practice of spending the recitation hour in quizzes on assigned texts. And, to make sure that his instruction would not consist in "the transmission of ideas from the note-book of the lecturer to the note-book of the student without passage through the mind of either," he would stop to explain points raised in his lectures and question his students on their grasp of what he was saying.

He enlivened his lectures with epigrams, some of which have come down, in revised form, to our own day. To one group of students he delivered himself thus: "Lads, if it should fall to the lot of any of ye, as it may do, to appear upon the theater of public life, let me impress upon your mind two rules in oratory that are never to be departed from—Ne'er do ye speak unless ye ha' something to say, and when ye are done, be sure and leave off."

It might have been expected that a man so strait-laced as Witherspoon would be a strict college disciplinarian. And so he was, but he did not carry discipline to the point of undue severity. "Govern always, but beware of governing too much," was his motto. And he knew how to temper justice with mercy. . . . As he was leaving the college building one morning, a boy threw from a window a bucket of water intended for a fellow-student who was just coming out at that moment. This student, however, courteously drew back to let Witherspoon pass, and the college president was drenched. Looking up, Witherspoon spotted the prankster leaning from the window to see the effect of his work, and mounted to the culprit's room to confront him. No doubt the student cringed in expectation of an outburst of righteous indignation, but all the president said was, "D'ye see, young man, how ye wet my new coat?" The boy apologized, and the incident was forgotten. . . .

Under Witherspoon's vigorous and enlightened leadership the college flourished. Its constituency was enlarged to include not only the Scottish-Irish of America, but also the sons of Southern planters. And whereas before his day Princeton had prepared men mainly for the ministry, it now also trained its students for public office. James Madison, one of Witherspoon's students, became the fourth President of the United States. Another became

Vice-President, ten became cabinet members, sixty were elected to Congress, twelve became governors, and three were appointed to the Supreme Court.

When Witherspoon was called to America it was to be expected that he would play an important role in the Presbyterian Church as well as in the field of education. Matthew Arnold once remarked that "Presbyterianism is born to division as the sparks fly upward." Near the middle of the 18th Century American Presbyterianism had split into "New Side" and "Old Side" groups. Though these united in 1758 to form the Synod of New York and Philadelphia, they still had to be welded together and prepared for fresh efforts of expansion. Witherspoon, as an outsider in the American church dispute, and as an able and experienced church leader in his native Scotland, came naturally into the leadership of the Presbyterian Church in America. . . .

The Revolutionary War drew Witherspoon out from school and church into the realm of national politics. His college work slowed down, for when relations between Great Britain and the American Colonies became strained, some Princeton students found drilling with muskets more exciting than drilling with grammars. As early as the autumn of 1775 there was a decrease in enrollment, and this continued for several years thereafter. During the early years of the War, Princeton, as a battleground, witnessed more exchanges of bullets than of ideas; its beds were apt to be occupied by soldiers rather than by students.

Witherspoon threw in his lot with the colonists—as did the vast majority of American Presbyterians. He was elected delegate to the New Jersey Provincial Congress in 1775, and voted for the imprisonment of Governor William Franklin and the renunciation by New Jersey of its allegiance to the British crown. In 1776 he was appointed a delegate from New Jersey to the Continental Congress at Philadelphia. He had the distinction of being the only clergyman to sign the Declaration of Independence.

In the Congress he rendered yeoman service on many committees. One of his duties, for example, was to help with the prosaic but necessary task of raising the money with which to fight the War. As one of the Board of War he was partly responsible for military affairs. As a member of the Committee of Secret Correspondence he played a part in the vital negotiations with France. And, realizing the necessity of "a perpetual union" of the thirteen colonies, he entered actively into the debates over the Articles of Confederation, and helped to organize the executive department of the infant American republic.

But political service, however important, was for Witherspoon incidental to the main business of his life, that of combined minister and educator. So with peace and victory attained, he retired from the Congress in 1782 and returned to his church and college duties.

The Presbyterian Church in America, now solidly united, reorganized itself to meet its new nation-wide responsibilities more adequately. In this movement of Presbyterian reorganization between 1785 and 1789, Witherspoon played a leading part. . . . In 1788 the Westminster Confession, in line with the newly-created position of the United States, was amended by Witherspoon's committee to "proclaim the religious liberty and legal equality of all Christian denominations," and to state that the civil magistrate should "protect the Church of our common Lord, without giving the preference to any denomination of Christians above the rest." In this revised form the Westminster Confession was adopted by the Presbyterian Church. . . .

Witherspoon's outstanding eminence was recognized by his being appointed to preside until a regular Moderator should be duly elected. Thus it may be claimed with substantial truth that Witherspoon was the chief architect of the constitution of the Presbyterian Church in the United States of America as it exists today.

President Witherspoon found the college in a dilapidated condition, due to the ravages, physical and financial, of the War. To its rehabilitation he now gave himself with characteristic devotion—even journeying to Britain in search of funds, a search which did not prove very fruitful. But though post-war conditions in the Princeton College were difficult, Witherspoon before his death in 1794 had justified the opinion that he was "perhaps the greatest educator of the 18th Century as well as the greatest ecclesiastical leader." He deserves honorable mention along with Washington, Jefferson, Franklin, and John Adams as one of the founding fathers of the United States of America. John Witherspoon helped create the Declaration of Independence. His hand was strong in the building of religious freedom.

Benjamin Franklin

*"It is too probable that no plan we propose will be adopted. . . .
If, to please the people, we offer what we ourselves disapprove,
how can we afterward defend our work? Let us raise a standard
to which the wise and honest can repair: the event is in the hand
of God."*

*So did Washington admonish the wrangling delegates to the
Constitutional Convention in 1787, when state jealousies and individual interests threatened doom to any concrete plan.*

*For over a month the bitter debate seesawed. Then at a
crucial moment, aged Benjamin Franklin laboriously heaved his
body from a chair. Generally regarded as among the most scepti-
cal of men, one concerned primarily with scientific and political
matters, he rebuked the members for their neglect of prayer.
"God," he said, "governs in the affairs of men." The tensions thereafter began to lessen, and the Constitution slowly evolved. Here,
in the abbreviated notes of James Madison's Journal, are Franklin's stirring words.*

Franklin Proposes Prayer

BY JAMES MADISON

Doctor Franklin to Mr. President

The small progress we have made after 4 or five weeks close
attendance & continual reasonings with each other—our different
sentiments on almost every question, several of the last produc-
ing as many noes as ays, is methinks a melancholy proof of the
imperfection of the Human Understanding. We indeed seem to
feel our own want of political wisdom since we have been running about in search of it. We have gone back to ancient history
for models of Government, and examined the different forms of

those Republics which having been formed with the seeds of their own dissolution now no longer exist. And we have viewed Modern States all round Europe, but find none of their Constitutions suitable to our circumstances.

In this situation of this Assembly, groping as it were in the dark to find political truth, and scarce able to distinguish it when presented to us, how has it happened, Sir, that we have not hitherto once thought of humbly applying to the Father of lights to illuminate our understandings? In the beginning of the Contest with G. Britain, when we were sensible of danger we had daily prayer in this room for the divine protection. Our prayers, Sir, were heard, and they were graciously answered. All of us who were engaged in the struggle must have observed frequent instances of a Superintending providence in our favor. To that kind providence we owe this happy opportunity of consulting in peace on the means of establishing our future national felicity. And have we now forgotten that powerful friend? or do we imagine that we no longer need his assistance? I have lived, Sir, a long time, and the longer I live, the more convincing proofs I see of this truth—*that God governs in the affairs of men.* And if a sparrow cannot fall to the ground without his notice, is it probable that an empire can rise without his aid? We have been assured, Sir, in the sacred writings, that "except the Lord build the House they labour in vain that build it." I firmly believe this; and I also believe that without his concurring aid we shall succeed in this political building no better than the Builders of Babel; We shall be divided by our little partial local interests; our projects will be confounded, and we ourselves shall become a reproach and bye word down to future ages. And what is worse, mankind may hereafter from this unfortunate instance, despair of establishing Government by Human Wisdom and leave it to chance, war and conquest.

I therefore beg leave to move—that henceforth prayers imploring the assistance of Heaven, and its blessings on our deliberations, be held in this Assembly every morning before we proceed to business, and that one or more of the Clergy of this City be requested to officiate in that service—

Mr. Sherman seconded the motion.

Mr. Hamilton & several others expressed their apprehensions that however proper such a resolution might have been at the beginning of the convention, it might at this late day, 1. bring on it some disagreeable animadversions. & 2. lead the public to believe that the embarrassments and dissentions within the convention, had suggested this measure. It was answered by Docr. F. Mr. Sherman & others, that the past omission of a duty could not justify a further omission—that the rejection of such a proposition would expose the Convention to more unpleasant animadversions than the adoption of it: and that the alarm out of doors that might be excited for the state of things within, would at least be as likely to do good as ill.

Mr. Williamson observed that the true cause of the omission could not be mistaken. The Convention had no funds.

Mr. Randolph proposed in order to give a favorable aspect to ye measure, that a sermon be preached at the request of the convention on 4th of July, the anniversary of Independence,—& thenceforward prayers be used in ye Convention every morning. Dr. Frankn. 2ded. this motion. After several unsuccessful attempts for silently postponing the matter by adjourning, the adjournment was at length carried, without any vote on the motion.

George Washington

Side by side with his interest in good government went Washington's awareness of the value of "genuine vital religion." His intuitive comprehension of the keenly significant role of faith in a man's life seemed to mount as increasing public responsibilities pressed upon him. This is reflected in his declaration that "The blessing and protection of Heaven are at all times necessary, but especially so in times of public distress or danger." Accordingly, the pictures of the commander-in-chief on his knees during the terrible winter at Valley Forge are true to life, expressing a devotion which the world cherishes.

His own reverence included a warm understanding of divergent expressions of faith. It is clearly evident in these words: "I have often expressed my sentiments that every man conducting himself as a good citizen, and being accountable to God alone for his religious opinions, ought to be protected in worshiping the Deity according to the dictates of his own conscience."

Washington Irving and John Fiske show how Washington, speaking in New York on April 30, 1789—the day of his first inauguration—established a pious tradition for future presidents.

The Inauguration

BY WASHINGTON IRVING
AND JOHN FISKE

AT NINE o'clock in the morning there were religious services in all the churches, and prayers put up for the blessing of Heaven on the new government. At twelve o'clock the city troops paraded before Washington's door; and soon after, the committees of Congress and heads of departments came in their carriages. At half-past twelve the procession moved forward, preceded by the

47

troops; next came the committees and heads of departments in their carriages; then Washington in a coach-of-state, his aide-de-camp, Colonel Humphreys, and his secretary, Mr. Lear, in his own carriage. The foreign ministers and a long train of citizens brought up the rear.

About two hundred yards before reaching the hall, Washington and his suite alighted from their carriages, and passed through the troops, who were drawn up on each side, into the hall and senate chamber, where the Vice-President, the Senate, and House of Representatives were assembled. The Vice-President, John Adams, recently inaugurated, advanced and conducted Washington to a chair-of-state at the upper end of the room. A solemn silence prevailed, when the Vice-President rose, and informed him that all things were prepared for him to take the oath of office required by the Constitution.

The oath was to be administered by the Chancellor of the State of New York, in a balcony in front of the senate chamber, and in full view of an immense multitude occupying the street, the windows, and even roofs of the adjacent houses. The balcony formed a kind of open recess, with lofty columns supporting the roof. In the centre was a table with a covering of crimson velvet, upon which lay a superbly bound Bible on a crimson velvet cushion. This was all the paraphernalia for the august scene.

All eyes were fixed upon the balcony, when, at the appointed hour, Washington made his appearance, accompanied by various public functionaries, and members of the Senate and House of Representatives. He was clad in a full suit of dark-brown cloth, of American manufacture, with a steel-hilted dress sword, white silk stockings, and silver shoe-buckles. His hair was dressed and powdered in the fashion of the day, and worn in a bag and solitaire.

His entrance on the balcony was hailed by universal shouts. He was evidently moved by this demonstration of public affection. Advancing to the front of the balcony, he laid his hand upon his heart, bowed several times, and then retreated to an arm-chair near the table. The populace appeared to understand that the scene had overcome him, and were hushed at once into profound silence.

After a few moments Washington rose and again came forward. John Adams, the Vice-President, stood on his right; on his left the Chancellor of the State, Robert Livingston; somewhat in the rear were Roger Sherman, Alexander Hamilton, Generals Knox, St. Clair, the Baron Steuben and others.

The chancellor advanced to administer the oath prescribed by the Constitution, and Mr. Otis, the Secretary of the Senate, held up the Bible on its crimson cushion. The oath was read slowly and distinctly, Washington at the same time laying his hand on the open Bible. When it was concluded, he replied solemnly, "I swear—so help me God!" Mr. Otis would have raised the Bible to his lips, but Washington bowed down reverently and kissed it.

The chancellor now stepped forward, waved his hand and exclaimed, "Long live George Washington, President of the United States!" At this moment a flag was displayed on the cupola of the hall, on which signal there was a discharge of artillery on the Battery. All the bells of the city rang out a joyful peal, and the multitude rent the air with acclamations.

Washington again bowed to the people and returned into the senate chamber where he delivered, to both houses of Congress, his inaugural address, characterized by his usual modesty, moderation, and good sense, but uttered with a voice deep, slightly tremulous, and so low as to demand close attention in the listeners. After this he proceeded with the whole assemblage on foot to St. Paul's church, where prayers suited to the occasion were read by Dr. Prevost, Bishop of the Protestant Episcopal Church in New York, who had been appointed by the Senate one of the chaplains of Congress. So closed the ceremonies of the inauguration.

The whole day was one of sincere rejoicing, and in the evening there were brilliant illuminations and fireworks.

TWO

The Blessings

of Liberty

". . . and to secure the blessings of liberty for ourselves and our posterity."

Both the Declaration of Independence and the Constitution with its Bill of Rights spell out our Founding Fathers' concern that the blessings of freedom should accrue to generations hence. In many ways, however, the Constitution proved to be ahead of its time; its words and promises had to be tested, sometimes in blood on the battlefield, and sometimes in arduous debate in courts and in Congress, before the liberty we live by could become real.

James Madison

"In terms of American history," writes the distinguished authority, Saul K. Padover, "Madison lived in a period that may be described as heroic. Among his friends, colleagues, and collaborators were a number of remarkable men who struck a spark in him. One need only mention George Washington, George Mason, John Adams, Alexander Hamilton, James Wilson, Benjamin Franklin, and Thomas Jefferson to sense the impact of Madison's environment. Most important of all these contemporaries, insofar as Madison's public and intellectual life is concerned, was Jefferson . . ."

Jefferson had immense regard for "the great little Madison," for his knowledge of divinity, the Scriptures, and philosophy as well as history, economics, and law. It was to the lean, stooped fourth president of the United States that Jefferson went when the University of Virginia needed suggestions for its theological library.

Madison was convinced that freedom under the law must include liberty in religion as well as in government. In the securing of those freedoms he has been called "our greatest constructive legal statesman." In the following portrait of James Madison and the times in which he lived, Saul K. Padover explains why he deserves that title.

Champion of Religious and Intellectual Freedom

BY SAUL K. PADOVER

MADISON and Jefferson first met at Williamsburg in the historic year 1776, when the latter was on his way to the Continental Congress and immortality. Thereafter their lives became politically intertwined. Up to March, 1809, Madison was Jefferson's lieutenant, adviser, collaborator, organizer, and, ultimately, successor. Together they helped to build America's first political party, the Republican [now Democratic]; together they fought and defeated the Federalists and planned campaigns that gave the Jeffersonians the Presidency of the United States for an unbroken twenty-four years. Madison was Jefferson's Secretary of State for eight years and succeeded him both in the Presidency and in the rectorship of the University of Virginia. Upon retirement from office in 1817, Madison remained in constant contact with Jefferson, exchanging letters and visits, some of the latter lasting two or three weeks at a time.

Their last correspondence, fifty years after they first met, dwelt on their long friendship and on the hope that posterity, for which both had labored so consciously and devotedly, would not forget them. . . .

Despite their intimacy, however, it would be misleading to assume that Madison was a mere follower or carbon copy of Jefferson. The truth is that not only was Madison a great personality in his own right but that he also differed from Jefferson in a number of subtle and significant ways. The first and most obvious difference was physical. Jefferson was tall—about 6 feet, 2 inches —rangy and vigorous; Madison was tiny, frail, and hypochondriacal. As Washington Irving said of "poor Jemmy Madison," he is "but a withered little apple-john.". . . Where Jefferson often looked what in many ways he was—a Western pioneer on horseback—Madison gave the impression of a sober and studious ecclesiastic. . . .

They differed, too, in manner. . . . "I thought Mr. Jefferson more of a statesman and man of the world than Mr. Madison," wrote Sir Augustus Foster, the British Minister to Washington, who knew both men; ". . . yet the latter was better informed, and, moreover, a social, jovial, and good humoured companion, full of anecdote, . . . of a political and historical interest. He was a little man with small features, rather wizened when I saw him, but occasionally lit up with a good-natured smile." . . .

[Madison] shared with Jefferson a lifelong passion for religious freedom and distrust of any and every kind of clericalism. History taught him that established churches, relying upon the power of the state, created "ignorance and corruption." The exercise of religion, he insisted, should be completely separated from government so that every person would be free to worship, or not to worship, where, how, and what he pleased. Man, he said, "is accountable to his God alone," and not to any priest or hierarchy. Complete religious liberty for every individual and every sect, Madison argued, would not only free the human mind from that "religious bondage [that] shackles and debilitates it, and unfits it for every noble enterprise," but would also lead to harmony in society. Instead of any one church, Madison, therefore, favored a multiplicity of sects, because the existence of a large number of religions would, among other things, prevent any one from dominating the others.

Madison was, to a large extent, instrumental in establishing "freedom of religious opinions and worship" in the United States. In the first Virginia Constitution, which he helped to draw up, he inserted the provision for the "free exercise of religion according to the dictates of conscience." In 1785, when an attempt was made in the Virginia legislature to impose a tax on the people for the support of "teachers of the Christian religion," Madison led a masterful and successful attack on the bill. In the course of that conflict he wrote A *Memorial and Remonstrance Against Religious Assessments*, which still remains a classic statement of religious freedom.

"We remonstrate against the said bill," he wrote in his *Memorial and Remonstrance*—

Because we hold it for a fundamental and undeniable truth "that religion or the duty which we owe to our Creator, and the manner of discharging it, can only be directed by reason and conviction, not by force or violence." The religion, then, of every man must be left to the conviction and conscience of every man; and it is the right of every man to exercise it as these may dictate. . . .

Because, finally, "the equal right of every citizen to the free exercise of his religion, according to the dictates of conscience," is held by the same tenure with all our other rights. If we recur to its origin, it is equally the gift of nature; if we weigh its importance, it cannot be less dear to us. . . . Either, then, we must say that the will of the legislature is the only measure of their authority, and that in the plenitude of that authority they may sweep away all our fundamental rights, or that they are bound to leave this particular right untouched and sacred. Either we must say that they may control the freedom of the press, may abolish trial by jury, may swallow up the executive and judiciary powers of the state . . . or we must say that they have no authority to enact into a law the bill under consideration.

We, the subscribers, say that the General Assembly of this commonwealth have no such authority. And in order that no effort may be omitted on our part against so dangerous an usurpation, we oppose to it this remonstrance; earnestly praying . . . that the Supreme Lawgiver of the Universe . . . may . . . guide them . . . (to) establish more firmly the liberties, the prosperity, and the happiness of the commonwealth.

A few years later, in 1789, it was Madison, as a member of the first Congress of the United States, who led the movement for the passage of the Bill of Rights which was to guarantee, forever, the basic liberties, including religious, of all Americans.

Madison's views of religious liberty formed an integral part of his whole philosophy of freedom, which embraced both material and spiritual objects. He argued that the possession of property could not, and should not, be separated from the possessions of opinions, whether intellectual or religious. A human being, he insisted, must have a right to property and a property in rights. As no just society can deprive a citizen of his material property, so it cannot take away his freedom of expression, which Madison regarded as a fundamental property right. For he conceived of property not merely as merchandise or money but as a totality of possessions which "embraces every thing to which a man may attach a value and have a right." In a remarkable essay on property and liberty, Madison thus formulated his theory:

A man has property in his opinions and the free communication of them.

He has a property of peculiar value in his religious opinions, and in the profession and practice dictated by them.

He has property very dear to him in the safety and liberty of his person. . . .

In a word, as a man is said to have a right to his property, he may be equally said to have a property in his rights.

In sum, Madison may be described as a striking historic figure, deserving to rank among the very great Americans who created this republic. He was a man of almost classic virtues—a statesman, a selfless patriot, and a political philosopher who was in the fortunate position of being able to translate his thought into living institutions. As one of the major architects of the American democracy, he deserves to be better known than he is.

"Let Freedom Ring"

In 1751, when Pennsylvania was celebrating the Golden Jubilee of William Penn's "Charter of Privileges," the Assembly sent to England for a bell to be hung in the steeple of the State House. Cracked during its first test, it was later recast.

Tradition has it that this bell pealed in proud proclamation of the Declaration of Independence, and that thereafter it announced other events of national importance. Writer Struthers Burt memorably tells us that while not all the aspects of this traditional story are true, the bell as a symbol of freedom has remained untarnished and pure.

The Liberty Bell

BY STRUTHERS BURT

AT FIFTH and Chestnut Streets, in Philadelphia, a most important thing had been happening, far more important than anyone at the time knew. The most historic building in America had been built.

In March, 1729, the Assembly had passed an appropriations bill for £50,000, and of this, £2,000 was to be used for a Provincial State House. Work was begun in July, 1732, and the central portion was about done by 1736; enough, at least, for a state banquet, the first to be given in the East Room.

Franklin's *Pennsylvania Gazette* speaks of, this as the "most grand and elegant entertainment that has been made in these parts of America."

Fourteen years later, it was suggested that a bell be hung in the tower and a clock affixed to the tower wall. The bell, cast in London, arrived in 1752 and, when tested, cracked. Two young brass founders, John Stow and John Pass, who had a foundry on

Third Street above Market, or High, offered to break up the bell and recast it, adding an ounce and a half of copper to each pound of the old bell. An April 17, 1753, the new bell, found satisfactory, was raised into place.

Four blocks away, diagonally across the State House square, not yet called Independence Square, and then across another open space, not yet called Washington Square, ground was being readied for the building of the Pennsylvania Hospital. When the cornerstone of the main building was laid in 1755, this was carved on it:

> In the year of Christ MDCCLV,
> George the second happily reigning,
> (For he sought the happiness of his people)
> Philadelphia flourishing,
> (For its inhabitants were public-spirited)
> This building
> By the bounty of the government
> And of many private persons,
> Was piously founded
> For the Relief of the sick and the miserable.
> May the God of Mercies bless the undertaking.

Twenty-one years later, across the intervening squares, across the whole town, across the entire country and the world, the bell of the State House clamored its denial of the pious cornerstone of the Pennsylvania Hospital.

But unfortunately for tradition—and why does this have to happen so often, for tradition as a rule is so much more right, philosophically and dramatically, than the facts?—it was not the great bell, now known as the Liberty Bell, which Isaac Norris ordered from London, and John Stow and John Pass had mended, which rang. To the contrary, it was a smaller bell, which now hung in the tower of the State House, and which was known as the "Province Bell."

The big bell had rung for the last time before the Revolution, in 1765, when it had called the citizens together to protest against the Stamp Act. But even by then it had become a symbol, and a name, and a tradition. During the British occupancy of 1777-1778 it was taken north to Allentown for safekeeping, being returned to Philadelphia later.

About the Liberty Bell, you see, there was an odd occurrence, a coincidence, an eerie second sight. Around its top ran these words: "Leviticus XXV, 10—Proclaim Liberty throughout all the Land unto all the Inhabitants thereof."

And Isaac Norris had ordered the bell in 1750, twenty-six years before the Revolution.

That's interesting, isn't it?

After all, it makes little difference which bell actually rang so long as the big one, the great full-throated one, and the verse from Leviticus, still ring in the hearts of the American people. It seems to me they do.

Freedom of the Press

> I honor the man who is willing to sink
> Half his present repute for the freedom to think,
> And when he has thought, be his cause strong or weak,
> Will risk t'other half for the freedom to speak.

James Russell Lowell wrote these words in 1848; but for a hundred years before, and for more than a hundred years after, Americans have been saying the same thing in a thousand different ways. Throughout our history we have been fighting for this freedom to speak—with stirring words in some instances, with life itself in others. In the following account, historian Carl Carmer graphically tells of the first major test on these shores of a free press—the trial of John Peter Zenger.

The Trial of John Peter Zenger

BY CARL CARMER

One of the rights Americans have guarded most zealously through the years is that of telling people what we think in print. Let your imagination take you back through the years to a little, hot printing-house in the town of Boston in June of the year 1722.

A boy of seventeen is trying to get out a newspaper. The title at the top of the sheet reads *The New England Courant*. His older brother, owner of the paper, has been put in jail, for printing criticism of government authorities. The boy knows that he himself may go to prison for the words he is printing—yet he does not hesitate.

Without freedom of thought there can be no such thing as wisdom—and no such thing as public liberty without freedom of speech.

That the words were not his own but a quotation from the *London Journal* did not lessen the force of the argument of the boy printer, Benjamin Franklin. But an obstinate government across the sea continued to suppress the printing of critical comment in the American colonies. Arrogant governors influenced the King of England, George II, to prohibit freedom of the press in the great province of New York: "Forasmuch as great inconvenience may arise by the liberty of printing within our province of New York, you are to provide that no person keep any press. . . . nor that any book, pamphlet or other matters whatsoever be printed without your especial leave and license be first obtained."

Nevertheless, enemies of Governor Cosby's dictator-like rule in old New York started a newspaper—the *Weekly Journal*—and chose as editor John Peter Zenger, immigrant from the banks of the Rhine. Zenger set about printing strong criticism of the governor and was arrested and thrown into jail. Then Governor Cosby really went to work to assure the prisoner's conviction on charges of libel. He had the two lawyers who dared to represent Zenger disbarred for challenging the jurisdiction of the court. And he kept Zenger in jail for nine months. But the dauntless printer kept on editing the *Weekly Journal*. Each day his wife came to the prison and John Peter Zenger told her—through a hole in the door of his cell—what he wanted published in the next issue: "It is the great design of this paper to maintain and explain the glorious principles of Liberty and to expose the art of those who would dark or destroy them."

John Peter Zenger was tried in midsummer in the old City Hall. It stood on Wall Street where the Sub-Treasury Building now stands. The attorney general, a favorite of the Governor's little court, denounced the editor bitterly and the Governor's judge nodded his head in agreement.

The cause of freedom of the press seemed hopelessly lost when the time came for the defense to present its case. Then the courtroom audience gasped. An old man had risen. He was Andrew Hamilton—the finest lawyer in all the colonies. Though his body was weak with years he had come all the way from Philadelphia to speak for the rights of John Peter Zenger and the rights of all men:

> It is a privilege—I will go further, it is a right which all free men claim, to complain when they are hurt; they have a right publicly to remonstrate against abuses of power. . . . to put their neighbors upon their guard against craft or open violence of men in authority, and to assert with courage the sense they have of the blessings of liberty—and their resolution at all hazards to preserve it. Men who injure and oppress the people under their administration provoke them to cry out and complain, and then make that very complaint the foundation for new oppressions.
>
> The question before the court and you, gentlemen of the jury, is not of small or private concern; it is not the cause of a poor printer, nor of New York alone, which we are trying. No! . . . It is the best cause, it is the cause of liberty!

When the old man stopped speaking, there was stillness in the hot courtroom. Slowly the jury filed out and the crowd, knowing every one of them—for New York was a little city then—felt that they were trustworthy men who would give an honest verdict. There was a long wait. The sultry August day moved slowly toward its close. Then—there was the jury marching back again. Their foreman spoke out for all people everywhere who love freedom and hate tyranny: *"We find the defendant, John Peter Zenger, not guilty!"*

There was no silence after that speech. The crowd's yell shook the courtroom. While the enraged judge fumed and spluttered, the waiting people outside in Wall Street took up the exulting cry. It spread over the city like a flame—the flame of freedom. New York rejoiced that it had won a round in the everlasting conflict men must wage to keep their civil rights.

Andrew Hamilton, being a wise man, knew that there would be other battles like this—in New York, in Boston, in his own city of Philadelphia—but he had fought a good fight and he had won it.

But there was one great and glorious fact that he could not know. It was that, through battles such as his own, and those that had gone before in this land which he loved, a new nation would be born—a nation whose very foundation would rest on human rights. Benjamin Franklin and Andrew Hamilton had fought for the same thing—and it was because they kept the love of freedom alive in this country that eventually that part of our Constitution known as the Bill of Rights was born. Old Andrew Hamilton did not know it, but his courageous fight helped make it possible that more than half a century later, the very first session of our Congress wrote into our Constitution one of its most sacred scriptures. Hear the voice of James Madison reading to that Congress the words which have become our precious heritage: "Congress shall make no law respecting an establishment of religion, or prohibiting the free exercise thereof, or abridging the freedom of speech, or of the press, or the right of the people peaceably to assemble, and to petition the government for a redress of grievances."

Adams and Jefferson

In 1800 John Adams was so sure he would be reelected to the Presidency that his defeat by Jefferson infuriated him; he sped away from Washington without waiting to greet his former friend and associate, without even taking part in Jefferson's inauguration. Adams was the only President to so openly show his resentment of his successor.

Years later, Dr. Benjamin Rush persuaded Adams to resume a long-interrupted correspondence, one that he knew would not only give pleasure to the two aging statesmen, but would also provide a rich treasury of learning for future readers. Thus in 1812 began the famous, regular, and prolonged series of letters in which Jefferson and Adams exchanged the broad cultural beliefs of the North and the South, reviewing the difficulties they had overcome to help create a new, free nation.

Catherine Drinker Bowen, with her distinctive flair for the high pageantry of history, begins her narrative of John Adams and the American Revolution on July 4, 1826—the day when death came to both of these great Americans. Then, in our selection, she takes us back fifty years to the signing of the Declaration of Independence.

Adams and Jefferson—Not Alone in Their Faith

BY CATHERINE DRINKER BOWEN

On the Fourth of July, 1826, America celebrated its Jubilee—the Fiftieth Anniversary of Independence. John Adams, second President of the United States, died that day, aged ninety, while

64

from Maine to Georgia bells rang and cannon boomed. And on that same day, Thomas Jefferson died before sunset in Virginia.

In their dying, in that swift, so aptly celebrated double departure, is something which shakes an American to the heart. It was not their great fame, their long lives or even the record of their work that made these two seem indestructible. It was their faith, their bounding, unquenchable faith in the future, their sure, immortal belief that mankind, if it so desired, could be free.

They were not alone in their faith. Theirs was the eighteenth century. The *Century of Enlightenment,* men called it proudly —the *Age of Reason,* when knowledge of the natural world was to break the bonds of man's primordial guilt, revealing that God himself was reasonable. . . . The riddle of his destiny was man's own to solve, by the joyful exercise of his free will. The awful catechism was reversed. God put the questions now, and in hope and eagerness men searched out answers, conquered the smallpox with a needle, threw down kings, and fashioned governments to their very liking. "You will think me transported with Enthusiasm but I am not," John Adams wrote his wife the day after Independence was declared—"I am well aware of the Toil and Blood and Treasure it will cost Us to maintain this Declaration, and support and defend these States.—Yet through all the Gloom I can see the Rays of ravishing Light and Glory. I can see that the End is more than worth all the Means. And that Posterity will triumph in that Day's Transaction, even altho We should rue it, which I trust in God We shall not."

Abigail Says Amen

Thomas Jefferson, sitting next to Dr. Franklin in Congress, shifted his position for the fifth time in as many minutes. It was the morning of July the fourth, and the delegates in Committee of the Whole were discussing the Declaration. They had been at it since late afternoon of July second, when the vote on independence was announced.

The process was quite obviously painful to the author. From time to time, Franklin glanced at him quizzically. The thing was not going at all as Jefferson had expected. It was in the Preamble that he—and John Adams too—had looked for most trouble. The Preamble contained extremely dangerous doctrines:

all men are created equal was a hard morsel for patrician land-holders to swallow. But somehow, Congress let it through, and with it the statement that men are endowed by their Creator with the right to *life, liberty and the pursuit of happiness.*

Life, liberty and property was the old revolutionary slogan. For denying it, Tories had lost their lives. *Property* was included even in the very radical Virginia Declaration of Rights, published in Philadelphia newspapers less than a month ago. Jefferson preferred his own phrase, "the pursuit of happiness."

It was when Harrison reached the indictments against the King that Jefferson began truly to suffer. He had composed twenty separate clauses, twenty fierce "reasons" to let the world know that America was justified in what she did. Battering their way through all twenty, Congress cut and slashed, deleted, contracted, changed words and phrases—and then took out, entire, Jefferson's most cherished outburst against the slave trade. (*This assemblage of horrors,* Jefferson had called it; *this market where men are bought and sold.*)

Congress, plainly, saw no reason to lay on George Rex the blame for this deplorable but traditional trade. Had General Washington's slaves, John Hancock's slaves, been imported by order of George II? What about the late very lucrative Rhode Island traffic? New England's hands were far from clean. South Carolina and Georgia, moreover, were still importing slaves from Africa. . . . They made it instantly clear they had no slightest intention of letting CLAUSE 20 go through.

John Adams darted to his feet, shouted angrily at Rutledge—something about freedom being a mere masquerade in a country that sold humans in chains. John talked (Jefferson noted gratefully) much louder than the opposition—"fighting fearlessly for every word," Jefferson testified later. John banged with his hickory cane against the floor—and got, in the end, absolutely nowhere.

Calmly, with infinite and ruthless good sense, Congress drew the sting from Jefferson's expressed and ferocious desire for "eternal separation" from the British people as well as the British King. Why, said Congress, close the door on a people of whom a large proportion had shown great sympathy for the American cause? In the end, Harrison crossed out the word "eternal," crossed out indeed a whole page of angry accusation. America, he wrote above the lined-out sentence, would hold the British people, as she held the rest of mankind, *enemies in war, in peace friends.*

On the table before him, Harrison had one of Jefferson's copies of the Declaration. Above it the official pen hung poised as Harrison began to read aloud in a singsong, monotonous, well-bred voice. Jefferson sat near the front; his clear, steady gaze was fixed with awful intentness on the manuscript. His author's imagination reproduced each paragraph, each page with its horrid change and interlineation:

When in the course of human events it becomes necessary for

one   *dissolve the political bands which have connected*

a⋀ people to ⋀ ~~advance from the subordination in which they~~ *them with another, and to*

~~have hitherto remained, & to~~ assume among the powers of the

separate and equal

earth the ⋀ ~~equal & independent~~ station to which the laws of nature's god entitle them, a decent respect to the opinions of mankind requires that they should declare the causes which

the separation

impel them to ⋀ ~~the change~~.

self-evident;

We hold these truths to be ⋀ ~~sacred & undeniable;~~ . .

That last change was Dr. Franklin's. Grudgingly, Jefferson confessed to himself that one word, even hyphenated, was better than three.

Congress, in point of fact, improved the document by every single alteration. Moreover they shortened rather than expanded it, a feat seldom if ever achieved by parliamentary critics. In the end however, it was still Jefferson's composition; no one could doubt it. His pen had written it, his spirit brooded over it, giving light to the whole . . . Now he sat listening as Harrison's voice droned on. This was the final reading. When it was over, the Declaration would be voted on in full Congress. There was no question of signing the document today; this mutilated copy was not fit for formal signature. It must be properly printed, "engrossed on parchment." Congress moreover possessed no official seal or stamp to honor such a document; for a hundred years the colonies had used only the King's great seal. A stamp must be invented, and quickly.*

* Late that day, a committee was named: Dr. Franklin, Mr. J. Adams and Mr. Jefferson, to bring in a device for a seal of the United States of America.

We therefore [read Harrison], *the Representatives of the
United States of America in General Congress assembled . . .
do solemnly* PUBLISH *and* DECLARE, *That these United Colonies
are and of right ought to be,* FREE AND INDEPENDENT STATES . . .
with FULL POWER *to levy War, conclude Peace, contract Alliances, establish Commerce, and to do all other Acts and Things
which* INDEPENDENT STATES *may of right do.*

*And for the support of this Declaration, with a firm reliance
on the protection of divine Providence, we mutually pledge to
each other our Lives, our Fortunes, and our sacred Honour.*

In the State House Yard there stood a round scaffold about
twenty feet high, with a little railed platform on top. From this
"awful stage," as John called it, the Declaration was first proclaimed on Monday, July eighth, at noontime. Colonel Nixon
of the Philadelphia Associators read it to a crowd that filled the
State House Yard. Troops, drawn up in formation, saluted, the
people gave three great huzzas. Forty-nine members of Congress, standing just below the platform, cheered too, then filed
through the State House door and went back to work.

It was not a big celebration nor a loud one. Pennsylvania had
made more noise, rung more bells and lighted more bonfires
when she held her first Provincial Conference. But there was no
question that people felt deeply the significance of the Declaration. As the days passed and post riders carried it north and
south, the country everywhere responded. In towns and hamlets
men gathered, cheering as the Declaration was read from Meeting-house steps; then ran to tear down the King's Arms from
their courthouse doors. The Lion and the Unicorn would prance
no more in these American States.

American States . . . People tried the phrase, turning it over
on their tongue. . . . *God bless the American States!* "This
Declaration has had a glorious effect," wrote Whipple of New
Hampshire, who had voted for it in Congress. "It has made these
colonies all alive." . . . A hundred King Streets changed their
name to State Street; Queen Street became Congress Way. In
their dwelling houses, men turned the King's portrait to the wall.
Even the halfpenny that bore the royal face was degraded to a
farthing. On Bowling Green, New Yorkers pulled down the
dashing equestrian statue of George Rex and melted it into—
the account was pleasingly specific—"42,500 bullets." Worcester,
Massachusetts, had a grand banquet: "24 Toasts were drank,"
reported the *Worcester Spy*—"Perpetual itching and no scratch-

ing to America's enemies. . . . May the freedom and independency of America endure, till the sun grows dim and this earth returns to chaos!"

On the nineteenth of July, 1776, the Declaration was proclaimed in Boston from the State House balcony. Abigail Adams was there. She had followed the crowd into King Street and stood across from the State House, waiting, her eyes fixed on the balcony that opened from the old Council Chamber. Troops stood at attention. The square, the streets leading from it were jammed with people. People perched on the rooftops; every window was filled with heads.

Here on this small square balcony, Thomas Hutchinson had stood on Massacre Night, pleading with the multitude . . . A thousand angry faces upturned in the moonlight, a thousand hands ready for the shedding of blood . . .

In the bright July noon sun the crowd began to shout as a man stepped on the balcony. Abby recognized him at once. It was Tom Crafts, the house painter, Sam Adams's right-hand man since 1764. "Colonel" Crafts, he was now. . . . It was Crafts who had led the little crowd of liberty boys that night when they serenaded John below the bedroom window in Cold Lane . . . JOHN ADAMS *dear, we sing to you, May heav'n its blessing show'r* . . .

The foolish, friendly words came back to Abby as clearly as if the scene were yesterday. "Why Abby," John had cried in astonishment, "they are singing my name!" Remembering, Abby felt tears start in her eyes. How long ago it was! A terrible dream, all this. Yet somehow, by God's mercy, terrible no longer. . . .

Tom Crafts had begun to read; the crowd was very still. The plain, flat Yankee voice reached easily across the square. ". . . Endowed by their Creator with sart'in . . ." Crafts stumbled, went back. ". . . By their Creator with sart'in unalienable rights; that among these are life, liberty and the pursuit of happiness . . ."

It did not take him long to finish. "God save the American States!" a voice shouted from the balcony. Crafts flung up both arms and the crowd surged forward, cheering.

"The Bells rang [*wrote Abigail that night to her husband*] the privateers fired the forts & batteries, the cannon were discharged the platoons followed & every face appeared joyfull. . . . After dinner the kings arms were taken down from the State House

& every vestige of him from every place in which it appeared &
burnt. . . . Thus ends royal Authority in this State, and all the
people shall say Amen."

Three hundred miles to the southward, John Adams sat in
Philadelphia City Tavern. It was dinnertime, and John had a
table to himself in a far corner; Sam Adams and McKean had
promised to join him. John was early; he had a full twenty
minutes to wait. From a pocket he took his wife's letter and
reread it. Abby, he thought with satisfaction, was a great hand
at a description: . . . *every vestige of the King from every place
where it appeared, and burnt.* He could see her face as she
wrote—intent, serious, the lips drawn in, the fine nostrils spread
a little: *and all the people shall say Amen.*

John looked up, his expression thoughtful, his blue eyes calm.
James Otis should be here tonight, he told himself with a little
pang of sadness. Otis had worked hard and long in this business
and had shared no reward. . . . A scene came back to John with
sudden clarity: the old Council Chamber in Boston, with the
Stuart kings framed in gold against the wall, and Otis speaking.
*This writ is against the fundamental principles of English law!
An act against the constitution is void.* How many men had
conspired beforehand, to make that speech possible, make it
come to pass! . . . Jeremiah Gridley—*I raised up two young
eagles*—On the day when John first went to see him, Gridley's
office had been quiet in the dark winter morning. *Pursue the
study of the law rather than the gain of it,* the old man had
advised. *Do not marry early.* Well, he had taken the advice on
both counts. . . . Benjamin Pratt had stood in the library of his
fine house, crutch under his arm. His voice had been cold as
iron. *Were you sworn at Worcester, Mr. Adams? Have you read
Fortescue? How far have you gone with Coke-Littleton?*

How far, John wondered now—how far with Sir Edward
Coke? How far with the law, with right and wrong, with sinning
and learning, with praying, rejoicing, with the cursing of God
in a man's own heart? . . . Through John's mind a thousand
scenes revolved, blotting out the tavern room, the tables crowded
with diners, the colored waiters moving back and forth. . . .
He saw his Boston office near the Town-house and the Irish
Infant offering a guinea in his outstretched palm; heard his own
voice: *I will defend Captain Preston and the soldiers. Mr. For-
ester, you may count on me.* . . . In Boston Court House, the

prisoners' room had been crowded after the trial. A soldier had lifted his branded thumb. *A small price to pay for our lives, Mr. Adams.*

How far with Coke-Littleton, how far with life? What was it that young man, that young minister, declared from Braintree pulpit long ago? Briant, his name was. Lemuel Briant. *The doctrines of civil liberty, inherited from our fathers.* A wild young man, John's father had said. A man of most insidious doctrine. . . . Lemuel Briant's face was dim now, his words slipped the memory. It was another, older face John saw tonight in Braintree pulpit . . . Dr. Hancock, benign, familiar as one's father . . . *Lord, make us to see our end, that we may know the measure of our days.* . . . There had been a hymn, a Psalm they had sung often in the Meeting-house. John's mind groped for the words. Something about a people redeemed and *freed from th' enemies' hands.* . . . Great-uncle Peter used to sing it, back of the malt house when he was cleaning his gun, roaring it out full basso. *Then did they to Jehovah cry* . . . Ah, that was it!

> *Then did they to Jehovah cry*
> *When they were in distress,*
> *Who did them set at liberty,*
> *Out of their anguishes.*
>
> *In such a way that was most right*
> *He led them forth also,*
> *That to a city which they might*
> *Inhabit they might go.*

Abby knew that hymn; she liked to think it was written for New England people. . . . New England? *Where are now your landmarks,* Patrick Henry had demanded—*Where are your boundaries? I am not a Virginian but an American.*

"Thus ends royal Authority," Abby's letter said. . . . Thus ends a way of living, a way of thinking. "A new empire has arisen, styled the United States of America." Judge Drayton of Carolina had declared it from the bench, in full court assembled. The United American States. There was great power in a name, a phrase. Yet before the world would recognize this name, a terrible war must be fought. . . . *"I am well aware of the Toil and Blood and Treasure it will cost Us to maintain this Declara-*

*tion, and support and defend these states." John's own words
came back to him. "Yet through all the Gloom I can see the
Rays of ravishing Light and Glory."*

*I can see that the end is worth all the means. This is our day
of deliverance. With solemn acts of devotion to God we ought
to commemorate it. With pomp and parade, with shows, games,
sports, guns, bells, bonfires and illuminations from one end of
the continent to the other from this time forward forevermore . . .*

A hand fell on John's shoulder. He looked up. "Cousin John,"
Sam Adams said cheerfully. "You are in a very brown study. I
said your name three times. . . . Is it well with you tonight?"

John smiled, filled suddenly with happiness, gratitude, a flood
of deep feeling he could not have defined. With a wide, sweeping gesture of hospitality he pulled out a chair. "It is very well
with me tonight, Cousin," he said.

Jefferson and the Press

Jefferson wrote it in a letter to George Washington: "No government ought to be without censors; and, where the press is free, no one ever will."

Such censors Jefferson had aplenty. Their attacks against him bristled with phrases like "arch traitor and rogue." Margaret Bayard Smith, a leader of Washington society during its first forty years, recalls Jefferson's reaction when the free press used its freedom to cut and thrust at him.

"Why Are These Libels Allowed?"

BY MARGARET BAYARD SMITH

M R. JEFFERSON was known in Europe as much, if not more, as a philosopher, than as a politician. Mr. Jefferson's acquaintance in this wide and distinguished circle in Paris made him well known throughout Europe, and when he became President his reputation as a philosopher and man of letters brought many literary and scientific foreigners to our country. Among others, Baron Humboldt one day, in answer to some inquiries addressed to this celebrated traveler, replied, "I have come not to see your great rivers and mountains, but to become acquainted with your great men." Of these, he held Mr. Jefferson in the highest situation. Soon after the Baron's arrival on our shores, he hastened to Washington and, during his visit to our city, passed many hours of every day with Mr. Jefferson. . . .

His visits at the President's House were unshackled by mere ceremony and not limited to any particular hour. One evening he called about twilight, and being shown into the drawing room without being announced, he found Mr. Jefferson seated on the floor, surrounded by half a dozen of his little grand-

73

children, so eagerly and noisily engaged in a game of romps that for some moments his entrance was not perceived. When his presence was discovered, Mr. Jefferson rose up and shaking hands with him said, "You have found me playing the fool, Baron, but I am *sure* to you I need make no apology."

Another time he called of a morning and was taken into the cabinet. As he sat by the table, among the newspapers that were scattered about, he perceived one that was always filled with the most virulent abuse of Mr. Jefferson, calumnies the most offensive, personal as well as political. "Why are these libels allowed?" asked the Baron, taking up the paper. "Why is not this libelous journal suppressed, or its editor at least fined and imprisoned?"

Mr. Jefferson smiled, saying: "Put that paper in your pocket, Baron, and should you hear the reality of our liberty, the freedom of our press, questioned, show this paper and tell where you found it."

He Died for Freedom

Elijah P. Lovejoy is said to be the only editor of an American religious periodical who gave his life for the right to express liberal social news. It was in the columns of a little Presbyterian journal, the St. Louis Observer, *that the young minister first championed the gradual abolition of slavery with what he termed "the freedom of a republican and the meekness of a Christian."*

Later, as publisher of the Alton, Illinois, Observer, *he was to see his printing press destroyed three times by mobs before he himself was killed defending it.*

John Quincy Adams called Elijah Lovejoy "the first American martyr to the freedom of the press and the freedom of the slave." His heroic death was widely commemorated, not only at the time, but again in 1937 during its centenary. He has come to epitomize, as Supreme Court Justice William Douglas shows us, the evangel of the American ideal.

The Martyrdom of Elijah P. Lovejoy

BY WILLIAM O. DOUGLAS

At Alton, Illinois, is the grave of Elijah P. Lovejoy, whom Irving Dilliard of the St. Louis *Post-Dispatch* has called "the first martyr to freedom of the press in the United States," an editor "who knew no compromise on right or wrong as his conscience understood them."

Alton was divided on the issue of slavery. Lovejoy, an abolitionist editor, was outspoken. An aroused community destroyed several of his presses. Finally a public meeting was called at which a resolution was adopted demanding that Lovejoy end his career as editor in Alton. Lovejoy addressed the gathering on November 3, 1837.

75

Have I, sir, been guilty of any infraction of the laws? Whose good name have I injured? When and where have I published anything injurious to the reputation of Alton?

What, sir, I ask, has been my offense? Put your finger upon it—define it—and I stand ready to answer it. If I have committed any crime, you can easily convict me. . . . But if I have been guilty of no violation of the law, why am I hunted up and down continually like a partridge upon the mountains?

If the civil authorities refuse to protect me, I must look to God; and if I die, I have determined to make my grave in Alton. I have sworn eternal opposition to slavery and by the blessings of God I will never turn back. With God I cheerfully rest my cause. I can die at my post but I cannot desert it.

Four nights later a mob attacked the warehouse where Lovejoy's new printing press was stored. Lovejoy was killed in the encounter.

Recently American journalists erected bronze markers at the place where Lovejoy fell. By that act they illustrated a trait in the American character. At times we indulge in violent excesses. But the American conscience usually speaks up, and on a later day pilgrimages are made to atone for the injustice.

John Quincy Adams

*Like so many early American statesmen—including his father,
our great second president—John Quincy Adams excelled in
various fields. But in one honor he stands alone: he is the only
person in our history to retire from the Presidency and then be
elected to the House of Representatives. He served there as a
Massachusetts Congressman for seventeen years, until the moment
of his death; and the two causes to which he gave utmost devotion were the abolition of slavery and the constitutional right of
petition, a question then even more momentous than that of free
speech.*

   *Henry Cabot Lodge, another Bay State statesman, presents a
warmly perceptive account of Adams as the champion of free
speech and the right to petition. He reveals how religious faith
gave Adams true courage, "that virtue which champions the
cause of right."*

The Right of Petition

BY HENRY CABOT LODGE

THE lot of ex-Presidents of the United States, as a rule, has
been a life of extreme retirement, but to this rule there is one
marked exception. When John Quincy Adams left the White
House in March, 1829, it must have seemed as if public life
could hold nothing more for him. He had had everything apparently that an American statesman could hope for. He had
been Minister to Holland and Prussia, to Russia and England.
He had been a Senator of the United States, Secretary of State
for eight years, and finally President. Yet, notwithstanding all
this, the greatest part of his career, and his noblest service to

his country, were still before him when he gave up the Presidency.

In the following year (1830) he was told that he might be elected to the House of Representatives, and the gentleman who made the proposition ventured to say that he thought an ex-President, by taking such a position, "instead of degrading the individual would elevate the representative character." Mr. Adams replied that he had "in that respect no scruples whatever. No person can be degraded by serving the people as Representative in Congress, nor, in my opinion, would an ex-President of the United States be degraded by serving as a selectman of his town if elected thereto by the people." A few weeks later he was chosen to the House, and the district continued to send him every two years from that time until his death. He did much excellent work in the House, and was conspicuous in more than one memorable scene; but here it is possible to touch on only a single point, where he came forward as the champion of a great principle, and fought a battle for the right which will always be remembered among the great deeds of American public men.

Soon after Mr. Adams took his seat in Congress, the movement for the abolition of slavery was begun by a few obscure agitators. It did not at first attract much attention, but as it went on it gradually exasperated the overbearing temper of the Southern slaveholders. One fruit of this agitation was the appearance of petitions for the abolition of slavery in the House of Representatives. A few were presented by Mr. Adams without attracting much notice; but as the petitions multiplied, the Southern representatives became aroused. They assailed Mr. Adams for presenting them, and finally passed what was known as the gag rule, which prevented the reception of these petitions by the House. Against this rule Mr. Adams protested, in the midst of the loud shouts of the Southerners, as a violation of his constitutional rights. But the tyranny of slavery at that time was so complete that the rule was adopted and enforced, and the slaveholders undertook in this way to suppress free speech in the House, just as they also undertook to prevent the transmission through the mails of any writings adverse to slavery. With the wisdom of a statesman and a man of affairs, Mr. Adams addressed himself to the one practical point of the contest. He did not enter upon a discussion of slavery or of its abolition, but turned his whole force toward the vindication of the right of petition. On every petition day he would offer, in constantly increasing numbers, petitions which came to him from all parts of the country for the abolition of slavery, in this way driving the Southern representatives almost to madness, despite their rule which prevented the reception of such documents when offered. Their hatred of Mr. Adams is something difficult to conceive, and they were burning to break him down, and, if possible, drive him from the House. On February 6, 1837, after presenting the usual petitions, Mr. Adams offered one upon which he said he should like the judgment of the Speaker as to its propriety, inasmuch as it was a petition from slaves. In a moment the House was in a tumult, and loud cries of "Expel him!" "Expel him!" rose in all directions. One resolution after another was offered looking toward his expulsion or censure, and it was not until February 9, three days later, that he was able to take the floor in his own defense. His speech was a masterpiece of argument, invective, and sarcasm. He showed, among other things, that he had not offered the petition, but had only asked the opinion of the Speaker upon it, and that the petition itself prayed that slavery should not be abolished. When he closed his speech, which was quite as savage as any made against him, and infinitely abler, no one desired to reply, and the idea of censuring him was dropped.

The greatest struggle, however, came five years later, when, on January 21, 1842, Mr. Adams presented the petition of certain citizens of Haverhill, Massachusetts, praying for the dissolution of the Union on account of slavery. His enemies felt that now, at last, he had delivered himself into their hands. Again arose the cry for his expulsion, and again vituperation was poured out upon him, and resolutions to expel him freely introduced. When he got the floor to speak in his own defense, he faced an excited House, almost unanimously hostile to him, and possessing, as he well knew, both the will and the power to drive him from its walls. But there was no wavering in Mr. Adams. "If they say they will try me," he said, "they must try me. If they say they will punish me, they must punish me. But if they say that in peace and mercy they will spare me expulsion, I disdain and cast away their mercy, and I ask if they will come to such a trial and expel me. I defy them. I have constituents to go to, and they will have something to say if this House expels me, nor will it be long before the gentlemen will see me here again." The fight went on for nearly a fortnight, and on

February 7 the whole subject was finally laid on the table. The
sturdy, dogged fighter, single-handed and alone, had beaten all
the forces of the South and of slavery. No more memorable
fight has ever been made by one man in a parliamentary body,
and after this decisive struggle the tide began to turn. Every
year Mr. Adams renewed his motion to strike out the gag rule,
and forced it to a vote. Gradually the majority against it dwin-
dled, until at last, on December 3, 1844, his motion prevailed.
Freedom of speech had been vindicated in the American House
of Representatives, the right of petition had been won, and the
first great blow against the slave power had been struck.

Four years later Mr. Adams fell, stricken with paralysis, at his
place in the House, and a few hours afterward, with the words,
"This is the last of earth; I am content," upon his lips, he sank
into unconsciousness and died. It was a fit end to a great public
career. His fight for the right of petition is one to be studied
and remembered, and Mr. Adams made it practically alone.
The slaveholders of the South and the representatives of the
North were alike against him. Against him, too, as his biographer,
Mr. Morse, says, was the class in Boston to which he naturally
belonged by birth and education. He had to encounter the bitter resistance in his own set of the "conscienceless respectability
of wealth," but the great body of the New England people was
with him, as were the voters of his own district. He was an old
man, with the physical infirmities of age. His eyes were weak
and streaming; his hands were trembling; his voice cracked in
moments of excitement; yet in that age of oratory, in the days
of Webster and Clay, he was known as the "old man eloquent."
It was what he said, more than the way he said it, which told.
His vigorous mind never worked more surely and clearly than
when he stood alone in the midst of an angry House, the target
of their hatred and abuse. His arguments were strong, and his
large knowledge and wide experience supplied him with every
weapon for defense and attack. Beneath the lash of his invective
and his sarcasm the hottest of the slaveholders cowered away.
He set his back against a great principle. He never retreated an
inch, he never yielded, he never conciliated, he was always an
assailant, and no man and no body of men had the power to
turn him. He had his dark hours, he felt bitterly the isolation
of his position, but he never swerved. He had good right to set
down in his diary, when the gag rule was repealed, "Blessed,
forever blessed, be the name of God."

The Gettysburg Address

Every American school child knows the story. How, for the dedication of Gettysburg cemetery, honoring so many fallen soldiers, the foremost speaker of his time was summoned to give the oration. How Edward Everett's expansive two-hour address was followed by a few brief sentences spoken by President Abraham Lincoln. How, incredibly, those ten immortal sentences were shrugged off by both the audience and the press of the day as disappointing.

Carl Sandburg, poet, novelist, and biographer, probably most highly esteemed for his writings on Lincoln, erases the years and permits us to stand on the field with Abraham Lincoln as he pays tribute, in everlasting words, to the dead—and to the living freedom of our great democracy, this "nation under God."

Lincoln Speaks at Gettysburg

BY CARL SANDBURG

A PRINTED invitation came to Lincoln's hands notifying him that on Thursday, November 19, 1863, exercises would be held for the dedication of a National Soldiers' Cemetery at Gettysburg. In the helpless onrush of the war too many of the fallen had lain as neglected cadavers rotting in the open fields or thrust into so shallow a resting-place that a common farm plow caught in their bones. Now by order of Governor Curtin of Pennsylvania, seventeen acres had been purchased on Cemetery Hill, where the Union center stood its colors on the second and third of July, and plots of soil had been allotted each State for its graves.

The sacred and delicate duties of orator of the day had fallen on Edward Everett, perhaps foremost of all distinguished

American classical orators. Serene, suave, handsomely venerable in his sixty-ninth year, a prominent specimen of Northern upper-class distinction, Everett was a natural choice of the Pennsylvania commissioners, who sought an orator for a solemn national occasion.

Lincoln meanwhile, in reply to the printed circular invitation, sent word to the commissioners that he would be present at the ceremonies. This made it necessary for the commissioners to consider whether the President should be asked to deliver an address when present.

And so on November 2 David Wills of Gettysburg, as the special agent of Governor Curtin and also acting for the several States, by letter informed Lincoln that the several States having soldiers in the Army of the Potomac who were killed, or had since died at hospitals in the vicinity, had procured grounds for a cemetery and proper burial of their dead. "These grounds will be consecrated and set apart to this sacred purpose by appropriate ceremonies on Thursday, the 19th instant. I am authorized by the Governors of the various States to invite you to be present and participate in these ceremonies, which will doubtless be very imposing and solemnly impressive. It is the desire that after the oration, you, as Chief Executive of the nation, formally set apart these grounds to their sacred use by a few appropriate remarks."

Lincoln's personal touch with Gettysburg, by telegraph, mail, courier, and by a throng of associations, made it a place of great realities to him. Just after the battle there, a woman had come to his office, the doorman saying she had been "crying and taking on" for several days trying to see the President. Her husband and three sons were in the army. On part of her husband's pay she had lived for a time, till money from him stopped coming. She was hard put to scrape a living and needed one of her boys to help.

The President listened to her, standing at a fireplace, hands behind him, head bowed, motionless. The woman finished her plea for one of her three sons in the army. He spoke. Slowly and almost as if talking to himself alone the words came and only those words:

"I have two, and you have none."

He crossed the room, wrote an order for the military discharge of one of her sons. On a special sheet of paper he wrote full and detailed instructions where to go and what to say in order to get her boy back.

In a few days the doorman told the President that the same woman was again on hand crying and taking on. "Let her in," was the word. She had located her boy, camp, regiment, company. She had found him, yes, wounded at Gettysburg, dying in a hospital, and had followed him to the grave. And, she begged, would the President now give her the next one of her boys?

As before he stood at the fireplace, hands behind him, head bent low, motionless. Slowly and almost as if talking to himself alone the words came and as before only those words:

"I have two, and you have none."

He crossed the room to his desk and began writing. As though nothing else was to do she followed, stood by his chair as he wrote, put her hand on the President's head, smoothed his thick and disorderly hair with motherly fingers. He signed an order giving her the next of her boys, stood up, put the priceless paper in her hand as he choked out the one word, "There!" and with long quick steps was gone from the room with her sobs and cries of thanks in his ears.

By many strange ways Gettysburg was to Lincoln a fact in crimson mist.

Fifteen thousand, some said 30,000 or 50,000, people were on Cemetery Hill for the exercises on November 19. On the platform sat governors, major generals, foreign Ministers, members of Congress, officials, together with Colonel Ward Hill Lamon, Edward Everett and his daughter, and the President of the United States.

The United States House chaplain offered a prayer while the thousands stood with uncovered heads.

Benjamin B. French, officer in charge of buildings in Washington, introduced the Honorable Edward Everett, orator of the day, who rose, bowed low to Lincoln, saying, "Mr. President." Lincoln responded, "Mr. Everett."

The orator of the day then stood in silence before a crowd that stretched to limits that would test his voice. Beyond and around were the wheat fields, the meadows, the peach orchards, long slopes of land, and five and seven miles farther the contemplative blue ridge of a low mountain range. His eyes could sweep them as he faced the audience. He had taken note of it in his prepared and rehearsed address. "Overlooking these broad fields now reposing from the labors of the waning year, the mighty Alleghenies dimly towering before us, the graves of our brethren beneath our feet, it is with hesitation that I raise my poor voice to break the eloquent silence of God and Nature. But the duty to which you have called me must be performed, —grant me, I pray you, your indulgence and your sympathy." He spoke for an hour and fifty-seven minutes, some said a trifle over two hours, repeating almost word for word an address that occupied nearly two newspaper pages, as he had written it and as it had gone in advance sheets to many newspapers.

Everett came to his closing sentence without a faltering voice: "Down to the latest period of recorded time, in the glorious annals of our common country there will be no brighter page than that which relates THE BATTLES OF GETTYSBURG." It was the effort of his life and embodied the perfections of the school of oratory in which he had spent his career. His erect form and sturdy shoulders, his white hair and flung-back head at dramatic points, his voice, his poise, and chiefly some quality of inside goodheartedness, held most of his audience to him, though the people in the front rows had taken their seats three hours before his oration closed.

Having read Everett's address, Lincoln knew when the moment drew near for him to speak. He took out his own manuscript from a coat pocket, put on his steel-bowed glasses, stirred in his chair, looked over the manuscript, and put it back in his pocket. Ward Hill Lamon rose and spoke the words "The President of the United States," who rose, and holding in one hand the two sheets of paper at which he occasionally glanced, delivered the address in his high-pitched and clear-carrying voice:

> Fourscore and seven years ago, our fathers brought forth upon this continent a new nation, conceived in liberty and dedicated to the proposition that all men are created equal.
>
> Now we are engaged in a great civil war, testing whether that nation—or any nation, so conceived and so dedicated—can long endure.
>
> We are met on a great battle-field of that war. We are met to dedicate a portion of it as the final resting place of those who have given their lives that that nation might live.
>
> It is altogether fitting and proper that we should do this.

But, in a larger sense, we cannot dedicate, we cannot consecrate, we cannot hallow, this ground. The brave men, living and dead, who struggled here, have consecrated it, far above our power to add or to detract.

The world will very little note nor long remember what we say here; but it can never forget what they did here.

It is for us, the living, rather, to be dedicated, here, to the unfinished work that they have thus far so nobly carried on. It is rather for us to be here dedicated to the great task remaining before us; that from these honored dead we take increased devotion to that cause for which they here gave the last full measure of devotion; that we here highly resolve that these dead shall not have died in vain; that the nation shall, under God, have a new birth of freedom, and that government of the people, by the people, for the people, shall not perish from the earth.

The applause, according to most of the responsible witnesses, was formal and perfunctory, a tribute to the occasion, to the high office, to the array of important men of the nation on the platform, by persons who had sat as an audience for three hours. Ten sentences had been spoken in five minutes, and some were surprised that it should end before the orator had really begun to get his outdoor voice.

The ride to Washington took until midnight. Lincoln was weary, talked little. He had stood that day, the world's foremost spokesman of popular government, saying that democracy was yet worth fighting for. He had spoken as one in mist who might head on deeper yet into mist. He incarnated the assurances and pretenses of popular government, implied that it could and might perish from the earth. What he meant by "a new birth of freedom" for the nation could have a thousand interpretations. The taller riddles of democracy stood up out of the address. It had the dream touch of vast and furious events epitomized for any foreteller to read what was to come. He did not assume that the drafted soldiers, substitutes, and bounty-paid privates had died willingly under Lee's shot and shell, in deliberate consecration of themselves to the Union cause. His cadences sang the ancient song that where there is freedom men have fought and sacrificed for it, and that freedom is worth men's dying for. For the first time since he became President he had on a dramatic occasion declaimed, howsoever it might be read, Jefferson's proposition which had been a slogan of the Revolutionary War—"All men are created equal"—leaving no other inference than that he regarded the Negro slave as a man. His outwardly smooth sentences were inside of them gnarled and tough with the enigmas of the American experiment.

Emma Lazarus

More than the Liberty Bell or any of the famous shrines in our nation's Capitol, the Statue of Liberty in New York harbor symbolizes for us, as for the world, the soul of America.

Emma Lazarus was a native American of Jewish descent who, through her poetry and her wide intellectual curiosity, won the interest of such distinguished men of letters as Ralph Waldo Emerson and John Burroughs. When, in answer to a special request, she sat down and wrote "The New Colossus," Emma Lazarus captured for all time the mission and message of our land. H. E. Jacob tells us here how that immortal sonnet came to be inscribed on the Statue of Liberty.

I Lift My Lamp

BY H. E. JACOB

EMMA had been back in New York only six weeks when an appeal came to her from a committee that was planning to set up, on Bedloe's Island in New York harbor, a colossal statue, "Liberty Enlightening the World." Some decades earlier two Frenchmen had conceived the idea of this statue, Laboulaye, the statesman, and Auguste Bartholdi, the sculptor. These two Frenchmen, apparently ashamed of the unfriendly policies the French Empire had pursued toward Lincoln's America, wished to "conciliate" the Americans. They therefore planned this gift which would remind America of the better France of Lafayette's time. The Americans were taken by surprise; they had no need of being "conciliated" because they had never been angry with France.

The statue, which was being built in Paris (it was really more of a construction job than sculptor's work), grew to incredible dimensions. How was it ever going to be transported? The famous

Trojan horse was a tiny mouse compared to it. Was not the handling of the statue an immigration problem in itself? But the very vastness of the conception ("the biggest statue in the world") inflamed the ambitions of the Americans. Overnight, everyone was in favor of it. "Liberty Enlightening the World" entered the arena of politics like a kind of golem before it was ever set up. New York, which had originally been lethargic about the whole affair, stiffened its back when it saw that the other "cities of liberty," Philadelphia and Boston, were indicating a desire to obtain the colossus for themselves.

The request to Emma came from the chairman of the committee, her old friend, William M. Evarts. Money was needed to build the pedestal for the statue, and as one of the fund-raising projects an auction was to be held, in a gallery on the corner of Fourth Avenue and Twenty-third Street, at which manuscripts of Longfellow, Walt Whitman, Bret Harte and Mark Twain were to be sold. Evarts asked Emma to contribute a manuscript for this purpose, and after some hesitation she sent the committee a sonnet. Probably she hesitated because she saw in this request to write "to order," for a specific purpose, an infringement upon her cherished "liberty of invention." But was not the idea of Liberty in all its majesty more important than a petty set of artistic liberties? In any case, she sat down and, in the last week of November, 1883, wrote fourteen lines that have become immortal.

THE NEW COLOSSUS

Not like the brazen giant of Greek fame,
With conquering limbs astride from land to land;
Here at our sea-washed, sunset gates shall stand
A mighty woman with a torch, whose flame
Is the imprisoned lightning, and her name
Mother of Exiles. From her beacon-hand
Glows world-wide welcome; her mild eyes command
The air-bridged harbor that twin cities frame.
"Keep, ancient lands, your storied pomp!" cries she
With silent lips. "Give me your tired, your poor,
Your huddled masses yearning to breathe free,
The wretched refuse of your teeming shore.
Send these, the homeless, tempest-tost to me.
I lift my lamp beside the golden door!"

This poem has become a part of world literature. One of the most remarkable aspects of the poem was the fact that Emma had never seen the statue when she wrote the sonnet, had never seen the burning torch of liberty shedding its light through the salty air of New York harbor upon the "huddled masses" of immigrants. The statue stood in a shed in Paris and she knew it only from photographs and wooden models.

How did she know that the New Colossus would stand in forcible contrast to the classical Colossus of Rhodes alluded to in the first line? No matter—however it was that she knew, in the shadow of this poem all question of Emma's earlier weaknesses fades away. In this her strength sufficed; this was the *overflow* that William James required when he wrote her: "The power of *playing* with thought and language . . . ought to be the overflowing of a life rich in other ways." For it was the *experience* of the idea embodied in the statue that made the poem possible.

There were some who thought Emma's poem more articulate and architecturally greater than the planned statue itself. Old James Russell Lowell, at this time American ambassador to England, and a poet who had formerly not thought too highly of Emma, wrote to her: "I liked your sonnet about the Statue much better than I like the Statue itself. But your sonnet gives its subject a *raison d'être* which it wanted before quite as much as it wanted a pedestal. You have set it on a noble one, saying admirably just the right word to be said, an achievement more arduous than that of the sculptor." . . .

There is a shrine for Emma's memory which is well known to all Americans—even, curiously enough, to those who have never heard her name. In 1903, in an act "of loving memory," an admirer of Emma's, Georgiana Schuyler, arranged for her verses about the "huddled masses" to be engraved upon the pedestal of the Statue of Liberty. Since then a kind of kinship has existed between the Goddess of Liberty and Emma Lazarus' memory.

The Statue towers 305 feet above the sea, surpassing the legendary height of the Colossus of Rhodes. But the "halo" surrounding it must really be much greater than the actual light of its torch. What, otherwise, accounts for its being a beacon to the yearning masses in Europe, Africa, and Asia, to the "tired," the "poor," the "huddled," and the "tempest-tost?"

Around Bedloe's Island the winds sing, the waves slap, the seagulls screech. Since 1886 millions of immigrants have passed by the goddess with the torch. And since 1903 many hundreds of thousands of visitors have read the name of Emma Lazarus. Most of them have forgotten it again. . . . But what, after all, is a name? Names molder in libraries or wither in anthologies. Emma's name will not vanish so long as Liberty's statue stands; it is indissolubly joined with the mighty colossus on which her verses are graven.

Judge Learned Hand

One of the greatest jurists of all time, Judge Learned Hand stands in the proud tradition of our notable Supreme Court justices— Marshall, Holmes, Brandeis, and Cardozo—although he has never been a member of the High Court. Both his paternal grand-father and his own father were judges; an earlier forebear was the colonist John Hand, whose estate "consisted of a Bible, a Psalm Book, a sword, and a pistol."

During his forty-two years on the bench (he retired from regular active service in 1951), Judge Learned Hand achieved renown as a vital, humane, and liberal interpreter of the spirit of the living law. The recognition which the bench and bar gave him from the beginning of his career, the public has accorded him in full measure since May, 1944, when he led a large number of new citizens in the pledge to the flag at the "I Am An American Day" ceremonies in Central Park, New York City. His words on that occasion belong to the ages. For he spoke of his faith in the spirit of liberty, the spirit of true democracy, with justice and brotherhood for all.

The Spirit of Liberty

BY JUDGE LEARNED HAND

WE HAVE gathered here to affirm a faith, a faith in a common purpose, a common conviction, a common devotion. Some of us have chosen America as the land of our adoption; the rest have come from those who did the same. For this reason we have some right to consider ourselves a picked group, a group of those who had the courage to break from the past and brave the dangers and the loneliness of a strange land. What was the object that nerved us, or those who went before us, to this choice? We sought liberty, freedom from oppression, freedom from want, freedom to be ourselves. This we then sought; this we now believe that we are by way of winning. What do we mean when we say that first of all we seek liberty? I often wonder whether we do not rest our hopes too much upon constitution, upon laws and upon courts. These are false hopes; believe me, these are false hopes. Liberty lies in the hearts of men and women; when it dies there, no constitution, no law, no court can save it; no constitution, no law, no court can even do much to help it. While it lies there it needs no constitution, no law, no court to save it. And what is this liberty which must lie in the hearts of men and women? It is not the ruthless, the unbridled will; it is not freedom to do as one likes. That is the denial of liberty, and leads straight to its overthrow. A society in which men recognize no check upon their freedom soon becomes a society where freedom is the possession of only a savage few; as we have learned to our sorrow.

What then is the spirit of liberty? I cannot define it; I can only tell you my own faith. The spirit of liberty is the spirit which is not too sure that it is right; the spirit of liberty is the spirit which seeks to understand the minds of other men and women; the spirit of liberty is the spirit which weighs their interests alongside its own without bias; the spirit of liberty remembers that not even a sparrow falls to earth unheeded; the spirit of liberty is the spirit of Him who, near two thousand years ago, taught mankind that lesson it has never learned, but has never quite forgotten; that there may be a kingdom where the least shall be heard and considered side by side with the greatest. And now in that spirit, that spirit of an America which has never been, and which may never be; nay, which never will be except as the conscience and courage of Americans create it; yet in the spirit of that America which lies hidden in some form in the aspirations of us all; in the spirit of that America for which our young men are at this moment fighting and dying; in that spirit of liberty and of America I ask you to rise and with me pledge our faith in the glorious destiny of our beloved country.

THREE

A More

Perfect Union

In no other land and at no other time had this audacious idea been dared—forging a union of such diverse, conglomerate colonies, peoples and religions as made up early America. But from these very differences came the pattern we ever seek to protect and perpetuate—living together in peace, proudly independent in spirit, firmly united in nation.

The Constitution Wins

The Bill of Rights, the cherished "backbone" of our Constitution, was actually an afterthought to that historic instrument. Strong passion marked the debate in Virginia on the adoption of the Constitution, with some—the redoubtable Patrick Henry among them—fearful that it smacked too much of monarchy: that a president could become, in effect, a king.

Blair Niles has explored widely and has made important contributions to geography, sociology, history, and fiction; but she is perhaps at her best when she writes, as in the next selection, of her native Virginia and its famous sons. Here she highlights those stormy sessions when, after vehement argument on both sides, the pro-Constitution forces finally swept the document to victory by a narrow margin.

Union

BY BLAIR NILES

IT HAPPENED in a long drought which had parched and killed the young tobacco plants. The day was Sunday, the first of June; a hot bright day. The delegates who were to debate the Federal Constitution arrived in Richmond thickly powdered with the dust which their horses' hoofs had raised in clouds along the way. The dust was white, grey, or red, according to the section of Virginia from which the men had come. All day they had been arriving; on horseback, in gigs, or in phaetons.

One of those who had journeyed by gig came up from south of the James. He was driving himself, and this man, they say, was dressed in the homespun of his own loom, and the dust which covered him was brick-red. They say, too, that as he drove his tall spare figure leaned forward in the gig, and that he seemed worn with travel; perhaps also worn with the anxiety concerning that battle which he was come to fight.

At the same time, from north of the James, another man was approaching, driven in a well-turned-out phaeton, and the dust which lay upon this man, upon his vehicle and his horse, was grey. Even before the phaeton stopped at the steps of Swan Tavern, and the traveler got out, you could see that he was lame, for he had crutches beside him. He was a tall man but his body was shrunken with age. Yet neither his age nor the fall from a horse which left him a cripple had taken from him the distinction of his bearing.

It was a little before sundown when these two men arrived at Swan Tavern, and on its steps met and greeted each other. The man who had arrived in the gig was Patrick Henry, the "Son of Thunder," come to oppose the Constitution. The man helped out of the phaeton and assisted up the steps was Edmund Pendleton, its ardent supporter.

Ever since Henry's speech against the Stamp Act, both he and Pendleton had played a great part in the momentous history of their time. Now they were come to Richmond as delegates to the convention that was to decide whether Virginia would accept the Constitution which would change the United States from a mere league of independent states to a union.

Before the Revolution the American colonies had been isolated, one from another. The war had temporarily related them, and they had then formed themselves into a confederation of separate states. But their league had been a ship without a captain, for the confederation had no president and no real power. It could make laws but could not enforce them. It was helpless before the problems which crowded upon it. The states must pay off their debts, must establish credit, must have treaty relations with the rest of the world. Without any central authority this was impossible, and in many parts of the country liberty had become license. Europe laughed at the chaos in America. "Let us act as a nation!" George Washington had cried. "Let us have a government by which our lives, liberties and properties will be secured."

In this crisis a Congress met in Philadelphia to discuss how the new states might be saved from ruin.

The difficulties of the Congress were great; opinion in the various states was divided. There was the question of abolishing the slave trade. Washington had long said he was "principled against slavery," that he wanted to see it abolished, but that the "one proper and effectual mode by which this can be accomplished is by legislative authority." George Mason, author of Virginia's Bill of Rights, called it a "diabolical trade . . . a disgraceful thing in America." Virginia delegates to the Congress voted the immediate abolition of foreign slave trade. New Jersey, Pennsylvania, and Delaware voted with her. The other states all voted no. In order to get consent to the Constitution there had to be compromise. At any cost the new system must quickly be adopted, for the captainless ship was headed for the rocks. The compromise was made: "The Migration or Importation of such Persons as any of the States now existing shall think proper to admit, shall not be prohibited by the Congress prior to the year one thousand eight hundred and eight . . ." Importation of slaves might, therefore, continue for twenty years more. This contented the rice and cotton planters of the deep South and those New England shippers engaged in importing slaves from Africa.

But of all the difficulties before the Congress, the most troublesome had been the problem of combining States' Rights with a strong central government.

Now at last the work was done. The Constitution was in process of being submitted to the states. Eight had already accepted it, though in Massachusetts it had won by a narrow margin. One more state was necessary for ratification. And in that June when on the Virginia plantations drought was killing the young tobacco plants, New York, New Hampshire, and Virginia were to debate on the Constitution and to make their decision.

Patrick Henry, though his affection and regard for Washington were "unalterable," was determined to fight against this system of government which Washington thought held the only salvation for the states. When Henry had gone home to Hanover after the first Continental Congress, the neighbors had crowded about, asking who was the greatest man at the Congress, and Henry had replied that for wisdom and solid judgment George Washington was the greatest man on the floor. Yet now Henry could not follow the judgment of this man whom he so admired.

Of the Virginians who had been delegates to that first Congress, Peyton Randolph, of the "Roman spirit," and Richard Bland, the "Antiquary," were dead. Of that group who had ridden up to Philadelphia to represent Virginia at the First Continental Congress, three more did not appear at the Convention in Richmond which was to vote on the New Constitution. Jefferson was in Europe. Richard Lee remained on his plantation, and Washington awaited the result at Mount Vernon. Of the original company only Henry, Pendleton, and Harrison were in Richmond now, but the great lawyers, George Wythe and John Marshall, were present, as were George Mason, Light-Horse Harry Lee, and two young men—James Madison and James Monroe.

The Constitution was debated in Richmond for three weeks. Patrick Henry spoke almost every day; often two or three times a day.

"I am but a poor individual," he said, "but I speak the language of thousands." To Henry's mind the new system would rob the states of their rights. "You will sip sorrow," he said, "if you give away your rights. . . . It is said that this Constitution has beautiful features, but . . . they appear to me horrible, frightful. Among other deformities is an awful squinting. It squints toward monarchy. Your president may easily become king . . . He will be a man of ambition and abilities, how easy for him to render himself absolute . . . we shall have a king . . ." Yes, the Constitution "squints toward monarchy."

During this speech Henry's eyes, sweeping the crowded hall, fell upon his son. Henry knew that he must have come with news from home, and he paused to ask a friend seated near him to take the boy out and question him. The boy's news was that his father's second wife had just given birth to a son. The cradle, as Hugh Grigsby had said, began to rock in Henry's house when he was eighteen; it continued rocking until his death at the age of sixty-three. So this latest birth was not startling news to Patrick Henry, and he continued his impassioned plea to "preserve the poor commonwealth of Virginia . . . to preserve," he told his audience, "your liberty and mine."

Day after day the debate went on. George Mason and James Monroe backed Henry. Madison, Marshall, Wythe, Light-Horse Harry Lee, and Edmund Pendleton argued for the Constitution.

And Washington waited at Mount Vernon. It was a choice, he felt, between anarchy and a "union under one federal head." The people must choose "whether they will be respectable and prosperous, or contemptible and miserable as a nation."

There came the last day of the debate before the vote was to be taken.

"The gentleman," Henry said, speaking of Madison, whose part in the drafting of the Constitution had been great, "the gentleman has told you of the numerous blessings which he imagines will be the result of this system. I see the awful immensity of the dangers with which it is pregnant. I see it. I feel it. When I see beyond the horizon that bounds human eyes . . . and see those intelligent beings which inhabit the ethereal mansions . . . I am led to believe that much will depend on what we now decide . . ."

A violent storm, ending the long drought, broke into Henry's speech. One who was present says that it shook the whole building, and that the spirits Henry had called seemed to come at his bidding. "It grew dark. The doors came to with a rebound like a peal of musketry. The windows rattled. The huge wood structure rocked. The rain fell from the eaves in torrents which were dashed against the window panes. The thunder roared, the lightning flashed."

But the "Son of Thunder" did not pause in his eloquent pleading. . . .

The next day the vote was taken. Henry had spoken with all his old magic. He had carried men on the tide of his profound sincere feeling. But he had been answered. And over the Convention there had hovered the spirit of the man who waited at Mount Vernon.

"We are either a united people, or we are not," Washington had insisted. "If the former, let us in all matters of general concern act as a nation which has a national character to support."

When the vote of the Richmond Convention was counted, the majority was not large; it was only ten. But that majority agreed with Washington that the world must not think that "we are a nation to-day, and thirteen States to-morrow. For who would treat with us on such terms?"

Patrick Henry, for the first time, had lost. But now that it was settled, he said, all must cherish the Constitution and give it a fair chance.

Yet he had not really lost. For certain amendments safeguarding the liberty of the individual states were to be added. And Virginia had still further qualified her vote by declaring the right to secede if ever she should feel her liberty to be threatened.

Pendleton, rising on his crutches, dissolved the Convention, in a voice tremulous with emotion. "We are brothers," he said, "we are Virginians. Our common object is the good of the country. . . ."

So, at Richmond beside the rushing waters of James River, Virginia voted for the Constitution and the Union.

Manasseh Cutler

In his career as a statesman, Manasseh Cutler consolidated a host of knowledges—he was a minister and a botanist, skilled in law and medicine, science and politics. He consummated a million-dollar real estate deal. His lifetime, from 1743 to 1823, spanned the crucial birth years of this republic, and his greatest contribution to his young country took place when the slavery issue was beginning to shake America's foundations.

Cutler helped formulate the Northwest Ordinance of 1787, which prohibited slavery "forever" in five states. Further, its third article promised that "Religion, morality and knowledge being necessary to good government and the happiness of mankind, schools and the means of education shall forever be encouraged."

The groundwork and the implications of the Northwest Ordinance are discussed by Joseph B. Clark, a well-known minister, as a compelling influence on our territorial system and on the leavening of the entire nation.

The Northwest Territory

BY JOSEPH B. CLARK

NEXT to the Declaration of Independence and the Constitution of the United States, no early event in American history is more significant or far-reaching in its influence than the famous Ordinance of 1787. The Declaration severed connection with the Mother Country. The Constitution laid the basis of a new confederation. The Ordinance was the beginning of government under the Territorial system. It applied specifically to the "Territory Northwest of the Ohio River," including the present States of Ohio, Indiana, Illinois, Michigan and Wisconsin.

No one man has a clearer claim to honor as the promoter of that

epoch-making ordinance than Manasseh Cutler. Born in Massachusetts, by turns a storekeeper, lawyer, clergyman, physician,
army-chaplain, an author of astronomical, botanical, and medical
treatises; a pioneer, a State legislator and member of Congress;
honored by Washington with a commission as Judge of the
Supreme Court of Ohio, which he declined, and rounding out
his busy life as a Congregational pastor in Eastern Massachusetts,
for the better part of seventy years, no finer illustration of that
New England vigor and versatility, to which the new country
stands so deeply indebted, could possibly be named.

It was as a member of the Ohio Company of 1786 that, with
prodigious energy, he raised and led a resolute band into Southeastern Ohio, after obtaining from the National Government the
grant of a million acres of land in the Northwest Territory, and
the passage of the Ordinance of 1787. Then and there the first
step in national expansion was taken which was to end only at
the Pacific. It is not too much to claim that the Ordinance of 1787
was the birth of American Nationalism. Yet it is doubtful if even
Mannasseh Cutler, seer as he was, had more than the dimmest
vision of the future of the Northwest Territory. . . .

A tract of 250,000 square miles, lying, wedge-shaped, between
the Great Lakes and the Mississippi and Ohio rivers, suddenly
opened its wide doors and invited the world to enter. The immediate government was Territorial with certain provisions for
future Statehood. Slavery was peremptorily forbidden by the
Ordinance. Vital to the future as this prohibition may have been,
there was another condition, "at least equally potential," namely,
"the guarantee that these new national possessions should not
be governed as independent provinces" but should be treated as
nascent States. Here was the initial of that policy, now familiar
to every American schoolboy, under which one Territory after
another has cast off its swaddling bands, and made good its claim
to full Statehood, until the raw material of States has become
practically exhausted. . . .

Early in 1788, a company of New England pioneers set out for
the Muskingum, headed by General Putnam of Revolutionary
fame. A little later, they were joined by Dr. Manasseh Cutler,
another leader who performed most of the journey in a sulky in
less than thirty days. Their course took them along the military
road across Pennsylvania and over the Alleghenies. They were
mostly soldiers, going West to draw their pay for military serv-

ices, in the shape of Ohio lands. Upon reaching the Youghiogheny they went into winter quarters, and waited for spring, before continuing the journey by water. Here they built a barge and christened it the *Mayflower*. It was the second of its name, and its builders had inherited something of the spirit of the Plymouth pilgrims. Reaching Fort Harmar on the 7th of April, 1788, they landed, forty-eight persons in all, and the new settlement of Ohio began.

It was a propitious beginning. "Respect for law, reverence toward God, love of country, unshaken faith in their own ability to do whatever they set their hands to, distinguished one and all."

Two of their first acts were to stake out a parsonage lot and to set apart two townships for a University. Before the end of June they had fixed on a name for the new city, calling it Marietta after Marie Antoinette and in gratitude for what France had done for America in the late war; and on the Fourth of July they celebrated Independence with a procession, speeches, and a barbecue. Their first county, which took in about one half of the present State, they named after Washington.

The chief peril of the colony came from the Indians who resented the advent of white faces on their ancestral hunting-grounds, and it required seven years of fighting, with the cost of many valuable lives, to secure a treaty with the natives, by which about two thirds of the State of Ohio was thrown open for peaceful settlement.

Meanwhile, in 1796, Moses Cleaveland and a company of about fifty persons reached Western Reserve on the shore of Lake Erie. Its settlement, however, proceeded slowly, owing to the continuing title of Connecticut, which was not considered as good as that of the United States. Later, Connecticut surrendered all claims to Western lands, and the settlement of the Erie shore began in earnest. Thus hopeful beginnings were made in Northeast and Southeast Ohio. Virginia had reserved certain lands between the Scioto and the Little Miami, known as the "Virginia Military District," which was being settled at this time by emigration from Kentucky and Virginia. Hence it happens that in different quarters of the State there began, and continues to this day, a marked distinction in the manners and customs of the people.

At the end of ten years from the passage of the Ordinance of 1787, there was a thin fringe of villages along the north bank of the Ohio with a white population of about 5,000, and these were the elements of a great State that was to be. Now began to be realized the beneficent provisions of the Ordinance. No slavery could enter, but "religion, morality, and the happiness of mankind" was "forever" to be encouraged. Nathan Dane and Manasseh Cutler built better than they knew when insisting upon these conditions, for no State ever began life under a grander charter, and, to their honor, let it be remembered that the first settlers of Ohio believed in and guarded these provisions, incorporating them, with the utmost vigilance, in the State constitutions of 1802 and 1851.

Conciliation

Party feeling in America had been at fever pitch for three years preceding the Presidential election of 1800. The Federalist party had attempted to legislate the opposition out of existence, but they lost the decision. Then, since the two Republican candidates, Thomas Jefferson and Aaron Burr, received an equal number of votes, the Federalist-dominated House of Representatives had to choose between them. A deadlock ensued, but a trend toward Burr began to develop. Behind the scenes Alexander Hamilton exerted his influence in favor of Jefferson, and in February, after thirty-six ballots, Jefferson emerged the winner.

The conciliatory tone of Jefferson's inaugural address, and the wise policies that he pursued, helped heal the bitterness of Federalists and Republicans alike. When he ran again for president in 1804, he was overwhelmingly reelected. Carl Van Doren, one of America's foremost historians and authors, brings to life the inaugural ceremony of 1801, in which Jefferson pledged himself to foster liberty, union and democracy.

Jefferson's Inaugural Address

BY CARL VAN DOREN

ON MARCH 4, 1801 Washington was not a city except in name and in hope. The Capitol and the White House were still unfinished. Pennsylvania Avenue, leading from one to the other, was a muddy road through an alder swamp. The town, what there was of it, looked less like a nation's capital than like a raw and not too prosperous real estate development.

But there was an idea back of this. The new nation wanted a new capital to grow up, as people said, with the country. And now the people had elected a new president who seemed to them to face the future as the new Capitol did.

He was Thomas Jefferson, who had written the Declaration of Independence twenty-five years before. Jefferson still believed that all men were created equal.

A good many Americans had in 1801 come to believe that this was a mere theory. The Federalists, the party in power, had recently seemed to be more interested in making the government strong than in keeping the people free. They had passed laws abridging the rights of free speech and a free press. But the people, resenting this, had overwhelmed the Federalists in the recent presidential election. A new people's party had elected Jefferson, the Republican [later Democratic] Party's founder and leader.

John Adams, the retiring President, was so much chagrined that he could not bear to see his successor inaugurated. Adams had slipped out of Washington in his coach at four o'clock that morning.

Across the square from the Capitol, on this bright March 4, 1801, was Conrad's boarding-house, where Jefferson lived. A company of militia artillery was drawn up in front of the door.

At noon Jefferson came out with a few friends. He was very tall and slender. His reddish hair was beginning to turn gray. He was plainly dressed in an ordinary coat, with green knee-breeches and gray woolen stockings. To the sound of guns fired by the artillery company, he walked with a lounging, unceremonious gait across the square to the completed north wing of the Capitol, where the Senate was sitting.

The senators were there, and the members of the House of Representatives had come in from their temporary quarters. The newly-elected Vice-President, Aaron Burr of New York, as president of the Senate, was in the chair. At his left sat John Marshall of Virginia, newly appointed Chief Justice of the United States Supreme Court. Marshall and Burr heartily disliked each other. Both disliked Jefferson, and Jefferson disliked both of them. But today Burr courteously gave up the vice-president's chair to Jefferson, and took another seat at his right. . . .

The Senate Chamber was full of animosities. Party spirit was still high and hot, after a campaign fought with terrible bitterness, political and personal. To many, the election of Jefferson seemed very close to a second revolution. The Federalists present were convinced that the government of their country had passed into the control of the rabble, led by a demagogue, and the new party had still to prove that they could safeguard liberty and yet prevent disorder.

In the circumstances, Jefferson was expected to speak like a triumphant and scornful revolutionary. But it was no partisan speech that the new chief executive made. He spoke merely as an American to and for all Americans:

Friends and Fellow-Citizens: . . . During the contest of opinion through which we have passed, the animation of discussions and of exertions has sometimes worn an aspect which might impose on strangers unused to think freely and to speak and write what they think; but this being now decided by the voice of the nation, announced according to the rules of the Constitution, all will, of course, arrange themselves under the will of the law, and unite in common efforts for the common good. All, too, will bear in mind this sacred principle, that though the will of the majority is in all cases to prevail, that will to be rightful must be reasonable; that the minority possess their equal rights, which equal law must protect, and to violate would be oppression. Let us, then, fellow-citizens, unite with one heart and one mind. Let us restore to social intercourse that harmony and affection without which liberty and even life itself are but dreary things. . . .

But every difference of opinion is not a difference of principle. We have called by different names brethren of the same principle. We are all Republicans, we are all Federalists. . . .

I know, indeed, that some honest men fear that a republican government cannot be strong, that this Government is not strong enough; but would the honest patriot, in the full tide of successful experiment, abandon a government which has so far kept us free and firm on the theoretic and visionary fear that this Government, the world's best hope, may by possibility want energy to preserve itself? I trust not. I believe this, on the contrary, the strongest Government on earth. I believe it the only one where every man, at the call of the law, would fly to the standard of the law, and would meet invasions of the public order as his own personal concern. . . .

Let us, then, with courage and confidence pursue our own Federal and Republican principles, our attachment to union and representative government. . . .

These principles form the bright constellation which has gone before us and guided our steps through an age of revolution and reformation. The wisdom of our sages and the blood of our heroes have been devoted to their attainment. They should be the creed of our political faith, the text of civic instruction, the touchstone by which to try the services of those we trust; and should we wander from them in moments of error or of alarm, let us hasten to retrace our steps and to regain the road which alone leads to peace, liberty, and safety.

I repair, then, fellow-citizens, to the post you have assigned me. . . . I ask so much confidence only as may give firmness and effect to the legal administration of your affairs. I shall often go wrong through defect of judgment. When right, I shall often be thought wrong by those whose positions will not command a view of the whole ground. I ask your indulgence for my own errors, which will never be intentional, and your support against the errors of others, who may condemn what they would not if seen in all its parts. . . .

Relying, then, on the patronage of your good will, I advance with obedience to the work, ready to retire from it whenever you become sensible how much better choice is in your power to make. And may that Infinite Power which rules the destinies of the universe lead our councils to what is best, and give them a favorable issue for your peace and prosperity.

When Thomas Jefferson ended his address, he turned to Chief Justice Marshall, who administered the oath of office. Then without any further ceremony, Jefferson walked with his friends back across the square to his boarding-house.

There is no use claiming that Jefferson's wise words about unity of spirit did away with party politics. The country during his administration was very much alive, very much divided on national aims and on the best means of achieving them. Where there is life in a democracy, there is difference of opinion. But the American government under Jefferson continued to be free and firm, in spite of disagreements among its citizens.

For when Jefferson said: "We are all Republicans, we are all Federalists," he was saying only what we are still saying: We are all Americans.

Uncle Tom's Cabin

Like all the Beechers, Harriet Beecher Stowe was early preoccupied with religious and humanitarian problems. After her marriage in 1836, she absorbed much of the anti-slavery sentiment flourishing at the colleges where her husband, Calvin E. Stowe, taught Biblical literature—particularly at Bowdoin College in Maine. Her son, Charles Edward, recalls in the next passage how his mother's strong feelings on abolition crystallized in Uncle Tom's Cabin, *written in answer to a friend's challenge. Despite the novel's melodrama and sentimentality, its impact was so tremendous that President Lincoln later greeted Mrs. Stowe as "the little woman who wrote the book that caused this great war."*

The Rushing of a Mighty Wind

BY CHARLES EDWARD STOWE

AFTER the passage of the Fugitive Slave Act, letter after letter was received by Mrs. Stowe in Brunswick from Mrs. Edward Beecher and other friends, describing the heart-rending scenes which were the inevitable results of the enforcement of this terrible law. Cities were more available for the capturing of escaped slaves than the country, and Boston, which claimed to have been the cradle of liberty, opened her doors to the slave-hunters. The sorrow and anguish caused thereby no pen could describe. . . .

Mr. Edward Beecher, in a letter to Mrs. Stowe's son, writing of this period, says:—

I had been nourishing an anti-slavery spirit since Lovejoy was murdered for publishing in his paper articles against slavery and intemperance, when our home was in Illinois. These terrible things which were going on in Boston were well calculated to rouse up this spirit. What can I do? I thought. Not much myself, but I know one who can. So I wrote several letters to your mother, telling her of various heart-rending events caused by the enforcement of the Fugitive Slave Law. I remember distinctly saying in one of them, "Now, Hattie, if I could use a pen as you can, I would write something that would make this whole nation feel what an accursed thing slavery is." . . . When we lived in Boston your mother often visited us. . . . Several numbers of *Uncle Tom's Cabin* were written in your Uncle Edward's study at these times, and read to us from the manuscripts.

A member of Mrs. Stowe's family well remembers the scene in the little parlor in Brunswick when the letter alluded to was received. Mrs. Stowe herself read it aloud to the assembled family, and when she came to the passage, "I would write something that would make this whole nation feel what an accursed thing slavery is," Mrs. Stowe rose up from her chair, crushing the letter in her hand, and with an expression on her face that stamped itself on the mind of her child, said: "I will write something. I will if I live." . . .

It was in the month of February [1851] . . . that Mrs. Stowe was seated at communion service in the college church at Brunswick. Suddenly like the unrolling of a picture, the scene of the death of Uncle Tom passed before her mind. So strongly was she affected that it was with difficulty she could keep from weeping aloud. Immediately on returning home she took pen and paper and wrote out the vision which had been, as it were, blown into her mind as by the rushing of a mighty wind. Gathering her family about her she read what she had written. Her two little ones of ten and twelve years of age broke into convulsions of weeping, one of them saying through his sobs, "Oh, mamma! slavery is the most cruel thing in the world." Thus Uncle Tom was ushered into the world, and it was . . . a cry, an immediate, an involuntary expression of deep, impassioned feeling. . . .

A few years afterwards Mrs. Stowe, writing of this story, said, "This story is to show how Jesus Christ, who liveth and was dead, and now is alive and forevermore, has still a mother's love for the poor and lowly, and that no man can sink so low but that Jesus Christ will stoop to take his hand. Who so low, who so poor, who so despised as the American slave? . . . He can do nothing, possess nothing, acquire nothing, but what must belong to his master. Yet even to this slave Jesus Christ stoops, from where he sits at the right hand of the Father, and says, 'Fear not, thou whom man despiseth, for I am thy brother. Fear not, for I have redeemed thee, I have called thee by my name, thou art mine.'"

Uncle Tom's Cabin is a work of religion; the fundamental principles of the gospel applied to the burning question of Negro slavery. It sets forth those principles of the Declaration of Independence that made Jefferson, Hamilton, Washington, and Patrick Henry anti-slavery men; not in the language of the philosopher, but in a series of pictures. Mrs. Stowe spoke to the understanding and moral sense through the imagination. . . . till human hearts could endure it no longer.

Robert E. Lee

Few men in our history so captivate the imagination as does Robert E. Lee. His was the dilemma of having to choose between conflicting loyalties, and he emerged as the American who "lost a war and won immortality." In the capsule biography which follows—it was originally published by the John Hancock Mutual Life Insurance Company—and in Lee's own exhortation for faithfulness to duty, we see elements of his creed of life.

He lost a war and won immortality

Even among the free, it is not always easy to live together. There came a time, less than a hundred years ago, when the people of this country disagreed so bitterly among themselves that some of them felt they could not go on living with the rest.

A test of arms was made to decide whether Americans should remain one nation or become two. The armies of those who believed in two nations were led by a man named Robert E. Lee.

What about Lee? What kind of man was he who nearly split the history of the United States down the middle and made two separate books of it?

They say you had to see him to believe that a man so fine could exist. He was handsome. He was clever. He was brave. He was gentle. He was generous and charming, noble and modest, admired and beloved. He had never failed at anything in his upright soldier's life. He was a born winner, this Robert E. Lee.

Except for once. In the greatest contest of his life, in the war between the South and the North, Robert E. Lee lost.

Now there were men who came with smouldering eyes to Lee and said: "Let's not accept this result as final. Let's keep our anger alive. Let's be grim and unconvinced, and wear our bitterness like a medal. You can be our leader in this."

112

But Lee shook his head at those men. "Abandon your animosities," he said, "and make your sons Americans."

And what did he do himself when his war was lost? He took a job as president of a tiny college, with forty students and four professors, at a salary of $1500 a year. He had commanded thousands of young men in battle. Now he wanted to prepare a few hundred of them for the duties of peace. So the countrymen of Robert E. Lee saw how a born winner loses, and it seemed to them that in defeat he won his most lasting victory.

There is an art of losing, and Robert E. Lee is its finest teacher. In a democracy, where opposing viewpoints regularly meet for a test of ballots, it is good for all of us to know how to lose occasionally, how to yield peacefully, for the sake of freedom. Lee is our master in this. The man who fought against the Union showed us what unity means.

Faithful to Duty

BY ROBERT E. LEE

NEARLY one hundred years ago, there was a day of remarkable gloom and darkness, still known as the Dark Day—a day when the light of the sun was slowly extinguished as if by an eclipse. The Legislature of Connecticut was in session, and as the members saw the unexpected and unaccountable darkness coming on, they shared in the general awe and terror. It was supposed by many that the last day, the day of judgment had come. Someone, in the consternation of the hour, moved an adjournment. Then there arose an old Puritan legislator, Davenport Stanford, who said that if the last day had come he desired to be found at his post of duty, and therefore moved that candles be brought so that the House could proceed with its business. So, my son, when in the conflict of life the cloud and the darkness come, stand unflinchingly by your post; remain faithful to the discharge of your duty.

"The Nation Is Immortal"

"Of all great Americans," says Carl Van Doren, "Lincoln has been the one most honored by American poets."

The name of Walt Whitman, in particular, is linked with that of the Great Emancipator. Although the two never met formally, a love of freedom, union, and democracy bound them together, and in chance street meetings in Washington while Lincoln was President, they would exchange bows. In "O Captain! My Captain!" and the stirring "When Lilacs Last in the Door-yard Bloomed," Whitman has paid eloquent tribute to Lincoln's role in our history. Less well known is this prose passage from his memoirs.

Lincoln, the Conservator

BY WALT WHITMAN

April 16, 1865—I find in my notes of this time, this passage on the death of Abraham Lincoln: He leaves for America's history and biography, so far, not only its most dramatic reminiscence— he leaves, in my opinion, the greatest, best, most characteristic, artistic, moral personality. Not but that he had faults, and show'd them in the Presidency; but honesty, goodness, shrewdness, conscience, and (a new virtue, unknown to other lands, and hardly yet really known here, but the foundation and tie of all, as the future will grandly develop,) UNIONISM, in its truest and amplest sense, form'd the hard-pan of his character. These he seal'd with his life. The tragic splendor of his death, purging, illuminating all, throws round his form, his head, an aureole that will remain and grow brighter through time, while history lives, and love of country lasts. By many has this Union been help'd; but if one name, one man, must be pick'd out, he, most of all, is

114

the conservator of it, to the future. He was assassinated—but the Union is not assassinated—*ça ira!* One falls, and another falls. The soldier drops, sinks like a wave—but the ranks of the ocean eternally press on. Death does its work, obliterates a hundred, a thousand—President, general, captain, private—but the Nation is immortal.

Joined by Rails

Before the Civil War, the West beyond the Mississippi had been opened up by explorers; next there followed a slow stream of pioneers, scouts, fur trappers, hunters, traders, and then settlers. And side by side with them rode the missionaries, who came to labor in their midst, building churches, courthouses, and schools.

With the population rush to California, there arose a pressing need for a railroad connection to link the Atlantic and the Pacific; and when the Central Pacific and the Union Pacific railroads were finally joined at Promontory Point, Utah, on May 10, 1869, the entire continent rejoiced.

Carl Van Doren here presents Thomas Hart Benton's fervent plea for railway expansion, and then describes the celebration which marked the end of the frontier era and the emergence of a new spirit of union.

The Transcontinental Railway

BY CARL VAN DOREN

THOMAS HART BENTON was a United States Senator from Missouri in the days of the covered wagon and the California Gold Rush.

Senator Benton seemed visionary to many people then, because he fought for something that we now take for granted. He fought for a transcontinental railroad—beyond Chicago and St. Louis to the Pacific. And with far-reaching vision he foresaw that railways from coast to coast would some day join the seas which separate America from those older worlds, the world of Europe and the world of Asia.

In a Convention Hall in St. Louis Senator Benton spoke prophetic words:

116

Three and a half centuries ago the great Columbus. . . . in the year 1492 departed from Europe to arrive in the East by going to the West. It was a sublime conception. . . . Two continents, not dreamed of before, arrested his voyage to India.

In the beginning, and in barbarous ages, the sea was a barrier to the intercourse of nations. It separated nations. . . . Mechanical genius, in inventing the ship, converted that barrier into a facility. The land and continents became the obstructions. . . . Now in our day, mechanical genius has again triumphed over the obstacles of nature. . . .

The steam car has worked upon the land. . . . among enlightened nations the miracle which the ship in barbarous ages worked upon the ocean. The land has now become the facility for the most distant communications. . . .

We hold the intervening land; we hold the obstacle which stopped Columbus; we are in the line between Europe and Asia. We have it in our power to remove that obstacle. . . . and to carry him on to his land of promise and hope, with a rapidity, a precision, and a safety unknown to all ocean navigation. A king and a queen started him upon his great enterprise. It lies in the hands of a republic to complete it. It lies in our hands.

We the people of the United States, of this first half of this nineteenth century, let us raise ourselves. Let us rise to the grandeur of the occasion. Let us complete the grand design of Columbus, by putting Europe and Asia into communication, and that to our advantage, through the heart of our country. Let us give to his ships, converted into cars, a continued course, unknown to all former times. Let us make the iron road, and make it from sea to sea.

Let us now, in this convention, rise above everything sectional, personal, local. Let us beseech the national legislature to build the great road upon the great national line which unites Europe and Asia—the line which will find, on our continent, the Bay of San Francisco at one end, and the national metropolis and great commercial emporiums at the other.

And let it be adorned with its crowning honor, the colossal statue of the great Columbus, whose design it accomplishes, hewn from the granite mass of a peak of the Rocky Mountains, overlooking the road—the mountain itself the pedestal, and the statue a part of the mountain, pointing with outstretched hand to the western horizon, and saying to the flying messenger: There is the East. There is India.

Thus Benton made his great plea for a railroad across America. We take such railroads as a matter of course today, but twenty years passed between the day of that speech and the day when the first railway line all the way from coast to coast was finished. Mountains had to be vanquished; deserts defeated; rivers spanned. Foot by hard-won foot, mile by back-breaking mile, the railroad crept from Omaha west, and from Sacramento east.

Then at Promontory Point at the northern end of the shores of Great Salt Lake came the meeting of the lines. It was a cold bright day in May, 1869. Two trains, one from the east, one from the west faced each other across a little gap in the track. About six hundred people were looking on. Officials from New York and San Francisco. Workers swarming on top of the two trains. A few Indians, Mexicans. Some soldiers in uniform. A photographer ready with his cameras. And telegraphers at their keys, ready to flash the news to both oceans.

The final tie was laid—polished laurel from California, with a silver plate commemorating the day. Chinese workmen in their best clothes brought up the last rail and put it in place. A clergyman from Massachusetts offered an invocation. The band of the 21st Infantry played *America*.

And then the last spike, of California gold. Leland Stanford, governor of the state and president of the Central Pacific, stood there, frock-coated, high-hatted, bearded, with a silver sledge. The telegrapher's hand was on his key. At each blow on the last spike he was to send a signal, so that the whole nation could share the ceremony.

Governor Stanford swung his sledge—and missed. Men who had driven spikes over all the miles from Omaha and Sacramento roared with laughter. But the alert telegrapher sent the signal anyway. The driving went on. Thomas Durant of New York, representing the Union Pacific, wearing a velvet coat, also swung the sledge. The two locomotives drew slowly up till their cowcatchers almost touched. The engineers climbed out and shook hands. Then each of them broke a bottle of champagne over the other's engine. The crowd shouted, the band played, the locomotive whistles drowned out all the other sounds.

But there was more to the ceremony than the small crowd at Promontory Point could see. For the telegraph made the ceremony nation-wide. At the signal a magnetic ball dropped on the pole on the dome of the Capitol at Washington. Bells rang in Independence Hall in Philadelphia. There was a salute of a hundred guns in City Hall Park in New York. In Chicago crowds fell into a volunteer procession, seven miles long. San Francisco, which had already been celebrating for two days, carried an exultant banner through the streets saying that "California Annexes the United States."

This was probably the most important and most exciting nonmilitary ceremony in the whole history of the American people. For it was railroads that did most to make the states, from east to west, united. Those early dreamers are gone but the railroads remain.

Ulysses S. Grant

"Nothing would afford me greater happiness [than] to know that, as I believe will be the case, at some future day, the nations of the earth will agree upon some sort of Congress which will take cognizance of international questions of difficulty, and whose decisions will be as binding as the decisions of our Supreme Court are upon us. It is a dream of mine that some such solution may be."

These words were spoken by a man who had achieved fame as a warrior, the man who led the Union forces to victory in the Civil War, and later became the chief executive of his nation. Paul H. Buck's prize-winning study, The Road to Reunion, *a social history of the United States during the contentious years of the Reconstruction period, explains how Ulysses S. Grant came to be known in the annals of America as a pacificator.*

The Pacificator

BY PAUL H. BUCK

GRANT was still a soldier when in 1868 he phrased a nation's yearning in his memorable "Let us have peace." The campaign for that elusive good, however, proved more difficult than the military problems of the war. From this point of view, his presidency was a failure, the magnanimity of Appomattox giving way to the excesses of Reconstruction. But in retirement the sturdy qualities of the soldier reappeared. There was something about Grant which suggested indifference to petty quarrels, the bigness of a man who once having fought deplores the indulgence of continued strife. His life closed as did his *Memoirs,* with a fervent prayer for good feeling between the sections. Gradually succumbing to an incurable disease, his tranquil and manly fortitude at Mount McGregor won the sympathy of the nation. Throughout

120

his suffering he gave evidence of a hearty and unreserved friendliness toward those who had fought against the Union. The magnanimity of his last words revealed a spirit which went far in composing lingering differences.

He would not have been displeased, therefore, had he been able to witness the union of the sections around his outworn body. The entire country felt the bereavement of his loss. Distinguished Confederate generals wearing gray sashes served as pallbearers with leading officers of the Union army. The spectacle was striking and sincere. One who was too young to know firsthand the story of the war has left his impressions of the scene in a leading New York hotel the night before the public funeral:

> The corridors were thronged with well known veterans of both armies, but what one chiefly noted in the great gathering was that while Union men met Union men like old friends, and Confederates met Confederates in the same manner, Union men and Confederates greeted one another like long-lost brothers. I lingered about for hours. . . . [When] I went home, it was with a feeling of pride I shall never forget. I had just witnessed a great sight—the kindly, open hearted meeting of men who had fought bitterly against one another.

It was no "sentimental effusion," therefore, but demonstrated sincerity which led representative men to interpret "the memorable pageant at the tomb of the great soldier" as the "virtual conclusion of sectional animosity in America."

If the North welcomed the idea of Confederate pallbearers, the South showed an equal willingness to bring tribute to her conqueror. The generous victor of Appomattox was remembered, his faults forgiven. One writer who may be taken as representative recalled Grant as the savior of the Union, in which capacity the South was now as grateful for his work as was the North. The manifestation of sympathy on the part of Southerners, it was generally observed, was spontaneous evidence of their loyalty, if not of their emotional attachment, to the government under which they lived.

A stately marble mausoleum now occupies a majestic site overlooking the Hudson. On its southern wall are inscribed the words by which its honored inmate is best remembered, LET US HAVE PEACE. Grant's wish was realized in his death. He entered the traditions of his country as a pacificator.

Division and Reunion

Factional feeling and the wounds of war were to last a long time following the North's defeat of the South. But the healing process was helped in strange and unexpected ways. In his book, Division and Reunion, *Woodrow Wilson describes an event that forwarded the cause of nationalism by giving Northerners and Southerners alike cause for national pride and a spirit of reconciliation. This was the International Industrial Exposition of 1876, marking the country's one-hundredth birthday.*

The Centennial Year

BY WOODROW WILSON

Soon after his inauguration, President Hayes wisely ordered the withdrawal of the federal troops from the South; and the Republican governments of South Carolina and Louisiana—upon whose *de facto* authority his election had turned—were quietly superseded by the Democratic governments which had all along claimed the right to occupy their places. In Florida, too, decisions of the courts effected the same result. . . .

May 10, 1876, had witnessed the opening of an International Industrial Exhibition at Philadelphia, which had been arranged in celebration of the centennial anniversary of the adoption of the Declaration of Independence. It was a fit symbol and assurance of the settled peace and prosperity which were in store for the country in the future. All the great commercial and industrial nations were represented in its exhibits, among the rest, of course, England, whose defeat the Exhibition was planned to celebrate. Her presence made it also a festival of reconciliation. It spoke of peace and goodwill with all the world. It surely is not fanciful to regard it, besides, as a type and figure of the reconstruction and regeneration of the nation. The Union was now restored, not only to strength, but also to normal conditions of government. National parties once more showed a salutary balance of forces which promised to make sober the arbiter of future policies. It showed the economic resources of the South freed, like those of the North, for a rapid and unembarrassed development. The National spirit was aroused, and conscious now at last of its strength. The stage was cleared for the creation of a new nation.

Grover Cleveland

Grover Cleveland's trustworthiness and courage when he entered public life as a sheriff led to his election as mayor of Buffalo. Sometime later, while he served as Governor of New York, his proud independence, sound reforms, and immense capacity for work gained nationwide attention. In the face of Tammany opposition, the Democrats nominated Cleveland for president. He won, despite a notably vicious campaign, reflecting particularly on his private life.

As chief executive Cleveland held to his own precept: "A public office is a public trust." He discarded the recriminatory politics of previous administrations, selecting two renowned Southerners for his first Cabinet in 1885. Robert McElroy, in his comprehensive biography, Grover Cleveland, The Man and the Statesman, *describes the implications of this historic decision.*

Cleveland Selects a Cabinet

BY ROBERT McELROY

I⊤ HAS been said that a President is known by the appointments he makes. And this is partly true. A small President is likely to choose small men to surround him, unwilling to invite the cooperation of great minds, lest his own be dwarfed by comparison. As an appointing agent Mr. Cleveland was not inerrant, but his mistakes came from no such petty jealousies. The average of his appointments is high as compared with any executive of his time, nor did he in his choice of men make secret concessions to standards which he was unable to profess openly.

He began selecting a Cabinet as soon as the November elections were over, his plan being to allow the names of contemplated appointees to reach the public early, in order that there might be the fullest criticism before they were sent to the Senate for confirmation. Like Lincoln, he had directed his friends to make no bargains which would bind him if elected. Like Lincoln, when elected, he found that bargains had been made which he now felt in honor bound to recognize, even against his own desires. . . .

For two of the . . . cabinet posts, the Department of the Interior and the office of Attorney General, Mr. Cleveland turned to the ranks of the late Confederate Government, thereby emphasizing his determination that, so far as his Administration was concerned, there should no longer be a North and a South. Lucius Q. C. Lamar, his choice for Secretary of the Interior, had drafted the Mississippi Ordinance of Secession in 1861, and had served for two years in the Confederate Army. But he had been wise enough to recognize the end when it came, and in his services to his reunited country had won a position which entitled him to recognition as a representative of the new South. The announcement that his name was considered for such a post was a signal for a flood of protests. "As a Union soldier," wrote one protestant, ". . . I beg to remind the President-elect that the Pension Bureau, with its three hundred thousand pension claims of Union soldiers still unsettled, is in this department, and I can imagine what will be said all through the North and at every Grand Army Post over such a selection." The President-elect was himself quite able to imagine what would be said, but he was not thinking in terms of Grand Army posts, but of a nation reunited after civil war. Lamar remained on the slate, and, as Cabinet officer and later as a Supreme Court Judge, he fully justified the courageous independence which had given him his chance. Of him, Chief Justice Fuller declared: "His was the most suggestive mind that I ever knew."

In the selection of Augustus H. Garland as Attorney General, President Cleveland did even greater violence to the opinions of such men as could not forget, such victors as thought it wise to be ungenerous. Garland, once Governor of Arkansas and now a United States Senator, had been a member of the Confederate Congress. But, like Lamar, he had accepted the verdict of trial by combat, and had worked wisely and effectively toward a reunion of hearts, North and South. "To him," wrote fifty members of the Arkansas Legislature, "we are most indebted for our restoration to an equal place in the Union, and equal representation in the national councils." And Samuel J. Tilden emphasized his fitness for office by expressing the opinion that he ought not to be taken out of the Senate at the beginning of a Democratic administration. . . .

The oath of office was administered by Chief Justice Waite, who used for the ceremony the little Bible which Mr. Cleveland kept always at hand, and upon the fly-leaf of which appear the words: "My son, Stephen Grover Cleveland, from his loving Mother." Colonel Lamont once said that he had first seen this Bible in Mr. Cleveland's law office in Buffalo. Later it was kept on the bureau in his bedroom; but while he was President it occupied the upper left-hand drawer of the desk that was presented to the President of the United States by the Queen of England as a memento of the Sir John Franklin expedition to the Arctic regions. Before returning this precious book to the President, the Clerk of the Supreme Court entered this record on the fly-leaf: "It was used to administer the oath of office to Grover Cleveland, President of the United States, on the fourth of March, 1885."

Cardinal Gibbons

"Brothers we are, whatever may be our nationality, and brothers we shall remain."

Cardinal Gibbons made this comment in the context of a matter involving Roman Catholics of various nationalities. But he could just as well have said it to a group of laborers and industrial leaders, or to an inter-faith assemblage. The cardinal was extraordinarily talented, but perhaps his greatest gift lay in his appreciation of people and their problems. And this extended to their religion, whatever it might be. Certainly no Roman Catholic churchman in our history has done more to foster understanding between men and women of various faiths.

It was to the city of his birth—Baltimore—that the future cardinal returned, after schooling and military service, to render his signal contributions to American life. In his masterly Church and State in the United States, *Anson Phelps Stokes has caught the essence of the cardinal's humanity, and gives us a glimpse of his many interests.*

"Our Watchword: Loyalty to Church and Country"

BY ANSON PHELPS STOKES

WHEN he was eighteen, after the death of his father, his mother returned to the United States [from Ireland] and settled in New Orleans, where the future Cardinal Gibbons was a clerk in a grocery store. There, when twenty years of age, he entered the priesthood. He studied at St. Charles College and at St. Mary's Seminary in Baltimore. He was ordained in 1861, and was given charge of a mission in Maryland near Fort McHenry, where he served as a chaplain, ministering to Federals and Confederates alike. His sympathies were with the Union cause, but he had a warm affection for the Southern people and took no part in the contest. . . . His stay in North Carolina had a vital effect upon his life, especially because it brought him into contact with so many people who were not accustomed to the Catholic tradition. He preached in Masonic lodge rooms and courthouses, and even in Protestant churches when no Catholic church was available.

This close contact with the people in a typically American state with a dominantly Protestant population gave him an understanding of American conditions and points of view that was to prove invaluable. He attended the Vatican Council of 1870, and in keeping with most other American prelates he did not question the truth of papal infallibility, though he did doubt the wisdom of declaring it at that time.

His trip to Europe was specially important to him as showing the conflicts between Church and State under the monarchical system, and this increased his conviction that the American plan of Constitutional religious freedom was wiser. It received his earnest support throughout his life.

In 1872 he was made bishop of Richmond, and in 1875 he became archbishop coadjutor in Maryland, succeeding to the archepiscopate later the same year. The year was also notable for the publication of his *The Faith of Our Fathers,* a book of which 2,000,000 copies were sold in his lifetime, and which did much, by its reasonable and tolerant attitude, to commend the Church to the people of the United States. At the age of forty-three he began his career in Baltimore, which was to make him for nearly half a century not only the leading Roman Catholic figure in the United States but one of its most respected citizens.

The proximity of Baltimore to Washington helped Gibbons to become the intimate friends of Presidents Cleveland, Theodore Roosevelt, and Taft; and he had friendly relations with all the other American presidents during his lifetime. He was not a partisan in national affairs, but took the deepest interest in helping to create wise public opinion in important issues. For instance, in 1881 he issued a circular letter to the clergy of the diocese expressing horror at Garfield's assassination. In the same year, when the observance of Thanksgiving Day was still far from general, he issued what is believed to have been the first direction by a Catholic prelate in the United States for the day's observance. He also took a leading part in the establishment of the Catholic University at Washington, which he served as head from its beginning until his death.

In 1887, after going abroad to receive the red biretta at the hands of his sympathetic friend Leo XIII, he preached a sermon in Rome in which he declared that the great progress of the Catholic Church in this country was in large part due to the liberty guaranteed by the American Constitution. He expressed his gratitude at being the citizen of a country "where the civil government holds over us the aegis of its protection, without interfering with us in the legitimate exercise of our sublime mission as ministers of the gospel of Christ," and added: "Our country has liberty without license and authority without despotism."

On this visit he devoted much attention to securing ecclesiastical support for the labor movement. He was able, as a result of his influence, to receive the assurance that the Knights of Labor would not be condemned in the United States, and secured the lifting of the ban against them in Canada.

In the last decade of the nineteenth century . . . he rendered perhaps his most significant public service by leading the opposition to the so-called Cahensly movement, which advocated the appointment of bishops in this country on the basis of the nationality of the groups they were to serve. In a famous sermon delivered in Milwaukee in 1899 . . . he said:

> Woe to him, my brethren, who would destroy or impair the blessed harmony that reigns among us. Woe to him who would breed dissension among the leaders of Israel by introducing a spirit of nationalism into the camps of the Lord. Brothers we are, whatever may be our nationality, and brothers we shall remain; we will prove to our countrymen that the ties formed by grace and faith are stronger than flesh and blood. This is our watchword—Loyalty to God's Church and to our country—this is our religious and political creed and faith . . .

American Catholics and all patriots may well be proud of the great cardinal.

Some idea of Cardinal Gibbons' place in American life may be had from a study of the accounts of the celebration in Baltimore in 1911 of the jubilee of his cardinalate. At a public meeting in the largest hall of the city, addresses praising his services both to his country and to the cause of religion were made by such representative Americans as President Taft, ex-President Roosevelt, Senator and former Secretary of State Elihu Root, and the British ambassador, the Honorable James Bryce.

During the early part of the twentieth century he also rendered service of importance in helping to adjust the difficulties between the friars in the Philippines and the United States government. During World War I he was president of the National Catholic War Council, and though past eighty he gave his country active support. A noticeable fact throughout his life was his friendly relations with Protestant leaders and the great respect in which they held him though he was always entirely loyal to his own Church and its doctrines.

A characteristic story is told by a Catholic authority of a civic function in Baltimore when the cardinal and Bishop William Paret of the Episcopal Diocese of Maryland met. The question was raised by someone as to precedence. The difficulty was solved by the cardinal's saying, "My dear brother, we will walk together." If that spirit were more common many church problems in the United States would disappear.

"Touching Elbows and Hearts"

President Woodrow Wilson's genius lay partly in his ability to voice the idealism of American traditions. In an address delivered at Convention Hall, Philadelphia, on May 10, 1915, before a gathering of recently naturalized citizens, he appealed to all to dedicate the best of their spirit and their dreams to this nation, because "America must have this consciousness, that on all sides it touches elbows and touches hearts with all the nations of mankind."

United by Ideals

BY WOODROW WILSON

. . . You have just taken an oath of allegiance to the United States. Of allegiance to whom? Of allegiance to no one, unless it be to God—certainly not of allegiance to those who temporarily represent this great government. You have taken an oath of allegiance to a great ideal, to a great body of principles, to a great hope of the human race. You have said, "We are going to America not only to earn a living, not only to seek the things which it was more difficult to obtain where we were born, but to help forward the great enterprises of the human spirit—to let men know that everywhere in the world there are men who will cross strange oceans and go where a speech is spoken which is alien to them, if they can but satisfy their quest for what their spirits crave; knowing that whatever the speech, there is but one longing and utterance of the human heart, and that is liberty and justice." . . .

We came to America, either ourselves or in the persons of our ancestors, to better the ideals of men, to make them see finer things than they had seen before, to get rid of the things that

131

divide and to make sure of the things that unite. It was but an historical accident no doubt that this great country was called the "United States"; yet I am very thankful that it has that word "United" in its title, and the man who seeks to divide man from man, group from group, interest from interest in this great Union is striking at its very heart. . . .

You have come into this great nation voluntarily seeking something that we have to give, and all that we have to give is this: We cannot exempt you from work. No man is exempt from work anywhere in the world. We cannot exempt you from the strife and the heartbreaking burden of the struggle of the day—that is common to mankind everywhere; we cannot exempt you from the loads that you must carry. We can only make them light by the spirit in which they are carried. That is the spirit of hope, it is the spirit of liberty, it is the spirit of justice.

The Decision to End Segregation

*The blessings of liberty have, sometimes vigorously and some-
times haltingly, come to virtually all the inhabitants of this land.
A stubborn area in which we have yet to attain success is in
affording the full rights of citizenship to 15,000,000 Negro Americans, in the North as in the South. With these fellow-country-
men we have mocked America's declared belief in the equality
of men as children of God.*

*Since World War II, giant steps have been made, even to
federal civil rights legislation passed for the first time since the
Civil War. But the landmark of our times has been the Supreme
Court decision outlawing, as unconstitutional, segregation in the
public schools. The forces of disunity which loomed threaten-
ingly immediately following the decision, have, with the passing
of time, given way in many sections to the stronger forces of
good will and brotherhood. In a concise summing-up, Life Magazine shows us what went into the making of this historic decision.*

Momentous Reversal in the Court

*No state shall make or enforce any law which shall abridge the
privileges or immunities of citizens of the United States . . . —*
from the Fourteenth Amendment, adopted in 1868.

The Fourteenth Amendment, like all parts of the Constitution,
is open to interpretation by the Supreme Court. As the Court
interprets, so goes the law. But the interpretations of the Court
are not static; they change as the will of the people changes.
From the Reconstruction period onward for many years, the
Court repeatedly interpreted the Fourteenth Amendment to
mean that segregation in public schools was constitutional—provided that "separate but equal" facilities were available for

133

Negroes. This was emphatically the will of the white South, and the other sections of the country acquiesced. But in the 1930s the opinion of the north, east and west, a majority of the people, began to change. Thereupon the Court too began to change. From the late 1930s onward it handed down a series of decisions which chipped steadily away at segregation in the schools. On May 17, 1954, the ultimate was reached. Chief Justice Earl Warren, announcing the Court's unanimous view, held that segregation in public schools does violate the Fourteenth Amendment and must end.

The Supreme Court's decision brought an end to public school segregation in law but not by any means in fact. To hasten the day of actual integration, Negroes turned to prayer.

FOUR

The Common

Welfare

Iₙ a nation where men and women know themselves to be children of God, the duties and privileges inherent in "insuring the common welfare" must be a sacred principle. We have not always abided by this principle; we have denied some of the best things of life to minorities, to the poor, to the ill and infirm, and for long years to the women of this country. But in each generation, there have been far-sighted men and dedicated women to give new meaning to these great words from the Preamble to our Constitution.

"Remember the Ladies"

At least two generations before women's rights became a national issue, they were a lively topic in some of the more progressive households of the new Republic. How Abigail Adams raised and pursued the question with her famous, but sometimes irascible, husband, John, is related in their Familiar Letters *during the Revolution, by a descendant of that illustrious family, the noted Charles Francis Adams.*

A Disputed Question*

BY CHARLES FRANCIS ADAMS

Even in the earliest days of the republic, women's rights were a disputed question. Among the remarkable letters of Abigail Adams (1744-1818)—remarkable because they display her vital interest in the course of public events, her cleverness in the management of her husband's farm and property, her loving devotion to family and friends, her buoyant spirit in isolation and adversity—there are several which show how keenly she felt about the position of her sex. Heartened by the British evacuation of Boston, she wrote John Adams on March 31, 1776, how she longed to hear that the Congress had declared an independency. And she went on to say:

> In the new code of laws which I suppose it will be necessary for you to make, I desire you would remember the ladies, and be more generous to them than your ancestors. Do not put such unlimited power into the hands of the husbands. Remember all men would be tyrants if they could. If particular care is not paid to the ladies, we are determined to foment a rebellion, and

* Excerpted and condensed

will not hold ourselves bound by any laws in which we have no voice or representation. . . . Why, then, not put it out of the power of the vicious and the lawless to use us with cruelty and indignity with impunity? Men of sense in all ages abhor those customs which treat us only as vassals of your sex; regard us then as beings placed by Providence under your protection, and in imitation of the Supreme Being make use of that power only for our happiness.

Charmed by his wife's *gaiété de coeur,* John replied promptly and definitely on April 14:

As to your extraordinary code of laws, I cannot but laugh. We have been told that our struggle loosened the bonds of government everywhere; that children and apprentices were disobedient, that schools and colleges are grown turbulent; that Indians slighted their guardians, and negroes grew insolent to their masters. But your letter was the first intimation that another tribe, more numerous and powerful than the rest, were grown discontented. . . . Depend upon it, we know better than to repeal our masculine systems. Although they are in full force, you know they are little more than theory. We dare not exert our power in full latitude. . . . In practice you know we are the subjects. We have only the name of masters, and rather than give up this, which would completely subject us to the despotism of the petticoat, I hope General Washington and all our brave heroes would fight. . . .

Abigail apparently had the last word on May 7, when she wrote that it seemed ungenerous to proclaim peace and goodwill to men, emancipating all the nations, but at the same time retaining absolute power over women. She reminded him that arbitrary power, like all very hard things, was liable to be broken: "Notwithstanding all your wise laws and maxims, we have it in our power, not only to free ourselves, but to subdue our masters, and, without violence, throw both your natural and legal authority at our feet;—

'Charm by accepting, by submitting sway,
Yet have our humor most when we obey.' "

Pioneer in Civil Rights

American history is filled with unsung heroes; some of them we never will know. A name that deserves to be revered by all Americans, and will ever be held in special esteem by freedom-loving American Jews, is that of Thomas Kennedy. A Scotch Presbyterian, he led a long struggle for the removal of political disabilities in Maryland. His celebrated "Jew Bill" passed in 1826 by a majority of one vote.

Nathan Ausubel, an authority on Jewish culture, offers a grateful acknowledgment to Thomas Kennedy, who did so much in laying the groundwork for the civil rights of minorities.

Thomas Kennedy and "The Jew Bill"

BY NATHAN AUSUBEL

THE most memorable battle for Jewish religious freedom in America was fought, not by Jews, but by Thomas Kennedy, a Scotch Presbyterian member of the Legislature of the State of Maryland. A decade after the Federal Constitution had been ratified, Solomon Etting, Barnard Gratz (for whom George Washington had once surveyed land) and several other Maryland citizens petitioned the State Legislature that "they are a set of people called Jews and that they are thereby deprived of many of the invaluable rights of citizenship, and praying that they be placed upon the same footing with other good citizens." Their "prayer," however, went unheeded.

But a generation later, Thomas Kennedy entered the lists against the bigots. He introduced what his opponents derisively dubbed "The Jew Bill." In defense of it he argued: "There are no Jews in the country from which I come, nor have I the slightest acquaintance with any Jew in the world. . . . There are few

Jews in the United States; in Maryland there are very few, but if there were only one, to that one we ought to do justice." It is perhaps an indication of the slow evolution of progressive ideas that the "Jew Bill" was defeated. Although defeated at the polls, Kennedy, nevertheless, remained in the political arena, tirelessly agitating for the cause of equal rights for the Jews. Before long he translated defeat into victory. Returned by an aroused electorate to the Legislature, he saw all religious and civil inequalities finally abolished in 1826.

Susan B. Anthony

"We never met without issuing a pronunciamento on some question," Elizabeth Cady Stanton writes of herself and Susan B. Anthony.

They were to share many defeats, these two hardy pioneers who rallied again and again, writing, lecturing, collecting pennies, moving from state to state to besiege the legislatures with their appeals for equal rights for women. No sacrifice, no activity was too much.

Susan B. Anthony died fifteen years before victory finally came. Others who worked with her—the saintly Quaker preacher Lucretia Mott, steadfast Mrs. Stanton, and such prominent men of the times as Horace Greeley, founder and editor of the New York Tribune, and Wendell Phillips, Boston lawyer, abolitionist, and lyceum lecturer—sensed the debt which the future would owe her. In this lively account by Mrs. Stanton, we see the tenacity, the power and the vision which sustained "Aunt Susan" during years of bitter campaigning.

The Napoleon of Woman's Rights

BY ELIZABETH CADY STANTON

THE reports of the conventions held in Seneca Falls and Rochester, N. Y., in 1848, attracted the attention of one destined to take a most important part in the new movement—Susan B. Anthony, who, for her courage and executive ability, was facetiously called by William Henry Channing, the Napoleon of our struggle. At the time she was teaching in the Academy at Canajoharie, a little village in the beautiful valley of the Mohawk.

"The Woman's Declaration of Independence" issued from those conventions startled and amused her, and she laughed

141

heartily at the novelty and presumption of the demand. But, on returning home to spend her vacation, she was surprised to find that her sober Quaker parents and sister, having attended the Rochester meetings, regarded them as very profitable and interesting, and the demands made as proper and reasonable. She was already interested in the anti-slavery and temperance reforms, was an active member of an organization called "The Daughters of Temperance," and had spoken a few times in their public meetings. But the new gospel of "Woman's Rights," found a ready response in her mind, and, from that time, her best efforts have been given to the enfranchisement of women. . . .

Mr. Anthony was a stern Hicksite Quaker. . . . He early offended by choosing a Baptist for a wife. . . . His coat soon became a cause of offence, . . . and he was finally disowned for allowing the village youth to be taught dancing in an upper room of his dwelling, . . . though his principles would not allow his own sons and daughters to join in the amusement. . . .

Susan Anthony was taught simply that she must enter into the holy of holies of her own self, meet herself, and be true to the revelation. She first found words to express her convictions in listening to the Reverend William Henry Channing, whose teaching had a lasting spiritual influence upon her. . . . Every energy of her soul is centered upon the needs of this world. To her work is worship . . . by the very laws of her being, she is a Reformer.

For the arduous work that awaited Miss Anthony her years of young womanhood had given preparation. Her father, though a man of wealth, made it a matter of conscience to train his girls, as well as his boys, to self-support. Accordingly Susan chose the profession of teacher, and made her first essay during a summer vacation in a school her father had established for the children of his employes. Her success was so marked, not only in imparting knowledge, but also as a disciplinarian, that she followed this career steadily for fifteen years [1834-1849] with the exception of some months given in Philadelphia to her own training. . . .

About the year 1850 Susan B. Anthony hid her ferrule away. Temperance, anti-slavery, woman suffrage,—three pregnant questions,—presented themselves, demanding her consideration. . . . Owing to early experience of the disabilities of her sex, the first demand for equal rights for women found echo in Susan's heart. And, though she was in the beginning startled that women had actually met in convention, and by speeches and resolutions had declared themselves man's peer in political rights, and had urged radical changes in State constitutions and the whole system of American jurisprudence, yet the most casual review convinced her that these claims were but the logical outgrowth of the fundamental theories of our republic.

At this stage of her development I met my future friend and coadjutor for the first time. How well I remember the day! George Thompson and William Lloyd Garrison having announced an anti-slavery meeting in Seneca Falls, Miss Anthony came to attend it. These gentlemen were my guests. Walking home, after the adjournment, we met Mrs. Bloomer and Miss Anthony on the corner of the street, waiting to greet us. There she stood, with her good, earnest face and genial smile, dressed in gray delaine, hat and all the same color, relieved with pale blue ribbons, the perfection of neatness and sobriety. I liked her thoroughly, and why I did not invite her home with me to dinner, I do not know. She accuses me of that neglect, and has never forgiven me, as she wished to see and hear all she could of our noble friends. I suppose my mind was full of what I had heard, or my coming dinner, or the probable behavior of three mischievous boys who had been busily exploring the premises while I was at the meeting. . . .

It is often said, by those who know Miss Anthony best, that she has been my good angel, always pushing and goading me to work, and that but for her pertinacity I should never have accomplished the little I have. On the other hand it has been said that I forged the thunderbolts and she fired them. Perhaps all this is, in a measure, true. With the cares of a large family I might, in time, like too many women, have become wholly absorbed in a narrow family selfishness, had not my friend been continually exploring new fields for missionary labors. . . .

Thus, whenever I saw that stately Quaker girl coming across my lawn, I knew that some happy convocation of the sons of Adam was to be set by the ears, by one of our appeals or resolutions. The little portmanteau, stuffed with facts, was opened and there we had what the Rev. John Smith and Hon. Richard Roe had said: false interpretations of Bible texts, the statistics of women robbed of their property, shut out of some college, half paid for their work, the reports of some disgraceful trial; injustice enough to turn any woman's thoughts from stockings and puddings. Then we would get out our pens and write articles for papers, or a petition to the legislature; indite letters to the faithful, here and there; stir up the women in Ohio, Pennsylvania, or Massachusetts; call on *The Lily, The Una, The Liberator, The Standard* to remember our wrongs as well as those of the slave. We never met without issuing a pronunciamento on some question. In thought and sympathy we were one, and in the division of labor we exactly complemented each other. . . .

In all our associations, ever side by side on the same platform, not one feeling of envy or jealousy has ever shadowed our lives. We have indulged freely in criticism of each other, and hotly contended whenever we have differed, but in our friendship of years there has never been the break of one hour. . . .

Night after night by an old-fashioned fireplace we plotted and planned the coming agitation, how, when, and where each entering wedge could be driven, by which woman might be recognized, and her rights secured. Speedily the State was aflame with disturbances in temperance and teachers' conventions, and the press heralded the news far and near that women delegates had suddenly appeared, demanding admission in men's conventions; that their rights had been hotly contested session after session, . . . Every right achieved, to enter a college, to study a profession, to labor in some new industry, or to advocate a reform measure was contended for inch by inch. . . .

Miss Anthony first carried her flag of rebellion into the State conventions of teachers, and there fought, almost single-handed the battle for equality. At the close of the first decade she had compelled conservatism to yield its ground so far as to permit women to participate in all debates, deliver essays, vote, and hold honored positions as officers. She labored sincerely in the temperance movement, until convinced that woman's moral power amounted to little as a civil agent, until backed by ballot and coined into State law. . . .

It was in 1852 that anti-slavery, through the eloquent lips of such men as George Thompson, Phillips, and Garrison, first proclaimed to Miss Anthony its pressing financial necessities. To their inspired words she gave answer, four years afterward, by becoming a regular employed agent in the Anti-slavery Society. For her espoused cause she has always made the boldest demands. . . .

There is scarce a town, however small, from New York to San Francisco, that has not heard her ringing voice. Who can number the speeches she has made on lyceum platforms, in churches, schoolhouses, halls, barns, and in the open air, with a lumber

wagon or a cart for her rostrum? Who can describe the varied
audiences and social circles she has cheered and interested?
Now we see her on the far-off prairies, entertaining, with ster-
ling common sense, large gatherings of men, women, and children; again, holding public debates in some town with half-
fledged editors and clergymen; next, sailing up the Columbia
River and, in hot haste to meet some appointment, jolting over
the rough mountains of Oregon and Washington; and then, before legislative assemblies, constitutional conventions, and congressional committees, discussing with senators and judges the
letter and spirit of constitutional law. . . .

Many times in traveling with her through the West, especially
on our first trip to Kansas and California, we were suddenly
called upon to speak to the women assembled at the stations.
Filled with consternation, I usually appealed to her to go first;
and, without a moment's hesitation, she could always fill five
minutes with some appropriate words and inspire me with
thoughts and courage to follow. . . .

One night, crossing the Mississippi at McGregor, Iowa, we
were icebound in the middle of the river. The boat was crowded
with people, hungry, tired, and cross with the delay. Some gentlemen, with whom we had been talking on the cars, started to
cry, "Speech on woman suffrage!" Accordingly, in the middle of
the Mississippi River, at midnight, we presented our claims to
political representation, and debated the question of universal
suffrage until we landed. Our voyagers were quite thankful that
we had shortened the many hours, and we equally so at having
made several converts and held a convention on the very bosom
of the great "Mother of Waters." Only once was Miss Anthony
taken by surprise, and that was on being asked to speak to the
inmates of an insane asylum. "Bless me!" said she, "it is as much
as I can do to talk to the sane! What could I say to an audience
of lunatics?" Her companion, Virginia L. Minor of St. Louis,
replied: "This is a golden moment for you, the first opportunity
you have ever had, according to the constitution, to talk to
your 'peers,' for is not the right of suffrage denied to 'idiots,
criminals, lunatics, and women?'" . . .

One of the greatest services rendered by Miss Anthony to the
suffrage cause was in casting a vote in the Presidential election
of 1872, in order to test the rights of women under the Fourteenth Amendment. For this offense the brave woman was arrested, on Thanksgiving Day, the national holiday handed down

to us by Pilgrim Fathers escaped from England's persecutions. She asked for a writ of habeas corpus. The writ being flatly refused, in January, 1873, her counsel gave bonds. The daring defendant finding, when too late, that this not only kept her out of jail, but her case out of the Supreme Court of the United States, regretfully determined to fight on, and gain the uttermost by a decision in the United States Circuit Court. Her trial was set down for the Rochester term in May. Quickly she canvassed the whole county, laying before every probable juror the strength of her case. When the time for the trial arrived, the District Attorney, fearing the result, if the decision were left to a jury drawn from Miss Anthony's enlightened county, transferred the trial to the Ontario County term, in June, 1873.

It was now necessary to instruct the citizens of another county. In this task Miss Anthony received valuable assistance from Matilda Joslyn Gage; and, to meet all this new expense, financial aid was generously given, unsolicited, by Thomas Wentworth Higginson, Gerrit Smith, and other sympathizers. But in vain was every effort, . . . for Judge Hunt, without precedent to sustain him, declaring it a case of law and not of fact, refused to give the case to the jury, reserving to himself the final decision. All the inconsistencies were embodied in that Judge, punctilious in manner, scrupulous in attire, conscientious in trivialities, and obtuse on great principles. . . . Behold him sitting there, balancing all the niceties of law and equity in his Old World scales, and at last saying, "The prisoner will stand up." Whereupon the accused arose. "The sentence of the court is that you pay a fine of one hundred dollars and the costs of the prosecution." Then the unruly defendant answers: "May it please your Honor, I shall never pay a dollar of your unjust penalty," and more to the same effect, all of which she has lived up to. The Judge had gained some insight into the determination of the prisoner; so, not wishing to incarcerate her to all eternity, he added gently: "Madam, the court will not order you committed until the fine is paid."

It was on the 17th of June that the verdict was given. On that very day, a little less than a century before, the brave militia was driven back at Bunker Hill—back, back, almost wiped out; yet truth was in their ranks, and justice, too. But how ended that rebellion of weak colonists? The cause of American womanhood, embodied for the moment in the liberty of a single individual, received a rebuff on June 17, 1873; but, just as surely as our Revolutionary heroes were in the end victorious, so will the inalienable rights of our heroines of the nineteenth century receive final vindication.

"A'n't I a Woman?"

The midwestern advance in all social reform was led by Frances D. Gage, a woman who had earned a distinguished reputation in humanitarian and literary groups. Chosen to preside at a woman's rights convention held in Akron, Ohio, in 1851, she saw the meeting threatened by a large number of men, including ministers, who had come to heckle and protest. Frances Gage herself relates how Sojourner Truth—an illiterate former slave who was highly regarded for her instinctive practicality, discernment, and profound religious faith—intervened at this riotous session and changed defeat into victory.

Sojourner Truth "Speaks in Meeting"

BY FRANCES D. GAGE

THE leaders of the movement trembled on seeing a tall, gaunt black woman in a gray dress and white turban, surmounted with an uncouth sun-bonnet, march deliberately into the church, walk with the air of a queen up the aisle, and take her seat upon the pulpit steps. A buzz of disapprobation was heard all over the house, and there fell on the listening ear, "An abolition affair!" "Women's rights and niggers!" "I told you so!" "Go it, darkey!"

. . . Morning, afternoon, and evening exercises came and went. Through all these sessions old Sojourner, quiet and reticent as the "Lybian Statue," sat crouched against the wall on the corner of the pulpit stairs, her sun-bonnet shading her eyes, her elbows on her knees, her chin resting upon her broad, hard palms. At intermission she was busy selling *The Life of Sojourner Truth*, a narrative of her own strange and adventurous life. Again and again, timorous and trembling ones came to me and said, with earnestness, "Don't let her speak, Mrs. Gage, it will ruin us. Every newspaper in the land will have our cause mixed up with abolition and niggers, and we shall be utterly denounced." My only answer was, "We shall see when the time comes."

The second day the work waxed warm. Methodist, Baptist, Episcopal, Presbyterian, and Universalist ministers came in to hear and discuss the resolutions presented. One claimed superior rights and privileges of man, on the ground of "superior intellect"; another because of the "manhood of Christ; if God had desired the equality of woman, He would have given some token of His will through the birth, life, and death of the Saviour." Another gave us a theological view of the "sin of the first mother."

There were very few women in those days who dared to "speak in meeting"; and the august teachers of the people were seemingly getting the better of us, while the boys in the galleries, and the sneerers among the pews, were hugely enjoying the discomfiture, as they supposed, of the "strong-minded." Some of the tender-skinned friends were on the point of losing dignity, and the atmosphere betokened a storm. Then, slowly from her seat in the corner rose Sojourner Truth, who, till now, had scarcely lifted her head. "Don't let her speak!" gasped half a dozen in my ear. She moved slowly and solemnly to the front, laid her old bonnet at her feet, and turned her great speaking eyes to me. There was a hissing sound of disapprobation above and below. I rose and announced, "Sojourner Truth," and begged the audience to keep silence for a few moments.

The tumult subsided at once, and every eye was fixed on this almost Amazon form, which stood nearly six feet high, head erect, and eyes piercing the upper air like one in a dream. At her first word there was a profound hush. She spoke in deep tones, which, though not loud, reached every ear in the house, and away through the throng at the doors and windows.

"Wall, children, whar dar is so much racket dar must be somethin' out o' kilter. I think dat 'twixt de niggers of de Souf and de womin at de Norf, all talkin' 'bout rights, de white men will be in a fix pretty soon. But what's all dis here talkin' 'bout?

"Dat man ober dar say dat womin needs to be helped into carriages, and lifted over ditches, and to hab de best place everywhar. Nobody eber helps me into carriages, or ober mud-puddles, or gibs me any best place!" And raising herself to her full height, and her voice to a pitch like rolling thunder, she asked, "And a'n't I a woman? Look at me! Look at my arm!"

(And she bared her right arm to the shoulder, showing her tremendous muscular power.) "I have ploughed, and planted, and gathered into barns, and no man could head me! And a'n't I a woman? I could work as much and eat as much as a man— when I could get it—and bear de lash as well! And a'n't I a woman? I have borne thirteen children, and see 'em mos' all sold off to slavery, and when I cried out with my mother's grief, none but Jesus heard me! And a'n't I a woman?

"Den dey talks 'bout dis ting in de head; what dis dey call it?" ("Intellect," whispered someone near.) "Dat's it, honey. What's dat got to do wid womin's rights or niggers' rights? If my cup won't hold but a pint, and yourn holds a quart, wouldn't ye be mean not to let me have my little half-measure full?" And she pointed her significant finger, and sent a keen glance at the minister who had made the argument. The cheering was long and loud.

"Den dat little man in black dar, he say women can't have as much rights as men, 'cause Christ wan't a woman! Whar did your Christ come from?" Rolling thunder couldn't have stilled that crowd, as did those deep, wonderful tones, as she stood there with outstretched arms and eyes of fire. Raising her voice still louder, she repeated, "Whar did your Christ come from? From God and a woman! Man had nothin' to do wid Him." Oh, what a rebuke that was to that little man!

Turning again to another objector, she took up the defense of Mother Eve. I cannot follow her through it all. It was pointed, and witty, and solemn; eliciting at almost every sentence deafening applause; and she ended by asserting: "If de fust woman God ever made was strong enough to turn de world upside down all alone, dese women togedder (and she glanced her eye over the platform) ought to be able to turn it back, and get it right side up again! And now dey is asking to do it, de men better let 'em." Long-continued cheering greeted this. "Bleeged to ye for hearin' on me, and now old Sojourner han't got nothin' more to say."

Amid roars of applause, she returned to her corner, leaving more than one of us with streaming eyes and hearts beating with gratitude. She had taken us up in her strong arms and carried us safely over the slough of difficulty, turning the whole tide in our favor. I have never in my life seen anything like the magical influence that subdued the mobbish spirit of the day, and turned the sneers and jeers of an excited crowd into the notes of respect and admiration. Hundreds rushed up to shake hands with her, and congratulate the glorious old mother, and bid her God-speed on her mission of "testifyin' agin concerning the wickedness of this 'ere people."

The Work of Reform

One of the outstanding women roused to action by the evils of the liquor traffic (which grew tremendously after the Civil War), Frances Willard joined in the "Woman's Crusade" after broad experience as a public school teacher, a university professor, president of Evanston College for Ladies, and dean of women at Northwestern University. When a group of women at Chautauqua decided in 1874 that the work of reform must be continued, she helped to organize the Women's Christian Temperance Union, serving as its secretary until 1879, and thereafter as its president. She threw her stalwart support behind other reform movements as well, especially that of woman suffrage.

Halford E. Luccock, in his inimitable way, tells of an amusing incident in Frances Willard's life.

Frances Willard Minds Her Own Business

BY HALFORD E. LUCCOCK

In a Middle Western city in the late 1890s, a woman had just finished speaking to a large audience which had sat enthralled by her eloquent attack on the alcoholic liquor traffic. She had a soft voice and a quiet manner, and did not look like a menace to anyone.

A large man came up to her in a belligerent mood, and wagging his finger and shaking his fist as though he were Julius Caesar, commanded her, "You mind your own business!" The woman looked at him with curiosity. She was not afraid of him.

"I *am* minding my own business," she replied. "Men, women, and children are my business because they are God's business. Anything that tramples on them, degrades them, and brings poverty, disease and shame to them, is the business of God their

152

Father, and of God's Church. You mind the Devil's business and yours, and I will mind God's business and mine!"

The woman was Frances E. Willard, talking back to a saloon keeper. She was one of the remarkable personalities of Methodism. She was the child of a Methodist home, and through the home and church gained a deep religious experience and conviction. She began her career as a school teacher, and by personality, eloquence, executive ability and sheer devotion, became an intrepid leader in two great struggles of her time, arousing the conscience of the nation against the liquor traffic, and the long battle for the rights of women. She was one of the earliest leaders in the work of the Women's Christian Temperance Union, becoming its national president in 1879. One of the most eloquent women of modern times, she exerted a wide influence. A bust of her placed in the Hall of Fame in 1923 offers tribute to this influence.

Her enemies called her "a busybody." She was that, all right. She was also a "busy mind" and a "busy heart," in carrying the matters of human welfare from the area of talk to the area of action. She operated on the theory that while it may be true, as declared in the Book of Proverbs, that "The wicked flee when no man pursueth," it is also true that "they make better time when someone is after them." She was "after them" for fifty years!

Legends have grown up around her, and the real woman has been somewhat obscured by clouds of adulation. But there is enough fact to make hers a remarkable life of influential leadership. Her achievement pictures two things: one, religious faith generating power for social action for human welfare; and the other, an example of the determined warfare of Methodism against the ravages of the liquor traffic, a 150 years' war still going on.

"My Prayer Has Been Granted"

Standing in our national capital is a magnificent medical center and army hospital, a fitting memorial to the inspired achievements of Dr. Walter B. Reed. The famous army surgeon and head of the Havana Commission for the study of yellow fever aimed always, we are told, "to do uncomplainingly the will of Him who gave us breath and life." The hardships of his own early years, along with medical service in underprivileged areas of New York City, had given him deep compassion for his fellow man.

Here, in his own words—recounted for us by Dr. Howard A. Kelly, a friend and colleague of Dr. Reed—we learn of the final yellow fever experiments, and see how Dr. Reed divulged the sensational news of the project's success to his wife.

Dr. Walter Reed's Work in Yellow Fever

BY HOWARD A. KELLY

At 11:55, December 21, 1900, [wrote Dr. Walter Reed in *The Propagation of Yellow Fever*] fifteen mosquitoes were freed in the larger room of the Infected Mosquito Building, which was divided into two compartments by a wire-screen partition. The interval that had elapsed since the contamination of these insects was as follows: one, twenty-four days; three, twelve days; four, eight days; and seven, five days. The only articles of furniture in this building consisted of three beds, one being placed in the mosquito room and two beyond the wire screen, these latter intended to be occupied by two "control" non-immunes. The articles of bedding as well as the bedsteads had been carefully disinfected by steam. At noon on the same day, five minutes after the mosquitoes had been placed therein, a plucky

154

Ohio boy, Moran by name, clad only in his night-shirt and fresh from a bath, entered the room containing the mosquitoes, where he lay down for a period of thirty minutes. On the opposite side of the screen were the two "controls" and one other non-immune. Within two minutes after Moran's entrance he was bitten about the face and hands by the insects that had promptly settled down upon him. Seven in all bit him at this visit. At 4.30 P.M. he again entered and remained twenty minutes, during which time five others bit him. The following day at 4.30 P.M. he again entered and remained fifteen minutes, during which three insects bit him, making the number fifteen that fed at these three visits. The building was then closed, except that the two non-immune controls continued to occupy the beds on the non-infected side of the screen. On Christmas morning at 11 A.M. this brave lad was stricken with yellow fever and had a sharp attack which he bore without a murmur. The period of incubation in this case was three days and twenty-three hours, counting from his first visit, or two days and seventeen and a half hours, if reckoned from his last visit. The two controls who had slept each night in this house, only protected by the wire screen, but breathing the common atmosphere of the building, had remained in good health. They continued to remain so, although required to sleep here for thirteen additional nights. As Moran had remained in strict quarantine for the period of thirty-two days prior to his attack, the source of his infection must be found in this house.

With this experiment the work for the time being came to a close. Dr. Reed's own sentiments regarding the blessing it had conferred upon the human race are expressed in the following letter to his wife:

Columbia Barracks,
Quemados, Cuba,
11.50 P.M., Dec. 31, 1900.

Only ten minutes of the old century remain. Here have I been sitting, reading that most wonderful book, *La Roche on Yellow Fever*, written in 1853. Forty-seven years later it has been permitted to me and my assistants to lift the impenetrable veil that has surrounded the causation of this most wonderful, dreadful pest of humanity and to put it on a rational and scientific basis. I thank God that this has been accomplished during the latter days of the old century. May its cure be wrought out in the early days of the new! The prayer that has been mine for twenty years, that I might be permitted in some way or at some time to do something to alleviate human suffering has been granted! A thousand Happy New Years. . . . Hark, there go the twenty-four buglers in concert, all sounding "Taps" for the old year.

Jane Addams

Many an American benefactor has begun life with the handicap of unusual frailty or illness. Theodore Roosevelt, for example, fought and finally overcame his early delicacy with rugged out-door living. Jane Addams was another whose life might have been one of retirement; but her Quaker father instilled in her the feeling of the "inner light," and she persevered against ill health to devote her life to the famous Hull House which she founded in Chicago in 1889. Here she made social service an expression of the spirit of true Christianity, and withal found time to write valuable books on sociology and reform.

This distinguished woman won the Nobel Peace Prize in 1931 for her dedication to the welfare of humanity; but perhaps her greatest reward was the reality her work gave to a favorite proverb: "Labor is the house that Love lives in . . ."

In the account which follows, Harry Hansen pays a personal tribute to the enduring achievements of Jane Addams.

Hull House: Monument to Love

BY HARRY HANSEN

WHEN my cab reached the brown, brick buildings of Hull House, at Halsted and Polk streets, I had the driver stop, and sat there and gazed at the plain lines and sharp gables of the institution as a flood of memories came over me. More than any other spot in Chicago, Hull House had seemed the place where the spirit bloomed in good works. It was the leaven in the lump, and no one could estimate the great good it had done, and still did, both practically and as an inspiration to people who fought privilege, political corruption, dishonest acquisitiveness and the ignorance of society's victims. Silently I saluted the memory of

157

Jane Addams, dead since 1935; Lillian D. Wald had called her "the finest expression of the American spirit of democracy."

. . . I had been in and out the doors of Hull House both as a student at the university and as a reporter, though never associated with its activities. In my first weeks at the university I went there with a classmate, a friend of Miss Addams. From the first moment Miss Addams exhibited her practical efficiency, and from then on I never entered Hull House without feeling that the spirit of getting things done, without fuss or window dressing, was in the very air of its rooms. The outcome of that first visit was a personal tour of the settlement, and what a tour! Miss Addams, determined to show her young visitors her domain, did not delegate the task; she led the way, but in double-quick time. We raced through the rooms: kitchen, theater, reading rooms, apartments, trying to keep pace with the energetic founder, who explained as she walked, and halted only to describe the murals of Lincoln and Tolstoy, both working with their hands.

Later, when I interviewed her at intervals, I came to respect her directness, her calm appraisal; she avoided guesses and dealt with concrete situations, and had a businesslike way of speaking, but always with deep courtesy. It was characteristic that she thought of solving social problems in terms of practical contact; her ideal never kept her in the library, among statistics, for she believed that "nothing so deadens the sympathies and shrivels the power of enjoyment as the persistent keeping away from the great opportunities for helpfulness and a continual ignoring of the starvation struggle which makes up the life of at least half the race."

When Jane Addams came to the Nineteenth Ward it was a congested district of small shops, saloons, factories, sweatshops and tenements, with many families living in rear houses on the alleys, where a faucet in the yard supplied water to all the tenants, and ashes and garbage lay heaped up under their windows. I had wandered in and out of this wilderness behind Hull House with a social worker and had seen washing strung out over the alleys on lines propelled on pulleys, while dust from the ashes swirled up around us.

To bring better housing into this world was a slow struggle, but Jane Addams and her associates put their energies into it. They arrived in 1889 at a melting pot that didn't melt. Huge migrations had crowded one nationality upon another. Italians,

Poles and Russian Jews jammed the meager housing facilities. The pushcart markets were only a few blocks away in Maxwell Street. Sweatshops were operated in lofts and basements while immigrant women carried huge bundles of cloth to their crowded homes for work far into the night. Children were exploited as workers; occupational protection was unknown; disease was not controlled. It was in this area that W. T. Stead, the London economist, found the material for his book, *If Christ Came to Chicago,* and co-operated with Hull House, just after the World's Fair of 1893, to stir the civic conscience.

What Jane Addams and Hull House accomplished cannot be put on memorial plaques, for it is merged in the history of social reform. Hull House took its valiant part in bringing about the first factory laws, abolishing sweatshops, fighting civic graft, curtailing child labor. Miss Addams knew how political corruption and exploitation of immigrant labor went hand in hand, and she has described her feeling of personal shame when an opponent of the bill to abolish sweatshops offered to donate $50,000 a year for two years to the settlement if she would withdraw her support of the bill. She supported the eight-hour day and the forty-eight-hour week when the trade-unions were still too weak to win; she stood behind the organization of a juvenile court. The girl who had been thrust out of home because of a misstep; the fiery radicals who needed a hall to blow off steam; the peddlers of foreign birth who were pushed around; the juvenile offenders who were not criminals, found help under these roofs. Jane Addams in turn praised "the kindness of the poor to each other" and recognized that dogmatic social theories have to be tested by experience if they are to alleviate the woes of mankind. Many other settlement houses and social service agencies followed Miss Addams's example in the congested districts of Chicago, important among them being Dr. Graham Taylor's Chicago Commons, Mary McDowell's University of Chicago Settlement, "back of the Yards," and the settlement house of Northwestern University. For her activities on behalf of international peace Miss Addams shared the Nobel Peace prize with Nicholas Murray Butler, and donated the money to the Women's Peace party. Only a short distance from Hull House, near Loomis Avenue, a district of poor habitations has yielded place to a modern housing project of fifty-two houses and 975 low-cost apartments; I thought it eminently proper that they should be called the Jane Addams Houses.

"The Sunlight Was Let In"

Jacob Riis came to the United States in 1870 as a penniless young emigrant from Denmark. For several years he was destined to know the worst experiences the new world had to offer—homelessness, hunger, the filth and degradation of the slums. Then opportunity met him halfway, and he found work as a police reporter. Thirty years later he was the famous and intimate friend of Theodore Roosevelt, a co-worker in the fight to tear down squalid tenements, build decent homes, establish parks and playgrounds, and improve the wretched conditions of overcrowded schools and municipal jails.

His autobiography, The Making of an American, *published in 1901, has become a classic of social literature. A gentle soul, Riis flamed into indignation at wrong. In the following account we see how his "consecrated pen"—and the faith that guided it—crusaded against rampant big-city graft and crookedness, and in this instance helped to transform a "pig-sty" into a park.*

A Consecrated Pen

BY JACOB RIIS

My scrap-book from the year 1883 to 1896 is one running comment on the [Mulberry] Bend, and upon the official indolence that delayed its demolition nearly a decade after it had been decreed. But it all availed nothing to hurry up things, until, in a swaggering moment, after four years of that sort of thing, one of the [New York] City Hall officials condescended to inform me of the real cause of the delay. It was simply that "no one down there had been taking any interest in the thing."

I could not have laid it out for him to suit my case better than he did. It was in the silly season, and the newspapers fell greedily upon the sensation I made. The Bend, moreover, smelled rather worse than usual that August. They made "the people's cause" their own, and shouted treason until the commission charged with condemning the Bend actually did meet and greased its wheels. But at the next turn they were down in a rut again, and the team had to be prodded some more. It had taken two years to get a map of the proposed park filed under the law that authorized the laying out of it. The commission consumed nearly six years in condemning the forty-one lots of property, and charged the city $45,498.60 for it. The Bend itself cost a million, and an assessment of half a million was laid upon surrounding property for the supposed benefit of making it over from a pig-sty into a park. Those property-owners knew better. They hired a lawyer who in less than six weeks persuaded the Legislature that it was an injury, not a benefit. The town had to foot the whole bill. But at last it owned the Bend.

Instead of destroying it neck and crop, it settled down complacently to collect the rents; that is to say, such rents as it could collect. A good many of the tenants refused to pay, and lived rent free for a year. It was a rare chance for the reporter, and I did not miss it. The city as landlord in the Bend was fair game. The old houses came down at last, and for a twelve-month, while a reform government sat at the City Hall, the three-acre lot lay, a veritable slough of despond filled with unutterable nastiness, festering in the sight of men. No amount of prodding seemed able to get it out of that, and all the while money given for the relief of the people was going to waste at the rate of a million dollars a year. The Small Parks Act of 1887 appropriated that amount, and it was to be had for the asking. But no one who had the authority asked, and as the appropriation was not cumulative, each passing year saw the loss of just so much to the cause of decency that was waiting without. Eight millions had been thrown away when they finally came to ask a million and a half to pay for the Mulberry Bend park, and then they had to get a special law and a special appropriation because the amount was more than "a million in one year." This in spite of the fact that we were then in the Christmas holidays with one year just closing and the other opening, each with its unclaimed appropriation. I suggested that to the powers that were, but they threw up their hands: that would have been irregular and quite without precedent. Oh, for irregularity enough to throttle precedent finally and for good! It has made more mischief in the world, I verily believe, than all the other lawbreakers together. At the very outset it had wrecked my hopes of getting the first school playground in New York planted in the Bend by simply joining park and school together. There was a public school in the block that went with the rest. The Small Parks Law expressly provided for the construction of "such and so many" buildings for the comfort, health, and "instruction" of the people, as might be necessary. But a school in a park! The thing had never been heard of. It would lead to conflict between two departments! And to this day there is no playground in the Mulberry Bend, though the school is right opposite.

It was, nevertheless, that sort of thing that lent the inspiration which in the end made the old Bend go. It was when, in the midst of the discussion, they showed me a check for three cents, hung up and framed in the Comptroller's office as a kind of red-tape joss for the clerks to kow-tow to, I suppose. They were part of the system it glorified. The three cents had miscarried in the purchase of a school site, and, when the error was found, were checked out with all the fuss and flourish of a transaction in millions and at a cost, I was told, of fifty dollars' worth of time and trouble. Therefore it was hung up to be forever admired as the ripe fruit of an infallible system. No doubt it will be there when another Tweed has cleaned out the city's treasury to the last cent. However, it suggested a way out to me. Two could play at that game. There is a familiar principle of sanitary law, expressed in more than one ordinance, that no citizen has a right to maintain a nuisance on his premises because he is lazy or it suits his convenience in other ways. The city is merely the aggregate of citizens in a corporation, and must be subject to the same rules. I drew up a complaint in proper official phrase, charging that the state of Mulberry Bend was "detrimental to health and dangerous to life," and formally arraigned the municipality before the Health Board for maintaining a nuisance upon its premises.

I have still a copy of that complaint, and, as the parting shot to the worst slum that ever was, and, let us hope, ever will be, I quote it here in part:—

> The Bend is a mass of wreck, a dumping-ground for all manner of filth from the surrounding tenements. The Street-cleaning Department has no jurisdiction over it, and the Park Department, in charge of which it is, exercises none.

The numerous old cellars are a source of danger to the children that swarm over the block. Water stagnating in the holes will shortly add the peril of epidemic disease. Such a condition as that now prevailing in this block, with its dense surrounding population, would not be tolerated by your department for a single day if on private property. It has lasted here many months. The property is owned by the city, having been taken for the purposes of a park and left in this condition after the demolition of the old buildings. The undersigned respectfully represents that the city, in the proposed Mulberry Bend park, is at present maintaining a nuisance, and that it is the duty of your honorable Board to see to it that it is forthwith abolished, to which end he prays that you will proceed at once with the enforcement of the rules of your department prohibiting the maintaining of nuisances within the city's limits.

If my complaint caused a smile in official quarters, it was short-lived, except in the Sanitary Bureau, where I fancy it lurked. For the Bend was under its windows. One whiff of it was enough to determine the kind of report the health inspectors would have to make when forced to act. That night, before they got around, some boys playing with a truck in the lots ran it down into one of the cellar holes spoken of and were crushed under it, and so put a point upon the matter that took the laughter out of it for good. They went ahead with the park then.

When they had laid the sod, and I came and walked on it in defiance of the sign to "keep off the grass," I was whacked by a policeman for doing it, as I told in the *Ten Years' War*. But that was all right. We had the park. And I had been "moved on" before when I sat and shivered in reeking hallways in that very spot, alone and forlorn in the long ago; so that I did not mind. The children who were dancing there in the sunlight were to have a better time, please God! We had given them their lost chance. Looking at them in their delight now, it is not hard to understand what happened: the place that had been redolent of crime and murder became the most orderly in the city. When the last house was torn down in the Bend, I counted seventeen murders in the block, all the details of which I remembered. No doubt I had forgotten several times that number. In the four years after that, during which I remained in Mulberry Street, I was called only once to record a deed of violence in the neighborhood, and that was when a stranger came in and killed himself. Nor had the Bend simply sloughed off its wickedness, for it to lodge and take root in some other place. That would have been something; but it was not that. The Bend had become decent and orderly because the sunlight was let in, and shone upon children who had at last the right to play.

"An Unpopular Righteous Cause"

Progressive and ahead of his time in so many ways, President Woodrow Wilson nevertheless for a long while balked at woman suffrage. First proposed at the Seneca Falls convention of 1848 by Elizabeth Cady Stanton, the crusade which led to final success had lasted more than seventy years when the Nineteenth Amendment, conferring the right of suffrage on women, became part of our Constitution on August 26, 1920.

Although the militant tactics of some suffragettes are well known, there were more leaders who trusted to their brains and their tongues rather than to sensational methods of fighting. Two such outstanding women, both of them close associates of the invincible Susan B. Anthony, were Dr. Anna Howard Shaw and Mrs. Carrie Chapman Catt.

Holding degrees in both theology and medicine, won with the utmost hardship, Dr. Shaw was a quick-witted, eloquent and persuasive speaker. She died with success almost in sight. Mrs. Catt, who succeeded Susan B. Anthony as president of the Suffrage Association, carried on the struggle by working for federal amendment rather than for individual state laws.

These two remarkable women, Dr. Shaw and Mrs. Catt, intrigued Secretary of the Navy Josephus Daniels, who here tells some amusing anecdotes of their "bombardment" of President Wilson.

The Woman-Suffragists Bombard Wilson

BY JOSEPHUS DANIELS

FOR many years, even before I entered the Wilson cabinet, I believed in woman suffrage. President Wilson once asked me why I was so strong for giving women the ballot. "I have two reasons that are convincing," I replied. "What are they?" he asked. "My mother and my wife," I said. "The first had the highest wisdom and soundest judgment of any inhabitant in the town where she lived and the most influence when she chose to exert it, and you know my wife and know how well qualified she is." I added, "Perhaps I am influenced by Emerson's advice: 'Attach yourself to an unpopular righteous cause.'"

That conversation took place shortly before the Democratic National Convention in 1916, when the President was renominated. Wilson was still standing "with reluctant feet." He had suggested a platform declaration that looked to action by the States. I pointed out that the States already could act and some of them had granted suffrage to the women, and that it should be uniform in all the States. He was slow to favor suffrage and he dictated the plank in 1916 which read: "We recommend the extension of the franchise to the women of the country by the States upon the same terms as to men."

. . . I had given little thought to woman suffrage prior to 1912. In North Carolina little or nothing was heard of the agitation that the great women leaders were making in other States. In the closing days of the Cleveland administration I chanced to be in Washington when Mrs. Carrie Chapman Catt was billed to speak on woman suffrage.

"Let's go and hear what the pussy cat will say," I remarked to a friend.

"I don't like her name," he said, "and moreover I do not care to hear a woman who wants to ape men."

The hall was small and crowded, and I had to stand in the rear. I went out of curiosity, perhaps to scoff, and was converted and always remained a real convert. Mrs. Catt spoke so logically, so clearly, and was so free from emotion that I could neither answer nor resist her arguments. Some time afterward I witnessed a woman suffrage parade on Fifth Avenue. In a spirit of badinage I wrote my wife: "I am now on the side of woman suffrage. Reason: Every woman in the parade wore a hat that cost only 39 cents. If that sort of hat will come to be universally worn when women get the ballot, husbands will save a lot of money." Upon my return home my wife asked me how the women in the parade looked. I said, "Fine." She banteringly replied, "I'll bet they looked like 39 cents." It was a long time before she was a convert, and she never did declare for it until she heard Dr. Anna Howard Shaw, whose eloquence and personal charm and reasoning power captivated her. "I got religion when she spoke," she often said afterwards. We were both converted to the suffrage for women by the eloquence of great women—she by Anna Howard Shaw and I by Carrie Chapman Catt.

In 1920 my wife was appointed by President Wilson as the delegate to represent the United States at the World Woman's Suffrage Conference at Geneva, and later was active in the cause both in Washington and in North Carolina.

The first Cabinet discussion touching women and the vote was in the spring of 1914. Protest had been made against Civil Service clerks taking part in woman-suffrage parades. There was heat between those who favored it and those who held that such action violated Civil Service rules and regulations. The President sought advice of some members of his Cabinet. Of course I advised him to give them the privilege—in fact, thought they should be encouraged in every proper way.

McAdoo agreed with me and was always an ardent suffragist. He had pioneered in Equal Rights to Women long before; after he had built the tunnel under the river in New York in 1907, he employed them as ticket sellers. The superintendent said, "We can secure the service of women at a much lower rate than we pay men." McAdoo said, "Employ the women, but we must pay them the same as we pay men." He added, "I want the road run with economy but not at the expense of justice."

Wilson asked Lane to give his views in writing. "I think," wrote Lane, "that I am a prejudiced partisan in this matter for I believe that women should have the right to agitate for suffrage." He said he believed they were going to get it, "and that it would be particularly unwise for the administration to create the impression that it was attempting to block the movement," and he added this sound observation: "What Civil Service clerks may do outside of the government offices is none of our business, so long as they do nothing toward breaking it down as a merit service, do not discredit the service, or render themselves unfit for it."

Wilson wrote to Chairman J. A. McIlhenny: "We ought to be as liberal as possible in the matter and I respectfully suggest a ruling like this: 'If the employees in a department conform to the regulations of the Civil Service governing such action, there is no reason why they should not join a suffrage society or take part in the work organized by such a society.'"

The advocates of the ballot gave Wilson many an uncomfortable hour. They moved in on Washington, and on the day before his inauguration staged a spectacular parade on Pennsylvania Avenue. Some became bitter because he did not at once father their cause, but the wiser ones were courteously insistent and persistent and lived to see him their champion. In his earlier years Wilson had opposed it, but its advocacy by his daughters softened him. And led by Dr. Anna Howard Shaw, the suffragists camped on the White House doorsteps until he was won to their cause. In November, 1913, they began to mobilize, and a delegation of seventy-three by "a good-humored show of force," invaded the executive office. The most Wilson promised was to give the subject "earnest consideration."

Dr. Shaw was not satisfied; she returned to the White House and told the President to his face that he was "dodging the issue." She secured his promise to approve a special committee of the House. But the suffragists never gave him any escape from their peaceful, and sometimes warlike, attitude. He once said that he might have to join hands with them lest their continual coming should leave him little time for what he regarded as more pressing matters.

The most winning and persistent advocate of suffrage camped in Washington was Helen Gardner, a rare personage. Wilson conceived a sincere admiration for her and rated her ability so high that he appointed her a member of the Civil Service Commission.

It was not until women did such yeoman service in the World War that Wilson was fully converted. He then made a strong argument for woman suffrage in an address in the Senate Chamber, but, unfortunately, the Senate delayed approval until Wilson went out of office.

Portrait of a Citizen

*"The man on the bench"—a Central Park, New York City, bench
—might very well be Bernard Baruch, financier and onetime
lawyer who has made his greatest mark in a career almost unique
with him: adviser to presidents. He has admittedly done some of
his best and most creative thinking on a certain Central Park
bench. During World War I, when he served as chairman of the
War Industries Board, he drew up the blueprint for economic
controls. A generation later, he authored the administration's
policy on the control of atomic energy. The plan, which is generally in accord with the attitudes of the religious forces of the
country, stresses three points: international control of the atom by
the United Nations or one of its agencies; development of atomic
power along medical, humanitarian, and economic lines; and cultivation of moral and spiritual forces for justice and peace
throughout the world.*

*Turning back the calendar to 1950, when Mr. Baruch was in
his eightieth year, we have W. L. White's sharply cut* Portrait of
a Citizen—*a citizen whose long life span has been devoted to
noble American leadership in humanitarian interests.*

Bernard Baruch

BY WILLIAM L. WHITE

. . . A CLOSER look now at this wind-blown, beady-eyed old
eagle today in his eightieth year. His fortune, which guesses once
put as high as 25 million, has largely (and quietly) been given
away, but "right up to the day they put the coffin lid on me," he
says with a grin, "I'll always have a dollar more than I need."

This even allowed for such an occasion as the thousands which
went (you would never learn this from him) to one of the late

President's children, bewildered and in financial difficulties. Perhaps he remembered those days when, a humble petitioner on that LaFayette Park bench, he was always received with high graciousness by Mrs. Roosevelt ("She's a brave woman. I don't know anybody I'd rather go lion-hunting with").

In his grey-carpeted Fifth Avenue apartment overlooking his park bench there is the dull glint of the English antique furniture and the delicate hand-hammered George II silver collected by Annie Griffen Baruch (she died in 1938). His present entourage consists of Miss Mary Boyle (his secretary since 1904) and Miss Elizabeth Navarro, a graduate nurse hand-picked for him several years ago by adoring Billy Rose. She jokes with him, picks lint off the lapels of his cutaway, restores his hearing-aid with fresh batteries ("My main job is stopping him from eating peanuts, and carrying his money for him").

He seldom accepts invitations, partly because "unless I dine at 7:30 sharp, I get cross and am poor company" and partly because he dislikes both opinionated bores and people with prying questions. In such crises his hearing aid (equipped with a secret cut-off) suddenly goes dead. Of one prominent politician he remarks with a grin, "I have heard nothing he has said to me since 1935."

Against any interviewer's questions which he considers improper, he has a stratagem which once wrung from the lyre of a lyrical *Fortune* writer an agonized twang when that baffled bard bitterly sang that "Baruch, squid-like, envelops himself in a dark cloud of self-revelation. The more he talks about himself, the more he obscures himself."

As for the Faith of his Fathers, in any era other than that of Adolf Hitler, he would have devoted no more time to considering the special problems of Jews than the late Calvin Coolidge devoted to those of Congregationalists. From boyhood Bernard Baruch has considered himself first an American, secondly a Southerner, thirdly a Confederate Democrat and lastly a Jew, this descending scale being a rough measure of the relative strength of his loyalties.

Yet, speaking from his heart and to his own people in his homeland (and this is not Tel Aviv, but Camden, South Carolina), he confessed last year: "I have had intolerance practiced against me and mine all my life. But I have never permitted it to rouse in me envy, jealousy or hatred, or to weaken in the slightest my faith in our form of government, its Constitution and its institutions."

Its effect instead may well have been to spur him to set an example of high service, not to the narrow interests of Jews, but to all his fellow-Americans, an example of broad and selfless patriotism perhaps unequalled since that other proud and brilliant Sephardic aristocrat, Benjamin Disraeli, became Prime Minister of Great Britain, to place upon the silvering head of England's little queen the golden diadem of that far-flung Empire upon which the Sun Never Set, until a less-far-sighted generation of drab Socialist statesmen started dribbling it away.

Since Bernard Baruch's three children have as yet given him no grandchildren, our Republic is the adored child which at eighty he now dandles on his knee, alternately spanking it with sound criticism and spoiling it with praise.

Sometimes, looking at the world from the perspective of these four-score years . . . [Mr. Baruch was born in 1870] . . . strange new trends disturb him, and he fears we are entering a period when civilization is on the downgrade like the time in the Third Century when Roman civilization lost faith in itself, and the masses from Central Asia went on the trek. At such moments he considers abandoning the rule of a lifetime to stump the country, making a last-ditch fight.

But his hope is that our youth will regain the rugged, self-confident faith of his own boyhood, and this is why the Man Who Never Seems Busy can find time out from advising Premiers and Presidents to answer the request of a little mid-western high school and, in dedicating their year-book, to remind the children that "the Ten Commandments and the Sermon on the Mount are still our best guides. And remember that this government is the best in the world. Improve it, but guard it well, and don't lean too heavily on it. You can and must do for yourself," says the tall man who, in all of these eighty years, has proudly stood alone.

FIVE

Crusade Across

a Continent

In America's epic sweep from the Eastern coastal states to the Pacific, the forces of religion took a decisive lead. Circuit-riding preachers chose to suffer and starve with the pioneers, "thankful . . . to plead the cause of God . . . where the banners of Christ were never before unfurled." In the freedom of the frontier, politics and religion shook off old traditions, reshaping the character and changing forever the destiny of the entire continent.

Francis Asbury

In his American Idealism, Dr. Luther A. Weigle speaks of Francis Asbury as a man suited to Paul's self-description: ". . . in journeyings often . . . in perils in the wilderness . . . in weariness and painfulness . . . that which cometh upon me daily, the care of all the churches."

Born in Birmingham, England, Asbury landed at Philadelphia in 1771, and began at once to travel up and down the colonies, from New Hampshire to Georgia, from the Atlantic coast to Kentucky and Tennessee. Asked by John Wesley to return to England after the Revolution, the fervent young preacher declined, so that he might devote the rest of his life to establishing the ways and doctrines of Methodism in the new land. He was, in effect, the first Methodist bishop.

In his fascinating volume, Endless Line of Splendor, Halford E. Luccock illustrates how the horizons of the missionary movement were continually expanding in America and elsewhere. In one of sixty sparkling episodes, he describes Asbury's forty-five years in America, spent tirelessly riding circuit and supervising the organization of this great fellowship in Christian life.

Wrap It Up in a Person

BY HALFORD E. LUCCOCK

ON September 4, 1771, a ship in the harbor of Bristol in England was ready to weigh anchor and set out on the long voyage to America. The last of the cargo was being loaded; the last of the passengers preparing to get on board. Among the passengers were two young men, Francis Asbury and Richard Wright. Asbury was twenty-six years of age. A few weeks earlier at the Methodist Conference at Bristol, John Wesley had called for

175

volunteers to go to America for the work there; those men had volunteered and been accepted. A slight hitch had occurred with Asbury's sailing. He arrived hurriedly at the ship and did not have a penny! A few friends gathered to see them off rallied round and gave Asbury ten pounds and some clothes. Not a penny to start with!

Forty-five years later, on March 3, 1816, an old man was lifted from his horse and carried into a small frame house, not much more than a cabin, belonging to a friend, a few miles from Fredericksburg, Virginia. He was Francis Asbury. Six weeks earlier he had preached his last sermon in Richmond, Virginia, sitting in a chair beside a table. He was in no condition to travel, but insisted on pushing on to Baltimore where a Conference was soon to meet. His strength ran out, and he died sitting in a chair, leaning against a young preacher traveling with him. "The prophet of the long road" had come to the end of the road. And he left America as he had started, without a penny! For thirty years he had labored as few men have ever toiled, at a salary of thirty dollars a year. His chief legacy was a pair of saddlebags, some books and clothes.

Between the penniless embarkment and the penniless end was packed almost a half-century of ardors and endurances which left a permanent influence on the whole of the United States.

A word recently written by Dr. J. Robert Oppenheimer, the atomic scientist, has a good chance of becoming a permanent addition to human wisdom. Pleading for funds for exchange students between different countries, he wrote, "The best way to send an idea is to wrap it up in a person." That, of course, is what God did in the Incarnation of our Lord Jesus Christ. "The Word became flesh and dwelt among us." Francis Asbury was the spirit and word of Methodism wrapped up in a person.

The record of his labor reads like the account of the labors of ten men. He outrode John Wesley himself, traveling in forty-five years, entirely on horseback or walking, over 275,000 miles, and mostly on wilderness trails. He crossed the Allegheny Mountains more than sixty times. From his *Journal* it has been computed that he preached over 16,000 sermons. When Asbury landed in America in 1771, there were only six Methodist preachers in all the thirteen colonies and only 600 members. At his death there were 700 preachers and more than 200,000 members on the roll.

He had the major share in the creation of an American Methodist Church, independent of England. His amazing practical capacity, his genius for organization, his all-consuming devotion to the spread of the gospel, his endless energy and courage—all contributed to his achievement. His insistence on itineracy kept the Church able to move swiftly and efficiently over the new continent being opened up. The inscription on the base of the noble statue in Washington, D. C., of Asbury astride a very tired horse, states part of the truth about the man: "If you would see the results of his labors, you will find them in our Christian civilization."

The Big Parade

With the Westward expansion, ministers of various Protestant denominations crossed the Alleghenies, riding abreast with the frontiersmen and serving their spiritual needs. Each Church made its distinctive contribution: austere Presbyterian clergymen set high standards of right and wrong, founding schools and churches in the towns. Methodism grew strong, appealing to people with its organization and its system of circuit riders. Baptists, often working with their flocks in primitive conditions, raised the level of daily life in the farming districts, villages, and small towns. Congregationalists, largely recruited from New England, brought their wisdom and ideals primarily to the field of education.

Smaller in number were the Episcopalians, Lutherans, Catholics, and Reformed Dutch. Thus, the Great Awakenings of 1799 and 1800 were carried on largely under the guidance of Presbyterians, Baptists, and Methodists. In his book, The Winning of the West, *Theodore Roosevelt paid special tribute to the accomplishments and fortitude of the Methodist missionaries, acknowledging as well the nation's vast debt to the leaders of these many other denominations who crossed the mountains into Kentucky and Tennessee and thence beyond. A man who well knew the hardships of a primitive and outdoor life, Teddy Roosevelt helps us understand the spirit of "the big parade" in this story of pioneer preachers.*

Pioneer Preachers and Settlers

BY THEODORE ROOSEVELT

As soon as the region between the Watauga and the Nolichucky grew at all well settled, clergymen began to come in. Here, as elsewhere, most of the frontiersmen who had any religion at all professed the faith of the Scotch-Irish; and the first regular church in this cradle-spot of Tennessee was a Presbyterian log meeting-house, built near Jonesboro in 1777, and christened Salem Church. Its pastor was a pioneer preacher, who worked with fiery and successful energy to spread learning and religion among the early settlers of the southwest. His name was Samuel Doak. He came from New Jersey, and had been educated in Princeton. Possessed of the vigorous energy that marks the true pioneer spirit, he determined to cast in his lot with the frontier folk. He walked through Maryland and Virginia, driving before him an old "flea-bitten grey horse," loaded with a sackful of books; crossed the Alleghenies, and came down along blazed trails to the Holston settlements. The hardy people among whom he took up his abode were able to appreciate his learning and religion as much as they admired his adventurous and indomitable temper; and the stern, hard, God-fearing man became a most powerful influence for good throughout the whole formative period of the southwest.

Not only did he found a church, but near it he built a log high-school, which soon became Washington College, the first institution of the kind west of the Alleghenies. Other churches, and many other schools, were soon built. Any young man or woman who could read, write, and cipher felt competent to teach an ordinary school; higher education, as elsewhere at this time in the west, was in the hands of the clergy.

As elsewhere, the settlers were predominantly of Calvinistic stock; for of all the then prominent faiths Calvinism was nearest to their feelings and ways of thought. Of the great recognized creeds it was the most republican in its tendencies, and so the best suited to the backwoodsmen . . . But backwoods Calvinism differed widely from the creed as first taught. It was professed by thorough-going Americans, essentially free and liberty-loving, who would not for a moment have tolerated a theocracy in their midst. Their social, religious, and political systems were such as naturally flourished in a country remarkable for its temper of rough and self-asserting equality. Nevertheless the old Calvinistic spirit left a peculiar stamp on this wild border democracy. More than anything else, it gave the backwoodsmen their code of right and wrong. Though they were a hard, narrow, dogged people, yet they intensely believed in their own standards and ideals. Often warped and twisted, mentally and morally, by the strain of their existence, they at least always retained the fundamental virtues of hardihood and manliness.

Presbyterianism was not, however, destined even here to remain the leading frontier creed. Other sects still more democratic, still more in keeping with backwoods life and thought, largely supplanted it. Methodism did not become a power until after the close of the Revolution; but the Baptists followed close on the heels of the Presbyterians. They, too, soon built log meeting-houses here and there, while their preachers cleared the forest and hunted elk and buffalo like the other pioneer settlers.

To all the churches the preacher and congregation alike went armed, the latter leaning their rifles in their pews or near their seats, while the pastor let his stand beside the pulpit. On week-days the clergymen usually worked in the fields in company with the rest of the settlers; all with their rifles close at hand and a guard stationed. In more than one instance when such a party was attacked by Indians, the servant of the Lord showed himself as skilled in the use of carnal weapons as were any of his warlike parishioners.

"God's Plowman"

Peter Cartwright spent all his days fighting evil. In a wilderness alive with hostile Indians, his fists were to count almost as much as his preaching in the battle for God. Settling in Logan, Kentucky, after harrowing experiences, Cartwright at seventeen felt a call to the strenuous life of a backwoods preacher. For the next seventy years he served the Methodist Episcopal Church, first as a circuit rider and then later as a Presiding Elder, covering Kentucky, Tennessee, Ohio, Indiana, and Illinois. As did so many other hardy pioneers, he disdained "educated preachers," whom he likened to "lettuce growing under the shade of a peach tree."

From the pen of Peter Cartwright came three colorful books about his life and times, true stories more thrilling than melodrama. He called himself "God's Plowman," and in these volumes, notably his Autobiography, he shows that "having put his hand to the plow, he never looked back."

Messengers of Salvation

BY PETER CARTWRIGHT

. . . SOMEWHERE between 1800 and 1801, in the upper part of Kentucky, at a memorable place called "Cane Ridge," there was appointed a sacramental meeting by some of the Presbyterian ministers, at which meeting, seemingly unexpected by ministers or people, the mighty power of God was displayed in a very extraordinary manner; many were moved to tears, and bitter and loud crying for mercy. The meeting was protracted for weeks. Ministers of almost all denominations flocked in from far and near. The meeting was kept up by night and day. Thousands heard of the mighty work, and came on foot, on horseback, in carriages and wagons. It was supposed that there were in attend-

181

ance at times during the meeting from twelve to twenty-five thousand people. Hundreds fell prostrate under the mighty power of God, as men slain in battle. Stands were erected in the woods from which preachers of different churches proclaimed repentance toward God and faith in our Lord Jesus Christ, and it was supposed, by eye and ear witnesses, that between one and two thousand souls were happily and powerfully converted to God during the meeting. . . . The heavenly fire spread in almost every direction. It was said, by truthful witnesses, that at times more than one thousand persons broke out into loud shouting all at once, and that the shouts could be heard for miles around.

From this camp-meeting, for so it ought to be called, the news spread through all the Churches, and through all the land, and it excited great wonder and surprise; but it kindled a religious flame that spread all over Kentucky and through many other states . . . this was the first camp-meeting ever held in the United States, and here our camp-meetings took their rise.

As Presbyterian, Methodist, and Baptist ministers all united in the blessed work at this meeting, when they returned home to their different congregations, and carried the news of this mighty work, the revival spread rapidly throughout the land. . . .

From the earliest of my recollection, up to this time, 1816, there were scarcely any books of any kind in this now mighty West; but especially was there a great scarcity of Bibles and Testaments. We were young and poor as a nation; had but a few years gained our liberty; had hardly begun to live as a republic after a bloody and devastating war for our independence; and although Congress, the very first year after the declaration of our independence, had wisely taken steps for furnishing the struggling infant for independence with the word of God, and did order that precious book, yet there was a great lack of the Bible, especially in the wilderness of the West; but this year the Lord put it into the hearts of some of his people to organize a Bible Society, which was done on the 11th of May, 1816; and although at first it was a feeble concern, yet God has prospered it, and millions upon millions of this precious book have been printed and circulated, and it is pouring streams of light, life, and knowledge upon almost every nation of this sin-stricken world. . . .

A Methodist preacher in those days, when he felt that God had called him to preach, instead of hunting up a college or Biblical institute, hunted up a hardy pony of a horse, and some traveling apparatus, and with his library always at hand, namely, Bible, Hymn Book, and Discipline, he started, and with a text that never wore out nor grew stale, he cried, "Behold the Lamb of God, that taketh away the sin of the world." In this way he went through storms of wind, hail, snow, and rain; climbed hills and mountains, traversed valleys, plunged through swamps, swam swollen streams, lay out all night, wet, weary, and hungry, held his horse by the bridle all night, or tied him to a limb, slept with his saddle blanket for a bed, his saddle or saddle-bags for his pillow, and his old big coat or blanket, if he had any, for a covering. Often he slept in dirty cabins, on earthen floors, before the fire; ate roasting ears for bread, drank butter-milk for coffee, or sage tea for imperial; took, with a hearty zest, deer or bear meat, or wild turkey, for breakfast, dinner, and supper, if he could get it. His text was always read, "Behold the Lamb of God," &c. This was old-fashioned Methodist preacher fare and fortune. Under such circumstances, who among us would now say, "Here am I, Lord, send me?"

Poet of the American Dream

Walt Whitman sang a song of America—the song of freedom—throughout his poetry and his life. And while he is regarded as the most American of poets, his philosophy and love of mankind leap national boundaries to encompass the world.

A poet draws his inspiration from many sources, some of them undoubtedly from half-forgotten memories out of his childhood. We can only guess the influence on an impressionable boy of the great individualistic Quaker saint, Elias Hicks, when Walt Whitman was taken to hear him "as a reward for being a good boy."

Biographer Frances Winwar colorfully portrays that dramatic incident, giving us at the same time the atmosphere of the Whitman home, where the poet learned to glorify the Inner Light and "hear America singing."

Walt Whitman's Family Stood With Elias Hicks

BY FRANCES WINWAR

ONE winter evening, toward the close of the year, Walter Whitman, returning home from his day's work, threw down on the kitchen floor the armful of kindling he had brought, and said to Louisa, "Come, Mother, Elias preaches tonight."

The name of Elias Hicks had often been mentioned in the Whitman family. Indeed, as a young man Grandfather Jesse had frequently been in the company of Elias, a carpenter at the time, fond of sleigh-riding and jovial songs, though much troubled in his mind about spiritual matters.

Not till he was twenty, however, did Hicks fully realize his mission, when he gave up his carpenter's trade and took up farm-

184

ing in the Hempstead section of Long Island where he was born. His parents were Friends, but until the crucial year he himself had taken little interest in religion. His closeness to the soil, however, and the solitary hours in the fields during which he came face to face with himself and his spirit, helped him to know the thing that was working within him. For years he wrestled with himself and the light pointing the way he should follow, but it was not till 1779, at the age of thirty-one, that he took his bundle and his Book and set out as an itinerant preacher.

From Vermont down to Maryland he went, rejecting openings leading to the ministry so that he might be free to express the God within him. Not everywhere was he well received, for although the persecutions that had marked the first landing of the Quakers in New England had ceased, there was still a difference of opinion on what a man might and might not utter as the promptings of the Inner Light. Like the New England Puritans whose General Court lost no time in pronouncing the Society of Friends "a blasphemouth sect," there were still many too ready to believe that if any voice spoke through an inspired man, it was not necessarily the voice of the Lord.

More generally than one might have expected in the enlightened nineteenth century, the Quakers were held suspect for having no set creed, no church and no ministers, and for holding their meetings as the spirit prompted them, under the direction of whatever member felt upon him the impulse of God. The feud, however, that had existed in the early days between the New England Church and the Quakers had ended. Devoted men and women no longer died by the rope for not worshiping God in the Puritan way. On the other side the Quakers, no longer exasperated by unjust laws, moderated their sometimes sensational protest. No prophets in winding sheets now broke in upon Church lectures, crying out upon the elders as hypocrites. No more bottles were broken over the heads of ministers as in the case of the Reverend John Norton of Boston, whom two Quaker women had treated to such summary symbolism "as a sign of his emptiness." No virgin, like the pure Deborah Buffrum of Salem, found it necessary to walk through the town naked, her face blackened with ashes, to expose the bareness of the religion of the Church. The Quakers were tolerated.

Although it was comparatively safe to worship as one pleased, it was another matter for even a man of God to interfere with economic tradition. Elias Hicks, therefore, showed remarkable

courage when he preached against slavery not only in the North
but in Maryland itself. For years he raised his voice like an angry
prophet, with such eloquence that even those who did not believe
with him agreed that a divine breath inspired him. Tall, majestic,
intense as a flame, he preached in a ringing voice, the deep black
eyes in the ascetic face suddenly glowing as if from the radiance
of the light within. He spoke simply, in the language of the Bible,
with a poetic figurativeness that all could understand. At times
his body was possessed by emotions so strong that those who sat
near him saw it quiver. Then, after he had spoken, he collected
himself with a brusque shock and became human.

At the time Walt was taken to hear him as a special reward
for having been a good boy, Hicks was a patriarch of eighty-one,
gaunt, spare, a taper consumed to the wick. The grand ballroom
of the Morrison Hotel on the Heights, resplendent with lights in
the crystal chandeliers, teemed with people, young and old, the
faithful and the curious. All of Brooklyn's fashionable and first
citizens—Pierrepont, Judge Furman, General Jeremiah Johnson—
fine ladies in their veils and furs, Navy Yard officers in uniform,
had turned out to hear the man, sitting there on the platform
amidst a group of elderly Friends, with his thin white hair over
his shoulders, and on his head the broad-brimmed hat which he
would take off for no man. How other-worldly he looked! How
grand and noble in the simplicity of his drab cloth!

Walt did not once take his eyes off him. Suddenly the old man
rose, stood for a moment silent while the people held their
breath, and then, his hat still on his head, he spoke slowly, in a
thrilling, resonant voice: "What is the chief end of man? I was
told in my early youth, it was to glorify God, and seek and enjoy
him forever. . . ." On and on he spoke, now pleading, now tender, now wrathful. At one point he took his broad-brim from his
head and dashed it on the seat behind him, speaking earnestly
all the while, as the people listened, many of them—the little
boy saw and marvelled—with tears in their eyes. The ten year
old could make little of the prophet's vehement speech, but he
never forgot the solemn and somber figure, lighting up miracu-
lously with the flame within him.

How much did the boy know of Hicks' story? He must have
been told of the preacher's humble origins, no better than his
father's, in fact, the same, but that Walter had farmed in West
Hills and Hicks in Jericho. He must have known that he had
helped to free the Negroes born in New York by preaching for

the passage of a certain act, just a few years before he, Walt, was born. Probably he had heard too of the prophet's personal sorrows, of the loss of his four sons, which perhaps gave his face that terrible, austere look. And, surely, in a house wherein both sides had connections with the Quakers, he must have heard talk of the split which Hicks had brought about in the Society because of his opposition to formalism. The Whitmans, though not really members, stood of course with the Hicksites, the liberal branch.

As he grew older, even more than the Sunday schooling to which he was exposed in the old gray Dutch Reformed Church on Joralemon Street, Walt was influenced by the winds of doctrine blown to him from the Hicksite quarter. The old prophet himself died a few months after that meeting at Morrison's hotel. His spirit, however, lived on in the Whitman household. Unwittingly, as he had been assimilating his experiences of nature, Walt was drinking in the outpourings of the prophetic fount, diluted, it is true, through his parents' comprehension, but still near enough to the source to retain their purity.

Vaguely at first, with a child's understanding, he apprehended what every good Quaker should believe—that the inner Deity is a surer guide than churches, doctrines, or even the teachings of the Bible. In a sense, therefore, every man is holy, and every body sacred for being the lamp through which the Inner Light may burn. All are sharers in the common divinity, the poor, the ignorant, for there is no vessel so mean that it may not receive the divine Host, and speak for Him. "The prophet . . ." Whitman was to write, "means one whose mind bubbles up and pours forth as a fountain, from inner, divine spontaneities revealing God . . . The great matter is to reveal and outpour the Godlike suggestions pressing for birth in the soul. This is briefly the doctrine of the Friends or Quakers."

Johnny Appleseed

"Johnny Appleseed" is more than a name, more even than a kindly wanderer in whose history fact and fiction strangely blend. He is an emblem of our national life in its pioneering days—of the faith, hope, and perseverance that caused the Western wilderness to blossom and bear fruit.

He carried no arms, no worldly goods save a few tattered religious books and his knapsack of precious seeds, which he planted and nurtured in myriad scattered places. He was greeted with joy everywhere, making friends of all whom he met. Poets like Vachel Lindsay celebrate him as "the symbol of the restless creative American spirit."

Walter Havighurst's fascinating volume, Land of Promise, *shows us in this account why Johnny Appleseed has become enshrined in our hearts as well as in our literature.*

Saint of the Busy West

BY WALTER HAVIGHURST

BEFORE the land was fenced and tamed, when there was room for a wanderer to tramp the meadows and tread the woods and steer his canoe in the running waters, a legend grew up in the new country. It is the only legend in a land that quickly filled with sober people. But Johnny Appleseed had his seasons when the settlements were still far apart on roads marked only by a white blaze on the bark of trees. Then a family in their clearing, hungry for a new face and a stranger's voice, would welcome a ragged man who planted apple trees while he talked of the road to heaven.

Johnny Appleseed was the name by which people knew him from Pittsburgh to the bends of the Wabash, from the Ohio River

to Lake Erie. He had a Christian name—Jonathan Chapman. He
was born in Massachusetts. There, in his boyhood, he often wandered off in quest of birds and flowers. In the autumn of 1801, he
floated down the Ohio in two canoes lashed together and laden to
the gunwales with apple pulp from the cider mills of western
Pennsylvania. He went west, not to locate land but to plant
apple orchards in the clearings where people would come. For
forty years he wandered the country with a deerhide sack rustling
on his shoulder. Along with apple seeds he scattered seeds of
healing herbs—catnip, hoarhound and pennyr'yle, to serve the
settlers of the future. Wherever he wandered he made friends—
with Indians and whites alike, with the men on the early traces,
teamsters, peddlers, itinerant preachers riding their forest cir-
cuits, with all the settlers, Yankee and Hoosier, Irish and German, and with little children playing dolls with corncobs and old
men sitting in sunlit doorways.

Johnny was something of a circuit rider himself, with the whole
country for his parish. He preached more often than any doctrine
a text of apple blossoms on the warm May wind. One story said
he was kicked in the head by a horse and had a vision of heaven
as a vast orchard of blooming apple trees. By belief he was a
Swedenborgian—among his apple seeds he carried ragged copies
of *Heaven and Hell* and left them for people to read till he should
call again. Sometimes he tore pages from his books to make them
go farther. So he circulated the visions of Immanuel Swedenborg
by installments, from cabin to cabin in the lonely country. When
night found him on the trail, he read his tattered texts by fire-
light and saved crumbs from his supper for the squirrels and
partridges. One rainy night he took refuge in a hollow log and
found it already occupied by a bear. The two slept peacefully
and in the morning parted on good terms. Some have called him
St. Francis of the West. He was the only saint the busy western
country ever bred.

No one knows certainly when Jonathan Chapman died—
though it was in the 1840s in Allen County, Indiana, not many
miles from the site of the old Battle of Fallen Timbers. But
Johnny Appleseed never died. He went on wandering the country, in people's memory. He was blessed every spring when the
orchards bloomed white on the hills and every autumn when the
ripe fruit bowed the branches down. Even after those orchards
were old and decaying by the rivers, his memory stayed green.
By that time he belonged to the whole Middle West, and an Illi-

nois poet, Vachel Lindsay, made a song about his crossing the
Appalachians to wander the wide country—*He ran with the rabbit and he slept with the stream*—and leave it blossoming behind
him.

Johnny Appleseed became a subject for stories. That is the way
he was remembered, and it is the way to tell about a man who
found a place in the affections of people who gave him a night's
lodging in return for his gentle gospel, and of others who never
heard his voice or saw him ragged in the twilight.

The Bride Wore Black

*The cultured young girl had read of missionary efforts in India
and Burma, and she decided that this was the way she would
spend her years. Beautiful, gifted Narcissa Prentiss enrolled with
the American Board of Missions.*

*Then she met Dr. Marcus Whitman. He was a physician and
teacher, a pioneer who shared her interest in missionary work.
Their marriage was a strange one: the bride wore black. Their
honeymoon was an incredible one—crossing the continent in a
covered wagon. Narcissa was the first white woman to make this
trip; from it, she never returned. She and her husband gave their
lives as missionaries, massacred by the Cayuse Indians whom
they were trying to Christianize and help. It is a tragic tale, yet
full of the splendor which falls on dedicated lives.*

*For more than a decade, Narcissa kept a Journal, recording in
it her activities and her inmost thoughts. Historian Carl Van
Doren brings us precious pages from that Journal, as he unfolds
Narcissa's story.*

Narcissa Whitman

BY CARL VAN DOREN

One of the most valiant of all Americans was a woman. She was
born Narcissa Prentiss at Angelica, New York. She was one of the
first pupils at Emma Willard's pioneering Seminary at Troy.
She was gentle, delicately brought up, surrounded with comfort
and conveniences.

Then she married Marcus Whitman in February, in 1836. Whitman was a medical missionary in Oregon. His bride was to spend
her honeymoon in a covered wagon, roughing it for the first
time in her life. She gave up her friends, her books, her comfort

to go to a country that was not even part of the United States. She was never to return.

Before Narcissa Whitman no white woman had crossed this continent. Her trip proved that women could cross from East to West. She left one of our cherished human documents: a diary which gives, day by day, a picture of what it meant to cross the rivers, plains and mountains of America, by wagon:

> Our manner of living is far preferable to any in the States. I never was so contented and happy before; neither have I enjoyed such health for years. As soon as the day breaks, the first that we hear is the words "Arise! Arise!" Then the mules set up such a noise as you never heard, which puts the whole camp in motion. You must think it very hard to get up so early after sleeping on the ground, when you find it hard work to open your eyes at seven o'clock. Just think of me. Every morning at the word "Arise!" we all spring. While the horses are feeding, we get breakfast in a hurry, and eat it. By this time the words "Catch up! Catch up!" ring through the camp for moving. We are ready to start usually at six, travel till eleven, encamp, rest and feed, start again about two, travel until six, or before, if we come to a good campground, then encamp for the night. . . .
>
> How do you think we manage to rest ourselves every noon, having no house to shelter us from the scorching heat? Perhaps you think we always encamp in the shade of some thick wood. Such a sight I have not seen, lo these many days. If we can find a few small willows or a single lone tree, we think ourselves amply provided for. But often our camping places are in some plain, and frequently a sand plain. But even here is rest and comfort. My husband, who is one of the best the world ever knew, is always ready to provide a comfortable shade, with one of our saddle blankets spread upon some willows, or sticks placed in the ground. How do you think you would like this?
>
> Just take a peep at us while we are sitting at meals. Our table is the ground, our table cloth is an India-rubber cloth used, when it rains, as a cloak. Our dishes are made of tin, basins for tea cups, iron spoons and plates for each of us, and several pans for milk and to put our meat in when we wish to set it on the table. Each one carries his own knife in his scabbard, and it is always ready for use. When the table things are spread, after making our own forks of sticks, we gather round the table.

Twelve miles a day was the prescribed distance to be made. The flour soon gave out, and bread was no longer available. The men and women lived on buffalo meat, and occasional berries.

There were no roads, and no bridges. What few rude sign posts there were pointed in only one direction—westward.

One day the Whitman party came to the Snake River. Whitman decided he could take only one wagon with him to the Columbia. Narcissa had to give up the one possession in the world that was her own. We know what it cost her from this letter to her sister:

Dear Harriet: The little trunk you gave me has come with me so far, and now I must leave it here alone.

Poor little trunk, I am sorry to leave thee. Thou must abide here alone, and no more by thy presence remind me of my dear Harriet. Twenty miles below the falls on Snake River—this shall be thy place of rest. Farewell, little trunk! I thank thee for all thy faithful services, and that I have been cheered by thy presence so long. Thus we scatter as we go.

The hills are so steep and rocky that my husband thought it best to lighten the wagon as much as possible, and take nothing but the wheels, leaving the wagon box with my trunk. I regret leaving everything that came from home, especially this trunk; but it is best. It would have been better for me not to have attempted to bring any baggage whatever, only what was necessary for use on the way. To pack and unpack so many times, and cross so many streams when the packs frequently get wet, requires no small amount of labor, besides the injury of the articles. Our books, what few we have, have been wet several times. The custom of the country is to possess nothing, and then you will lose nothing while traveling.

Early in September they reached the Columbia, near Fort Walla Walla, and found green vegetables from the fort's garden more exciting than gold. As soon as they could build it, they had a house . . . of one room. Blankets covered the windows. Green cotton-wood branches spread on the floor made their bed. There was no furniture.

For eleven years they maintained the mission station they had come west to serve. They were the first of the stream that followed them into Oregon. In 1847 came tragedy: measles struck down white children and Indian. Whitman's medicines cured the white children but had no effect on the Indians. The story spread that he was poisoning them. Angry Indians massacred the Whitmans.

But they had lived long enough to point the way. And in one of Narcissa Whitman's letters we find a few, simple words that reveal the spirit of all Americans who have helped to make our Scriptures:

> Sometimes my wicked heart has been disposed to murmur, thinking I should have no rest from the heat when we stopped. But I have always been reproved for it by the comfort and rest received. Under the circumstances I have never wished to go back. Such a thought never finds a place in my heart. "The Lord is better to us than our fears." I always find it so.

Savior of Alaska

Ten days before the Transcontinental Railroad was completed, Sheldon Jackson, in the company of two other ministers, climbed Prospect Hill—a high bluff near Sioux City, Iowa, from which four states could be seen. There the three men knelt in prayer for divine guidance, and then Sheldon Jackson as spokesman took possession of the land even beyond sight in Christ's name.

"What Francis Asbury, Methodist, was to the country east of the Mississippi," says Dr. Luther Weigle in American Idealism, *"Sheldon Jackson, Presbyterian, was to the Rocky Mountain frontier." The three presbyteries of Iowa had asked Jackson not only to organize churches throughout the vast unexplored region, but also to secure funds for the work. An enormous task—yet all had confidence in Sheldon Jackson, for he revealed the Word he preached, both in heart and in deed. Wherever he and his associates went, they brought mercy and goodness, law and decency, churches, schools, and a civilized way of life.*

When the West was well in hand, Sheldon Jackson received the call to Alaska, and until his death some twenty-three years later, the godly minister labored there selflessly. Helped by clergymen of other denominations who responded to his appeal, he built a magnificent missionary service, including an efficient system for medical care and schooling.

Frank S. Mead's On Our Own Doorstep *honors Sheldon Jackson and his fellow workers for their achievements, praising them as "saviors of Alaska."*

Sheldon Jackson

BY FRANK S. MEAD

W HEN the Americans came they found living conditions that were deplorably low. They found a handful of Christian Indians here and there, who had been converted by an Anglican, William Duncan, working across the line in Canada. An army private at Fort Wrangell was so concerned about it that he wrote a long letter to General Howard, his military commander, begging that something be done for these natives, that a missionary be sent, right away, to help the natives help themselves. History—even missionary history—tends to forget Private J. S. Brown, and that is too bad. For Brown started something. His letter fell into the hands of Sheldon Jackson, and in a matter of weeks Jackson had started for Alaska.

Jackson was a spiritual Cecil Rhodes, a diminutive kingdom builder who came to claim a great land and a great people for Jesus Christ. He had been building a string of Presbyterian churches all across the Rocky Mountain country and the Pacific Northwest when Private Brown's letter fell into his hands, so he was used to hardship. At Fort Wrangell he found a little school being held together by one of Duncan's converts. That school was his divine hint. It was schools, schools, schools with him, till he died. Far-visioned was Sheldon Jackson; he saw clearly that if the Eskimo and the Alaskan Indian were to be lifted up to a more abundant living, there must be intelligence for the mind as well as salvation for the soul.

He ran immediately into the same sort of white man opposition that the first Hawaiian missionaries met; he was threatened, heckled, badgered, persecuted, and even jailed by men who had come to Alaska only to exploit the native and get back home as soon as possible with their spoil. He was even told by one minister in the United States that he was wasting his time, that "even if all the people in Alaska were made Christian, they would not be worth one live Christian in Arizona, New Mexico, Utah, or Idaho!" The newspapers and the lobbyists in Washington hated him and fought him. They might as well have thrown pebbles at Gibraltar.

Tireless, he crossed mountains, crawled over glaciers, slept in the snow and on dog sleds and in hollow logs, hunting out isolated villages and settlements and giving them schools. Congress, finally convinced of the worth of Sheldon Jackson, made him Commissioner of Education for Alaska and gave him government cutters to sail around his "parish." He built an Industrial School for Boys at Sitka. At Kodiak, a village of log houses, he left a tiny school that one mother and two of her daughters traveled eighty miles to attend. At Afognak Island he put one hundred forty children and their parents in one school; at Karluk, one hundred eighteen children. At Unga, twenty-four. At Texikan, one hundred eighty-four.

He also made a trip now and then to the United States, talking in churches, talking in private homes, talking to anyone who would listen, talking about Alaska and the need for schools and schoolteachers and ministers and people who would help. He was a great recruiter. He could talk about a common weed and make you wish you had a weed like that in your front yard. He could talk of loneliness and cold and pioneering in Alaska and make men and women turn their backs on the comforts of civilization and go off into "the great white silence," teaching in schoolhouses that were shacks, burying themselves in isolated outposts where they hardly ever saw a white face and got their mail once a year.

He commuted to Washington, hounding Congress, buttonholing congressmen, inviting them to listen to his lectures, shoving articles he had written under their noses, following them on the streets and into their offices. Some liked him and some hated him. Enough liked him to present bills he suggested, and on July 8, 1880, he wrote in his diary, "Secured the passage of a resolution for schools in Alaska," which meant that the Federal government had taken over the schools. Five years later Congress voted him twenty-five thousand dollars to build more schools and maintain the old ones, appointed him United States Commissioner of Education for Alaska and gave him free passage on a revenue cutter. With the cutter *Bear* he ranged all the way from Nome to Point Barrow, which is the farthest north mission station in the world. He built schools and churches, broke his way through ice to relieve whites and natives trapped by famine, rescued shipwrecked sailors—a one-man army of the Lord against ignorance, suffering, despair, and sudden death.

He saw the whaling fleets of the Yankees drive the whale north
to the pole. He saw the walrus decimated almost to the vanishing
point, the sea lion and the salmon and the big game animals
slaughtered recklessly by men who didn't care whether the
natives—who lived on the flesh of these fish and animals—ate or
died. The natives *were* dying, fast; a trader in one village told
Jackson that the death rate in his area had become fifteen times
the birth rate. Jackson took it all in and made a most unusual
suggestion: why not make the Eskimos self-supporting and sure
of food by giving them herds of tamed reindeer—reindeer imported from Siberia? The white profiteers howled. This was like
suggesting socialism to Andrew Carnegie. Why feed a lot of
savages who were better off dead, anyway? Why didn't the missionary mind his own business? He was interfering all along the
line with men who were making fortunes out of the ignorant
Indian and Eskimo. Was Sheldon Jackson going to make a lot
of money out of this reindeer idea?

His enemies got to Congress, and Congress refused to appropriate money for such a wild scheme. Undisturbed, Jackson raised
two thousand dollars among his own friends, covered fifteen
hundred miles of Siberia and brought back sixteen reindeer, male
and female. A year later a somewhat shamed Congress helped
him get some more. As the herds increased, the native death
rate went down and the Eskimo smiled. Then the white capitalists
saw profit in the reindeer business, tried to get it away from the
Eskimo. It didn't work. Jackson went to work on the President,
the Cabinet and Congress, and laid the groundwork for a law
that put reindeer raising forever in the hands of the Eskimo.
Jackson was dead by the time that law was passed, but in his missionary's Valhalla, he must have said, "Amen!"

He built the first sawmill in the territory—a *mission* sawmill.
He taught the natives to build their own individual homes. Most
of the schools he built—and their name was legion—were built
with money he raised from Presbyterian churches and the government. The first reindeer money he raised in Presbyterian
churches.

It was Jackson who brought real law and government to the
territory. We find a notation in his diary, under date of May 17,
1884: "The President signed the bill for government in Alaska."
The act he referred to meant that Congress had adopted the laws
of the state of Oregon for Alaska; it provided for a governor ap-

pointed by the president, for a judge, a district attorney, a marshal, and four deputies.

He was a man "forever on the edge of things," forever looking ahead. He was no orator, no brilliant writer, but his concepts were bold and broad and he had the courage to fight for them. That was especially true of his religious faith. He was a Presbyterian, but he was also a happy warrior for interdenominational cooperation long before most contemporary Christians knew what those words really meant. He knew that no one denomination could ever do for Alaska what had to be done. So he filled his pockets with maps and pictures and figures and plans, came down to New York City, called a conference of Methodist, Baptist, Presbyterian, and Episcopalian leaders, and went to work on them. When he was through, they were as interdenominational as he was. They drew long lines across the map of Alaska, allotting territory. The Episcopalians took over the territory of the Yukon and northward. The Methodists said they would work in the Shumagin and Aleutian Islands and on the Alaska Peninsula. The Baptists were to send men to Cook Island and Prince William Sound, and the Presbyterians were to enlarge their work in Southeastern Alaska, where they were already settled. It was from the churches represented at this conference that Jackson recruited the teachers for his icebound schools. He didn't care much what church they went to, so long as they went to Alaska.

Inspired by Jackson and the new missionary interest, other church groups filtered in. Even before the New York conference, Jackson had talked with the Moravians, who had some few missionaries in Greenland and Labrador; he got them to take over the territory along the Kuskokium River. Then came the Norwegians, the Swedish Evangelical Church, the Friends. Heroes and heroines began to write their names in the brilliant missionary history of the day. Mrs. McFarland took her life in her hands working against the witch doctors and *shamans*, saving native girls from death and torture as witches. S. Hull Young, a young stripling just out of seminary, went over the land in dog sled and canoe, exploring, writing, teaching the natives to speak and write English, giving them grammars and Testaments in their own language. W. R. Corlies, a Baptist, buried himself in the icy wastes with one year's training in a medical school as his main equipment, and did for the sick of Alaska what Grenfell did for the sick of Labrador. . . .

There were others, too many to be mentioned here. By the end of the century there were American Protestant and Roman Catholic missionaries and missionary stations scattered from Metlakatla to Point Barrow. By 1905 they were infiltrating deep into the interior, building churches, schools, hospitals, homes; they were ministers, doctors, explorers, teachers. Sheldon Jackson looked at it and called it good, and died in 1909.

Twentieth-century Circuit-Rider

The North Carolina farm boy began to preach soon after he became a "real" Christian—soon after he experienced an out-and-out conversion. He has become the best-known, best-loved evangelist of his day.

Billy Graham's power-driven message, coupled with a sincerity which even his critics concede, has created a modern phenomenon. Multitudes gather wherever he speaks. He has been honored by the heads of state of several countries. Withal he remains the simple yet dynamic preacher of the old-time Gospel message.

"This is the ultimate spiritual energy that has always changed the world," a British journalist wrote after a Billy Graham meeting. Because he shares that sentiment, noted journalist Stanley High, son of a Methodist minister, wanted to find out for himself the story behind it all. To prepare his illuminating, authoritative biography of the young evangelist, he read all of Dr. Graham's private papers, studied the records of his organization, participated in Crusades here and abroad, and interviewed converts and local ministers. The dramatic and stirring bestseller which resulted, Billy Graham, *contains the following vivid summing-up of this modern circuit-rider's contribution to the religious revitalization of our time.*

Billy Graham's Crusades

BY STANLEY HIGH

Beginning with Los Angeles, Billy Graham's U. S. Crusades not only made religion front-page news. They tested Billy Graham. They sped his growth. They established his evangelism as no fly-by-night religious extravaganza, but as a sober, constructive, church-centered ministry, and they established Billy Graham as no hellfire-and-brimstone ranter but as an evangelist whose personal dedication and integrity merited comparison with the great evangelists of the past. It was such evidence—growing in weight and recognition with every U. S. Crusade—that opened the way for his expanding ministry in Great Britain, on the European continent and in Asia.

In many U. S. cities I have followed—from one to six years later—in the wake of Billy Graham. The evidence I gathered as to the permanence of the results of his Crusades is not statistical. I do not know and I did not make any particular effort to find out just what percentage of the "converts" in those cities are still carrying on. The statistical polls which I have seen for two cities were both made by amateurs obviously critical of Billy Graham. The results of both were somewhat negative.

Statistically, the churches of the United States do not need Billy Graham. Statistically, they are doing all right. But spiritually, as J. B. Phillips points out in the introduction to his stirring translation of the Acts of the Apostles, there has been a "deterioration in Christian faith and Christian living . . . The Church is very rarely making any considerable impact upon the modern pattern of living. It has unquestionably lost power; it has lost vision. . . ."

In every city I found, as I had found in Great Britain, men and women who, since the Billy Graham Crusade and because of it, were doing much more than carrying on; who had not only caught the Christian contagion, but had made it catching; individuals in the first-century tradition who, beginning with themselves, were turning their worlds—small worlds though they often were—"upside down." I do not know how many Christians of this kind would be required to make a total large enough to constitute "success" in the eyes of the critics of Billy Graham. The New Testament gives the impression that, in the eyes of the Lord, it would not take very many.

In September, 1949, when the Billy Graham Los Angeles Crusade began, Jim Vaus, an electronics expert, was established— and getting rich at it—as chief wiretapper for Mickey Cohen, Southern California's boss gangster. One night, on the eve of his departure on a Mickey Cohen mission to St. Louis, Vaus's wife, Alice, persuaded him—"lacking any good movies in the neighborhood"—to go with her to a Billy Graham meeting "just to see what this fellow's like." That night, Alice says, "Billy preached on God's judgment and God's mercy. When he gave the altar call I prayed, 'This is for me and for Jim, too, Lord, please.' Jim sat there unmoved. I prayed again, 'Lord, if this doesn't touch him, what will . . . ?'

"The crowd rose to sing, 'Almost persuaded, now to believe, almost persuaded, Christ to receive.' Again my heart cried, 'Persuade Jim, Lord, persuade him.'

"A wiry man with spare hair and a determined look on his thin face grabbed him by the arm. Jim glared at him. But he bowed his head to pray and when he raised his eyes, Jim muttered, 'I'll go.'"

To make restitution for electronic and photographic equipment he had stolen—there was some $15,000 of it—Jim Vaus sold his house and his automobile. He wrote, among others, to radio station KFWB, detailing what he had stolen, asking what he could do to make things right: "I want to right things with men that I may be right with God." The station manager's answer was: "Your unusual but courageous letter of December 8 received and we are happy to note your admission and your change of attitude. That in itself is payment in full as far as we are concerned. . . ."

When he turned up at the telephone company with a load of stolen goods, the manager there—instead of calling the police as Vaus expected—offered him a job.

He wrote to the district attorney confessing that, in a recent gangster case, he had committed perjury. He was promptly subpoenaed. The Court warned him: "You don't have to testify if your testimony will incriminate you." Vaus chose to testify and concluded his testimony with the Court's permission by giving his own account of what, as a result of "accepting Christ as my personal Savior," had happened to him. As a result of the evidence he gave, an officer of the Los Angeles police force was freed from charges pending against him. The indictment for perjury, which Vaus was certain would come, never materialized.

Now, Jim Vaus spends several months of every year conducting evangelistic services across the country. His crowds are large and so are the offerings. But all of the latter, save traveling expenses and his own $400-a-month salary, go into his Missionary Communication Service—a non-profit foundation he has established to provide electronic equipment for Christian missionaries in isolated stations around the world—"turning my specialty from crime to Christ's account." *Wiretapper,* a film produced in

1955 which dramatized the story of his underworld career and his conversion, was described by *Time* magazine as one of present-day evangelism's "most potent weapons."

Before World War II, Louis Zamperini was a track star at the University of Southern California. He was a miler on the U. S. team in the 1936 Olympics. In 1943 the plane in which he was a bombardier was shot down in the Pacific. When finally picked up by a Japanese fishing boat, he, with one other survivor, had floated forty-seven days in a rubber raft. Worse tortures were visited on him by guards in Japan's prison camps. When, at the war's end—a year after the War Department had declared him dead—he was released, he was rated as one of the half-dozen men "who suffered most in World War II."

Four years after the war's end, the "hero stuff" having worn thin, his marriage was near the rocks, his funds were running out, he had no settled job and "what's worse," he says, "no plan or purpose for my life."

It was his wife, Cynthia, herself a Crusade convert, who persuaded him to "give Billy Graham a one-meeting once-over." He left before Billy had finished preaching. When, on Cynthia's urging, he agreed to go a second time, it was on condition "that you will leave with me whenever I ask you to." She promised.

That night Billy Graham's text was: "For what shall it profit a man if he gain the whole world and lose his own soul? Or what shall a man give in exchange for his soul?"

"When he gave the invitation to accept Jesus as our Savior, I would not budge; I could not; I would not.

"'Don't you want to go forward?' asked Cynthia. . . . The moment had come; I stood at the top of a high wall; at the peak of conviction, I could still jump either way.

"'Let's leave,' I said and she rose slowly, her face very sad. But halfway down the aisle I stopped fighting and knew what I had to do. Turning around, I made my way to the prayer room. . . ."

Zamperini, too, made restitution: to the guards who, day after day, had tortured him in Japanese prison camps and toward whom, with the passing years, his hatred had not diminished. With friends helping to finance his trip, he went to Japan. He sought out as many of his torturers as he could find—some of them in prison. To each he gave his Christian testimony and offered, with his hand, his friendship.

"The six-year hate was over and I prayed my thanks. . . ."

Back in the United States, Zamperini was offered a lecture

contract: $50,000 a year for seven years—the only condition being that when it came to "talking about Christ," he would have to tone down a bit, agree not to "go overboard." Zamperini turned down the contract and "went to work, fulltime, for the Lord."

Today the dream which he and Cynthia had after their conversion is a reality: a Christian camp in the mountains not far from Los Angeles for juvenile delinquents, "Victory Boys' Camp." When the first "batch" of boys arrived the camp bank account was down to $50. "Faith," says Zamperini, "opened the camp and miracles have kept it going." Even greater miracles appear to have been worked in the lives of many of the confirmed delinquents he has taken in. The reality of those miracles is, I think, pretty well indicated by the wholehearted endorsement of his work by officials of the government of Los Angeles and of the state of California.

There are stories like these in every city where there has been a Billy Graham Crusade: of individuals who, as a result of that Crusade, became contagious Christians and for whom life's most important business has become the spreading of that contagion. I have enough such "case histories" in my own notes not merely to fill a chapter, but to make a substantial start toward a book. Yet I know that my inquiries hardly scratched the surface.

Five years after the Billy Graham Crusade there, I met the mayor of a Deep South city, a successful businessman.

"As a city," he said, "we've never been the same since, and, as a person, neither have I. It has made a difference for the better in the way business is carried on in our city that four groups of businessmen, organized as a result of the Crusade, meet regularly for Bible study and prayer. It has made for better labor-management relations that plant prayer meetings of employees and employers, begun during the Crusade, still meet, some of them daily.

"Today, in our city, interracial good will and cooperation are at an all-time high. Whites and Negroes, we are moving ahead together. When I appointed a Negro—the first—to our school board, the community accepted it, not as the necessary, but as the right thing to do. I don't think that would have happened without the new spirit engendered among our people during the Billy Graham Crusade. And, save for what happened to me, personally, in that Crusade, I doubt if I would have made such an appointment in the first place."

There is much more evidence, in high places and low, than I have space to recount:

In the fall of 1955 several young men were ordained for the Presbyterian ministry in Washington, D. C. Every one of these young men, according to Dr. Edward L. R. Elson, pastor of Washington National Presbyterian Church, was "brought to Christian experience in Billy Graham's Washington meeting."

One of the ministers of Southern California's largest Presbyterian church told me, "I personally know of more than a few young men and women who are now in seminaries or in church work here or in the mission field as a result of the 'decision for Christ' they made during the Los Angeles Crusade. Moreover, that Crusade was like a great bridge across the rift between the secular man and the churchman. Today the churches of this area are closer to the man in the street than ever before. That drawing together began with Billy Graham."

I called one day in Los Angeles at the office of one of the city's prominent real estate operators. "But this," he told me, "isn't the biggest thing in my life. The biggest thing in my life comes on Thursday night." Beginning with the Billy Graham Los Angeles Crusade, he had invited a few friends for Thursday evening Bible study. Now, after more than six years, that Bible class—taught by a well-known Los Angeles surgeon—has grown to an average attendance of more than 200. "To handle the crowd," he said, "my wife and I have built an addition to our house. If it continues to grow we'll gladly add another."

Riding through a residential area of Nashville, Tennessee, a friend called my attention to a sign on the front lawn of a lovely home. "There," he said, "is one of the permanent results of the Billy Graham Crusade." The sign read: "Neighborhood Prayer Meeting Here, This Morning." In preparation for the Crusade in 1954, Nashville women organized over 1,600 such neighborhood prayer groups. They met four mornings a week for four weeks. Now, more than two years later, scores of them are continuing to meet once a week. "If we stopped," the leader of one group told me, "every family in this street would be the loser. So would Nashville."

A Chattanooga newspaperman wrote me: "Interest has grown, not lessened since the end of the Crusade four years ago. Chattanooga may be the only city in America where students at the two largest high schools have organized prayer groups. It all began with Billy Graham. As for individuals, I could tick off for you the names of at least a half-dozen young men who made 'decisions' during the Crusade and are now studying for the ministry. Doesn't that sound pretty permanent?"

The minister of Chattanooga's largest Methodist church gave it as his conviction four years after the Billy Graham meetings that "the Crusade created a new spirit and environment in the city. . . . Prayer groups organized during the Crusade are more alive today than when they began. In my own church there are more than 200 prayer cells of from three to seven people each. Stirred by the Crusade many of our Methodist laymen have become lay preachers in small rural churches without pastors."

Two years after the New Orleans Crusade, the minister of the First Baptist Church reported that since Billy Graham's meetings there religion has had "a new lift" to it. The lasting consequence is not only still felt in the churches, but "extends to the whole moral life of New Orleans." In Memphis, says the minister of one of its largest churches, Billy Graham, three years after the Crusade, "is still refreshing to the religious life of the city. He was, and is, like a breeze in the desert. People are talking more about the church since he was here."

Three years after the 1952 Crusade in Pittsburgh, the editors of *Parade* magazine sent two reporters to that city to find the permanent effects of that Crusade, if any. An Episcopal bishop told that "the general awakening" stirred by Billy Graham was still being felt. The minister of a United Presbyterian church described the lasting results as "formidable"; a Methodist minister, as "tremendous." Among Pittsburgh's churchgoers, "there seems to be little doubt," said these reporters, "that a new spirit, engendered by Graham, is visible. Prayer groups and youth rallies started under the initial Graham enthusiasm, still meet weekly." Among all kinds of people—businessmen, schoolteachers, housewives, students, office workers—they found converts who were effectively and contagiously carrying on. Their conclusion:

"The question—Does Billy Graham's kind of religion 'stick'?—can be answered. The answer is Yes and No, with emphasis on the Yes."

Statistical appraisals of the permanence of the results of Billy Graham's Crusades will, I am sure, continue to be undertaken. The results of some of them, no doubt, will continue to serve as a means whereby the spiritually comfortable will seek to escape discomfiture. But there is another and, for Christians, a more conclusive kind of appraisal from which there is no such easy out:

"Another parable set he before them, saying, the kingdom of heaven is like unto a grain of mustard seed, which a man took and sowed in his field; which, indeed, is less than all seeds; but when it is grown it is greater than the herbs and becometh a tree, so that the birds of the heaven come and lodge in the branches thereof."

SIX

In God Is

Our Trust

Our nation's faith is inscribed even on its humblest coins: *In God we trust*. And this implicit belief in the power and presence of God, guided our early American statesmen not only in times of severe testing, but in their day-to-day responsibilities. Our great documents reflect trust in the Omnipotent, and awareness of the limitations of human nature. Again and again in our history our nation's leaders have found in their religious faith the necessary strength for the "impossible."

Our Second President

George Washington's voluntary retirement from the Presidency after eight years initiated a violent struggle between the two political parties organized during his administration.

John Adams, a controversial figure within his group, was chosen Washington's successor by the slimmest of margins. On the day that the votes were counted, and Adams, as vice-president, was required by law to announce himself president-elect, his devoted wife Abigail sent the following touching and inspiring letter, one of many she wrote to him during their long periods of separation.

An Understanding Heart

BY ABIGAIL ADAMS

Quincy, 8 February, 1797

"The sun is dressed in brightest beams,
To give thy honors to the day."

AND may it prove an auspicious prelude to each ensuing season. You have this day to declare yourself head of a nation. "And now, O Lord, my God, Thou hast made thy servant ruler over the people. Give unto him an understanding heart, that he may know how to go out and come in before this great people; that he may discern between good and bad. For who is able to judge this thy so great a people?" were the words of a royal Sovereign; and not less applicable to him who is invested with the Chief Magistracy of a nation, though he wear not a crown, nor the robes of royalty.

My thoughts and meditations are with you, though personally

211

absent; and my petitions to Heaven are that "the things which make for peace may not be hidden from your eyes." My feelings are not those of pride or ostentation upon the occasion. They are solemnized by a sense of the obligations, the important trusts, and numerous duties connected with it. That you may be enabled to discharge them with honor to yourself, with justice and impartiality to your country, and with satisfaction to this great people, shall be the daily prayer of your—

—A. A.

"What Hath God Wrought!"

Impetuous Samuel F. B. Morse was a man of varied talents. An artist by profession, and a politician, photographer, and writer by inclination, Morse achieved his place in history in yet another way, with his invention of the electro-magnetic telegraph. His device ultimately brought him honor throughout the world; first, however, he had to face attacks on this momentous new idea, defending his patent and even his own integrity.

At the request of a Pennsylvania churchman, Morse wrote with keen emotion of the event which made the telegraph "no longer the wild dream of a visionary, but an accomplished fact."

The First Telegraph Line

BY SAMUEL F. B. MORSE

Paris, November, 1866

I HAD spent at Washington two entire sessions of Congress, one in 1837-'38, the other in 1842-'43, in the endeavor so far to interest the Government in the novel Telegraph as to furnish me with the means to construct a line of sufficient length to test its practicability and utility.

The last days of the last session of that Congress were about to close. A bill appropriating thirty thousand dollars for my purpose had passed the House, and was before the Senate for concurrence, waiting its turn on the calendar. On the last day of the session (3d of March, 1843), I had spent the whole day and part of the evening in the Senate-chamber, anxiously watching the progress of the passing of the various bills, of which there were, in the morning of that day, over one hundred and forty to be acted upon, before the one in which I was interested

213

would be reached; and a resolution had a few days before been
passed, to proceed with the bills on the calendar in their regular
order, forbidding any bill to be taken up out of its regular place.
As evening approached, there seemed to be but little chance
that the Telegraph Bill would be reached before the adjournment, and consequently I had the prospect of the delay of another year, with the loss of time, and all my means already expended. In my anxiety, I consulted with two of my senatorial
friends—Senator Huntington, of Connecticut, and Senator
Wright, of New York—asking their opinion of the probability
of reaching the bill before the close of the session. Their answers
were discouraging, and their advice was to prepare myself for
disappointment. In this state of mind I retired to my chamber,
and made all my arrangements for leaving Washington the next
day. Painful as was this prospect of renewed disappointment,
you, my dear sir, will understand me when I say that, knowing
from experience whence my help must come in any difficulty,
I soon disposed of my cares, and slept as quietly as a child.

In the morning, as I had just gone into the breakfast-room,
the servant called me out, announcing that a young lady was
in the parlor, wishing to speak with me. I was at once greeted
with the smiling face of my young friend, the daughter of my
old and valued friend and classmate, the Hon. H. L. Ellsworth,
the Commissioner of Patents. On expressing my surprise at so
early a call, she said, "I have come to congratulate you." "Indeed, for what?" "On the passage of your bill." "Oh, no, my
young friend, you are mistaken; I was in the Senate-chamber
till after the lamps were lighted, and my senatorial friends assured me there was no chance for me." "But," she replied, "it is
you that are mistaken. Father was there at the adjournment, at
midnight, and saw the President put his name to your bill; and
I asked father if I might come and tell you, and he gave me
leave. Am I the first to tell you?" The news was so unexpected
that for some moments I could not speak. At length I replied:
"Yes, Annie, you are the first to inform me; and now I am going
to make you a promise: the first dispatch on the completed line
from Washington to Baltimore shall be yours." "Well," said she,
"I shall hold you to your promise."

In about a year from that time, the line from Washington to
Baltimore was completed. I was in Baltimore when the wires
were brought into the office, and attached to the instrument. I
proceeded to Washington, leaving word that no dispatch should

be sent through the line until I had sent one from Washington. On my arrival there, I sent a note to Miss Ellsworth, announcing to her that everything was ready, and I was prepared to fulfill my promise of sending the first dispatch over the wires, which she was to indite. The answer was immediately returned. The dispatch was, *"What hath God wrought!"* It was sent to Baltimore, and repeated to Washington, and the strip of paper upon which the telegraphic characters are printed, was claimed by Governor Seymour, of Hartford, Connecticut, then a member of the House, on the ground that Miss Ellsworth was a native of Hartford. It was delivered to him by Miss Ellsworth, and is now preserved in the archives of the Hartford Museum, or Athenaeum.

I need only add that no words could have been selected more expressive of the disposition of my own mind at that time, to ascribe all the honor to Him to whom it truly belongs.

"With Malice Toward None"

Ruth Painter Randall, a distinguished Civil War scholar, has specialized in the story of Lincoln and his family. She here sympathetically traces the course of the martyred President's religious pilgrimage, and points out how "in surmounting doubts and bitter trials he gathered a profound spiritual strength."

Lincoln's Faith Was Born of Anguish

BY RUTH PAINTER RANDALL

Abraham Lincoln reached his mature religion, as he did his statesmanship, by a process of growth. This development and the religious faith he achieved through the years can be traced in his own words. Stages in his progress were marked by certain deeply emotional experiences in his life. The first of these to be considered is the occasion when his engagement to Mary Todd was broken on what he called "that fatal first of Jany. '41." Lincoln fell into a torturing melancholia. "I am now the most miserable man living," he wrote. "To remain as I am is impossible; I must die or be better, it appears to me." Some of his friends described him as "crazy."

He soon got hold of himself enough to resume normal activities, but his depression and estrangement from Mary lasted through that year and far into the next. He himself traced his varying thoughts and emotions in a series of letters to his loved friend Joshua Speed. He and Joshua had been roommates in Springfield for four years. With the inquiring minds of young men they had had long discussions of such important subjects as marriage and religion and had raised skeptical questions about both. Then Joshua left Springfield and, some months after Lincoln's period of deepest melancholia, he, too, got himself

216

tied up in a psychological knot over a love affair. Lincoln tried to help Joshua by writing of his own experience and offering what would now be termed psychiatric advice.

When Joshua's courtship ended in marriage and he wrote his appreciation of his friend's help, Lincoln's reply showed he had reached a significant stage in his religious feeling. After months of mental conflict over perplexing factors in his broken engagement, he was ready to lay aside his struggle for a solution and rest passive while he awaited the revelation of divine guidance. "I always was superstitious," he wrote, "and as part of my superstition, I believe God made me one of the instruments of bringing your Fanny and you together, which union I have no doubt He had fore-ordained. Whatever he designs, he will do for *me* yet. 'Stand *still* and see the salvation of the Lord' is my text just now." It is a most satisfactory ending to Lincoln's love story to know that very close to this time, certain friends made themselves "the instruments" of bringing him and Mary Todd together and that four months to the day after he wrote this he and the woman he loved were married.

Lincoln's way with any problem was to examine it from all sides and reason it out intellectually. Such religion as he had known in his growing up in the backwoods was often mostly an orgy of emotionalism which could not meet the needs or command the respect of his mind. When he came to live in Springfield, which was well supplied with churches, he encountered the narrow orthodoxy of more than a century ago. He was a man of such scrupulous truthfulness that he would not use the conventional greeting, "I am delighted to see you," unless it were literally true. To have joined a church would have implied acceptance of doctrines which he could not accept, would have been acting out an untruth.

His not joining a church was used against him. In a political contest in 1846, a report was circulated that he was an open scoffer at Christianity. Lincoln wrote an answer to the charge: "That I am not a member of any Christian Church, is true; but I have never denied the truth of the Scriptures; and I have never spoken with intentional disrespect of religion in general, or of any denomination of Christians in particular." He admitted that "in early life" he had argued over a matter of doctrine, though he had never done so publicly, and he added: "The habit of arguing thus, however, I have entirely left off for more than five years.

"I do not think I could myself," he continued, "be brought to support a man for office, whom I knew to be an open enemy of, and scoffer at, religion."

Few people have been more loving and devoted parents than the Lincolns. When they lost their little son, Eddie, in Springfield, Lincoln in his agony of grief became closely acquainted with a Presbyterian minister, Dr. James Smith, who had written a book in which he dealt with religious questions on an intellectual level without loss of faith. He seems to have helped the bereaved father toward further maturity in his religious beliefs.

Dr. Smith became a loved friend of the Lincoln family and Mrs. Lincoln joined his church. Lincoln attended church with her, paid the rent on the family pew and served on church committees. In general, Lincoln cooperated with the ministers in Springfield. To one who was a close neighbor, he lent his horse and carriage for church work and when the minister's house was too crowded with visitors, the Lincolns put up the overflow at their house.

Mrs. Lincoln had an unquestioning faith and was devoted to her church. Something of the attitude which prevailed in the Lincoln home is disclosed in the fact that their little boy, Willie, wanted to be a preacher when he grew up.

A Springfield neighbor remembered Lincoln as often saying that when he discovered a church whose creed was the Golden Rule he would unite with it. Later he made a fuller statement. When he found, he said, a church whose sole qualification for membership was the injunction: "Thou shalt love the Lord thy God with all thy heart, and with all thy soul * * * and with all thy mind; and thy neighbour as thyself," that church he would join with all his heart and soul.

Lincoln lived in neighborly affection with his friends at Springfield. When his election to the Presidency brought the hour when he must leave them his farewell was like a prayer. He had before him, he said, a task "greater than that which rested upon Washington. Without the assistance of that Divine Being, who ever attends me," he continued, "I cannot succeed. With that assistance I cannot fail. Trusting in Him, who can go with me and remain with you and be everywhere for good, let us confidently hope that all will yet be well. To His care commending you, as I hope in your prayers you will commend me, I bid you an affectionate farewell."

In Washington Lincoln was soon at the storm center of war

in a divided country. Friends he loved were dying in battle; vicious abuse was being hurled at him from all sides; he was overwhelmed with mighty decisions. Then, in February, 1862, the Lincolns' beloved Willie, the child who had been born within the year after Eddie's death to comfort them, the son who was so like his father, sickened and died. The youngest son was also ill; Lincoln's wife was prostrated with grief.

A nurse was sent to the White House, a woman who had lost husband and two children and, finding strength and peace in her religious faith, was giving herself to the care of wounded soldiers in hospitals. Lincoln walked the floor in an agony of spirit as he questioned her as to how she had obtained her faith in God and the secret of placing herself in Divine hands. "Did you always feel that you could say, 'Thy will be done'? * * * This is the hardest trial of my life. Why is it? Oh, why is it?"

At Mrs. Lincoln's request a minister came to the White House to offer religious comfort. He repeated Biblical assurances of immortality which seemed to penetrate the frozen despair of the father, and Lincoln wept in his response to the thought that Willie's spirit was still alive. Later he referred to the "change" in his religious feeling after Willie's death. It marked another advance in his faith, another stage in what he called "a process of crystallization" going on in his mind.

He took up again the crushing burdens of the Presidency and the war for the Union. That spring, speaking of the dark state of the war to a friend, he said: "You know I am not of a very hopeful temperament. * * * But, relying on God for help, and believing that our cause is right, I think we shall conquer in the end."

But even with this reliance and belief, it was often hard to know what to do. A patriotic minister called on the President to urge him to "make a clean sweep for the Right." Lincoln replied: "Doctor, it's very hard sometimes to know what is right! You pray often and honestly, but so do those people across the lines. They pray and all their preachers pray devoutly. You and I do not think them justified in praying for their objects, but they pray earnestly, no doubt! If you and I had our own way, Doctor, we would settle this war without bloodshed, but Providence permits blood to be shed. It's hard to tell what Providence wants of us."

In 1862, Lincoln in effect asked Providence a question as to what to do. His Secretary of the Treasury, Salmon P. Chase, told of a meeting of the Cabinet at which the issuing of an emancipation proclamation was being discussed. Lincoln said: "When the rebel army was at Frederick, I determined, as soon as it should be driven out of Maryland, to issue a Proclamation of Emancipation such as I thought most likely to be useful. I said nothing to anyone; but I made the promise to myself, and (hesitating a little)—to my Maker. The rebel army is now driven out, and I am going to fulfill that promise."

Reading his letters and public statements from 1862 on, one finds running through them, like a low refrain slowly increasing in volume, expressions of his reliance on God's will. In May of that year, he said to a religious group: "You well know, gentlemen, and the world knows, how reluctantly I accepted this issue of battle forced upon me * * * that in taking up the sword thus forced into our hands this Government * * * declared that it placed its whole dependence upon the favor of God. I now humbly and reverently, in your presence, reiterate the acknowledgment of that dependence * * *"

In 1863, the middle year of the Civil War, this reiteration increased. In January, he said: "No one is more deeply than myself aware that without His favor our highest wisdom is but as foolishness and that our most strenuous efforts would avail nothing in the shadow of His displeasure." In February, he wrote in behalf of "* * * whatever shall tend to turn our thoughts from the unreasoning, and uncharitable passions, prejudices, and jealousies incident to a great national trouble, such as ours, and * * * strengthen our reliance on the Supreme Being * * *" In March: "* * * it is the duty of nations as well as of men, to own their dependence upon the overruling power of God * * *"

There is ample evidence that Lincoln read the Bible much and turned to it especially in his darkest hours. Its rhythm and the power of its phrasing permeate his writings. He found in it belief in the dignity of the individual and the underlying philosophy of democracy in which he had so great a faith. He called the Bible "the best gift God has given to man."

With the broad basis of his religion love of God and neighbor, Lincoln had consideration for the personal religious preferences of others. Shortly after he was nominated, a friend of his son, Robert, came to Springfield to see him. Lincoln casually took the young man home to dinner. As they walked into the dining room, the tall host asked the visitor if he said grace at meals.

The young man himself said a poetic grace while the Lincoln family, father, mother and children, bowed their heads.

We have President Lincoln's letter saying he had appointed as hospital chaplains three Protestant ministers and asking Archbishop Hughes to suggest "suitable persons of the Catholic Church, to whom I may, with propriety, tender the same service."

He did not care for the holier-than-thou approach. In his lecture on temperance he deflated those who felt too superior to associate with a reformed drunkard. "In my judgment," he said, "such of us as have never fallen victims have been spared more from an absence of appetite, than from any mental or moral superiority over those who have." In quite a different connection, he remarked: "Men are not flattered by being shown that there has been a difference of purpose between the Almighty and them."

When Lincoln was re-elected in 1864 he felt no elation, only humility. On the weary day following that night of listening to election returns he said to his friend, Noah Brooks: "I should be the veriest shallow and self-conceited blockhead upon the footstool, if in my discharge of the duties that are put upon me in this place, I should hope to get along without the wisdom that comes from God, and not from men." He dreaded the trials ahead, but declared simply: "I put my trust in God."

Joshua Speed came to Washington to see Lincoln in the summer of 1864 and found the President at the Soldiers' Home earnestly reading the Bible. The visitor remarked with a touch of sarcasm: "I am glad to see you so profitably engaged." "Yes," was the answer, "I am profitably engaged." Joshua then said: "Well, if you have recovered from your skepticism, I am sorry to say I have not." Lincoln put his hand on his friend's shoulder, his worn face calm and earnest. "You are wrong, Speed," he said. "Take all of this book upon reason that you can, and the balance on faith, and you will live and die a happier and better man."

The President talked freely to Noah Brooks about his matured religious beliefs. "His language seemed not that of an inquirer," wrote Brooks, "but of one who had a prior settled belief in the fundamental doctrines of the Christian religion * * * He [Lincoln] said, too, that after he went to the White House he kept up the habit of daily prayer." Brooks gained the impression that the President "was seriously considering the step which would formally connect him with the visible Church on earth."

Lincoln had "fought his doubts and gathered strength * * *
To find a stronger faith his own." As his service to his country
and his life itself drew near the end, he embodied his full-
rounded Christianity in the closing words of his second inaugural:

"With malice toward none; with charity for all; with firmness
in the right, as God gives us to see the right, let us strive on to
finish the work we are in; to bind up the nation's wounds, to
care for him who shall have borne the battle, and for his widow,
and his orphan—to do all which may achieve and cherish a just,
and a lasting peace, among ourselves, and with all nations."

Stonewall Jackson

The American soldier has always shown rare perception in the nicknames he accords his leaders. "Stonewall" Jackson was just that—one of the toughest-minded troopers of the Civil War, stern in discipline, yet adored by his men. At his best when danger was greatest, he won the respect of North and South alike through fearless performance of his duty.

But General T. J. Jackson was also a man of intense religious conviction, one who showed in many ways how he cherished his faith. Tolerant of all differences of opinion, he firmly believed in prayer, which was, even in battle, "the breath of his nostrils." David Macrae, a Scottish minister who toured America some years after the Civil War, brings to life memories of Jackson's noble spirit in both defeat and victory.

Jackson's Character Illustrated

BY DAVID MACRAE

TRAVELLING around the South I met so many of Jackson's friends, and heard him so often described by those who had known him and fought under him, that he rises before my mind as clearly as if I had seen him a hundred times myself. His old horse "Sorrel"; his faded gray uniform, discoloured with the smoke and dust of a hundred battle-fields; his long, stiff, lank figure; his strange walk, and occasionally abstracted look; his habit of sitting on his horse bent forward, with his knees cramped up and his old cadet-cap tilted so far forward that he had to keep his chin up to let him see—his luminous blue eye, clear and searching—his grave, stern look—the terrible kindling of his countenance when, in the midst of the battle, he rode up with what his men called his "war-look" on him—the strange motion of his right arm, lifted every now and then to heaven as if in prayer, and suddenly dropped again—all comes back to me with the vividness, not of description, but of sight.

It was said that the singularity of Jackson's appearance, and the oddness of his manner, made him at first the object of much ridicule and contempt. Jefferson Davis, who ought to have seen deeper into Jackson's character, is said to have gone so far at one time as to bring before his Cabinet a proposition for his removal.

It was very soon after this that Jackson's exploits in the Valley showed not only to Jefferson Davis, but to the world, that a great military genius had arisen in the South. After repulsing Banks, Jackson was retreating slowly up the Shenandoah, pursued by the converging columns of Frémont and Shields, when, turning suddenly at Cross Keys, he dealt Frémont a staggering blow, driving him back in wild confusion. The first news of this was received by Mr. Letcher at Richmond, who immediately went and read the dispatch to Davis. "There must be some mistake," said Davis. "That handful of men in retreat could never have turned and beat a strong army in pursuit."

Jackson, meantime, having disposed of Frémont, crossed the river rapidly, attacked Shields, who had been pursuing him on the other side, and routed him with great slaughter.

Again Letcher was the first to get the news, and hurried with it to Davis's house. He found Davis and his Cabinet at dinner.

"You would get my news of yesterday confirmed?" said Letcher.

"Yes, Jackson's despatch came in to-day, saying that, 'by the blessing of God,' he had gained the victory."

"Well," said Letcher, "here is another bulletin of victory"— and he handed Mr. Davis the telegram.

Mr. Davis started. "This is incredible!" he said. "It cannot be. It is unprecedented in military history—an army like that in full retreat turning on its track and vanquishing two stronger armies in pursuit!"

Still it turned out to be true. Mr. Davis never troubled his Cabinet with any proposal to remove Stonewall Jackson again.

Jackson was soon the idol of the South. When he passed with his command through towns or villages, people poured out eagerly to see him; women brought their children in their arms to point him out that they might tell in after life that they had seen the great soldier. His brother-in-law gave me an amusing instance of this popularity. A Virginian gentleman, on the Mechanicsville Turnpike, near Richmond, had given up his crops and pasture-fields to the Confederate Government, reserving one ten-acre lot of corn, which he guarded jealously. He was excited to fury one day by discovering a group of horsemen, whom he took for cavalry, riding straight through this ten-acre lot. He rushed out—"How dare you ride through my field?" he said. "You vagabonds, I'll report you—I'll report you to the President."

A horseman, in an old dusty gray coat and cadet-cap, rode up and said, "We are on urgent business, sir, and took the shortest cut."

"Do you command this company, sir?" cried the irascible Virginian.

"Yes, sir."

"Then I'll teach you a lesson. By thunder! I'll report you, sir. What's your name?"

"Jackson."

"Jackson? What Jackson?"

"T. J. Jackson, Major-General, Confederate Army."

"What! you ain't Stonewall Jackson?"

"They sometimes call me so," said the horseman.

"Bless my soul!" cried the Virginian, rushing forward and grasping the General's hand. "General Jackson! God bless you, sir! If I had known it was you! Ride where you like, sir—ride over my field; go back, sir, and ride over it, every inch of it."

Jackson's character and achievements excited even his enemies to admiration. Federal prisoners were always anxious to see him. At Harper's Ferry 11,000 of them, whom he had taken at one fell swoop in September, 1862, greeted him when he rode along the line with lusty cheers.

By his own men, Jackson was almost adored; and the sight of his faded coat and cadet-cap was always the signal for a cheer.

"They were terrible on us, them hard marches," said one of his soldiers, whom I met as far south as Vicksburg; "but oh, sir," he added, with the tears suddenly starting into his eyes, "how we loved him!"

Jackson himself was a man who disliked, and was ever afraid of adulation. He once said to a friend, "These newspapers make me ashamed."

When the editor of a public magazine wrote him for his photograph and a narrative of his achievements, with a view to publication, his reply was curt—"Sir, I have no photograph, and I have achieved nothing."

On another occasion he said—"The way in which press, army, and people seem to lean on individuals fills me with alarm. They are forgetting God in his instruments."

The Giver of Victory

Although devoted to the ideal of Union and hopeful for a successful compromise, Robert E. Lee could not accept President Lincoln's offer to appoint him field commander of the Union Army. Unable to fight against his beloved state of Virginia, he resigned his post, accepting first the command of the Virginia military forces, and later the generalship of all the Confederate armies.

After the tragic Battle of Gettysburg, Lee attempted to resign, but the whole South joined with Confederate President Davis in a plea that he stay on. Thus it was Robert E. Lee who finally surrendered at Appomattox, with General Grant showing him due deference for his honor, chivalry, and courage. The Reverend J. William Jones, who perhaps more than any other person knew this facet of Lee's character, relates how the great general gave the glory for his achievements to the God he so fervently worshiped and served.

The Christianity of Robert E. Lee

BY J. WILLIAM JONES

IN THIS age of hero-worship there is a tendency to exalt unduly the virtues of great men and to magnify the religious character of one professing to be a Christian. This is so well understood that there may be with those who never came in contact with this great man a lingering doubt as to the genuineness of his piety—a fear that, with him as with many others, his profession of religion was merely nominal. A few incidents, culled from the many that might be given, will serve to dissipate any such impression and to show beyond all cavil that with General Lee vital godliness was a precious reality. . . .

227

General Lee always took the deepest interest in the work of his chaplains and the spiritual welfare of his men. He was a frequent visitor at the chaplains' meetings and a deeply-interested observer of their proceedings, and the faithful chaplain who stuck to his post and did his duty could be always assured of a warm friend at headquarters.

While the Army of Northern Virginia confronted General Meade at Mine Run, near the end of November 1863, and a battle was momentarily expected, General Lee with a number of general and staff officers was riding down his line of battle when, just in the rear of General A. P. Hill's position, the cavalcade suddenly came upon a party of soldiers engaged in one of those prayer-meetings which they so often held on the eve of battle. An attack from the enemy seemed imminent; already the sharpshooting along the skirmish-line had begun; the artillery was belching forth its hoarse thunder and the mind and heart of the great chieftain were full of the expectant combat. Yet, as he saw those ragged veterans bowed in prayer, he instantly dismounted, uncovered his head and devoutly joined in the simple worship. The rest of the party at once followed his example, and those humble privates found themselves leading the devotions of their loved and honored chieftains.

It is related that as his army was crossing the James in 1864 and hurrying on to the defenses of Petersburg, General Lee turned aside from the road and, kneeling in the dust, devoutly joined a minister present in earnest prayer that God would give him wisdom and grace in the new stage of the campaign upon which he was then entering. . . .

General Lee's orders and reports always gratefully recognized "the Lord of hosts" as the "Giver of victory," and expressed a humble dependence upon and trust in Him.

He thus began his dispatch to the President the evening of his great victory [in 1862] at Cold Harbor and Gaines's Mill: "Profoundly grateful to Almighty God for the signal victory granted to us, it is my pleasing task to announce to you the success achieved by this army to-day."

His beautiful general order of congratulation to the troops on their series of splendid victories during the Seven Days' battles opened with these memorable words: "The commanding general, profoundly grateful to the Giver of all victory for the signal success with which He has blessed our arms, tenders his warmest thanks and congratulations to the army by whose valor such splendid results have been achieved."

His dispatch announcing the great victory at Fredericksburg contains the brief but significant sentence: "Thanks be to God."

In his dispatch to President Davis after Chancellorsville, he said: "We have again to thank Almighty God for a great victory." And in his general order to his troops he uses this significant language: ". . . While this glorious victory entitles you to the praise and gratitude of the nation, we are especially called upon to return our grateful thanks to the only Giver of victory for the signal deliverance He has wrought. It is therefore earnestly recommended that the troops unite on Sunday next in ascribing unto the Lord of hosts the glory due unto His name."

In his dispatch announcing the result of the first day's battle in the Wilderness he says: ". . . By the blessing of God we maintained our position against every effort until night, when the contest closed." . . .

He closes his dispatch concerning the first day at Spottsylvania by saying: "I am most thankful to the Giver of all victory that our loss is small"; and that concerning the action of June 3, 1864, with "Our loss to-day has been small and our success, under the blessing of God, all that we could expect."

In his order assuming the command of all the Confederate forces [in February 1865] he said: ". . . Deeply impressed with the difficulties and responsibility of the position and humbly invoking the guidance of Almighty God, I rely for success upon the courage and fortitude of the army, sustained by the patriotism and firmness of the people, confident that their united efforts, under the blessing of Heaven, will secure peace and independence."

. . . With the close of the war and the afflictions which came upon his loved land, the piety of this great man seems to have mellowed and deepened, and we could fill pages concerning his life at Lexington and the bright evidence he gave of vital, active godliness. He was a most regular attendant upon all of the services of his own church, his seat in the college chapel was never vacant unless he was kept away by sickness, and if there was a union prayer meeting or a service of general interest in any of the churches of Lexington, General Lee was sure to be among the most devout attendants. . . . He always devoutly knelt during prayer, and his attitude during the entire service was that of an interested listener or a reverential participant. . . .

He had also a most intelligent appreciation of the adaptation of religious services to particular occasions and of the appropriateness of prayers to the time and place in which they were offered. He once said to one of the faculty:

> I want you to go with me to call upon Mr. ——, the new minister who has just come to town. I want to pay my respects to him and to invite him to take his turn in the conduct of our chapel exercises and to do what he can for the spiritual interests of our young men. And do you think that it would be any harm for me to delicately hint to him that we should be glad if he would make his morning prayers a little short? You know our friend is accustomed to make his prayers too long. He prays for the Jews, the Turks, the heathen, the Chinese and everybody else, and makes his prayers run into the regular hour for our college recitations. Would it be wrong for me to suggest to the new minister that he confine his morning prayers to us poor sinners at the college, and pray for the Turks, the Jews, the Chinese and the other heathen some other time? . . .

General Lee was a member of the Episcopal Church and was sincerely attached to the church of his choice; but his large heart took in Christians of every name; he treated ministers of all denominations with the most marked courtesy and respect; and it may be truly said of him that he had a heart and hand ready to every good work. When once asked his opinion of a certain theological question which was exciting considerable discussion, he replied: "Oh, I never trouble myself about such questions. My chief concern is to try to be a humble, earnest Christian myself."

An application of a Jewish soldier for permission to attend certain ceremonies of his synagogue in Richmond was indorsed by his captain: "Disapproved. If such applications were granted, the whole army would turn Jews or shaking Quakers." When the paper came to General Lee he indorsed on it: "Approved, and respectfully returned to Captain —— with the advice that he should always respect the religious views and feelings of others." . . .

If I have ever come in contact with a sincere, devout Christian, one . . . whose piety constantly exhibited itself in his daily life, that man was General R. E. Lee.

"The Direct Handiwork of God"

On his father's Wisconsin farm, the eleven-year-old Scottish immigrant boy, John Muir, began to ponder on the marvels of nature, and meditated over the Bible he so loved to read and study. At twenty-nine he covered the country in a walk which extended from the Middle Border to the Gulf, making the first study of the flora, fauna, and physiography of the great Mississippi Valley. Later John Muir concentrated on the glaciers and the magnificent forests of California, and then pursued his study of nature on the icebound stretches of Alaska.

Enlisting the support of another nature-lover, Theodore Roosevelt, Muir laid the groundwork for America's first conservation project. At the same time he assumed its leadership through his impassioned writings. Edwin Way Teale, a kindred nature enthusiast, has caught the essence of Muir's feeling and philosophy in the following selection.

The Wilderness World of John Muir

BY EDWIN WAY TEALE

Among the rare books at the Yale University Library there is a rusty-brown volume with penciled notations running along the margins and spilling over onto the flyleaves at the back. The book is Volume I of *The Prose Works of Ralph Waldo Emerson*, published in 1870 by Field, Osgood & Company, of Boston. It was this book that John Muir carried with him, read and reread, during his mountain days in the high Sierra.

Emerson was one of the great admirations of Muir's life. The Concord philosopher replied in kind, for when, in his old age, he set down his list of "My Men," the ones who had influenced him most, he began it with Thomas Carlyle and ended it with

John Muir. Thus Muir's reflections on Emerson's words, especially points of divergence, have particular interest in revealing qualities of his mind and outlook.

In *Spiritual Laws*, Emerson declares: "The Vale of Tempe, Tivoli, and Rome are earth and water, rocks and sky. There are as good earth and water in a thousand places, yet how unaffecting." Beside these words, Muir has written, "They are not unaffecting." Again, in *Nature*, Emerson observes: "There is in woods and waters a certain enticement and flattery, together with a failure to yield a present satisfaction. This disappointment is felt in every landscape." Muir dissents: "No—always we find more than we expect."

Always, in truth, he found more than he expected in nature. Never did he get enough of wildness. Of those who have written of nature surpassingly well—Gilbert White, Henry Thoreau, Richard Jeffries, W. H. Hudson—John Muir was the wildest. He was the most active, the most at home in the wilderness, the most daring, the most capable, the most self-reliant. . . .

All he needed to do to get ready for an expedition, Muir said, was to "throw some tea and bread in an old sack and jump over the back fence." . . . While in the wilderness, he declared, he lived on "essences and crumbs" and his pack was as "unsubstantial as a squirrel's tail." Throughout his life—from his childhood in Scotland, with its brutality and floggings, his years of labor on the pioneer Wisconsin farm and his wanderings alone in the wilds of Canada, the South and among the mountains of the Far West—Muir was stoically indifferent to physical hardship.

He never carried a gun. Traveling alone and far from any other human being for weeks at a time, he never was harmed by bear or rattlesnake, never was seriously injured in an accident. Eliphaz the Temanite might well have addressed to Muir his words: ". . . thou shalt be in league with the stones of the field; and the beasts of the field will be at peace with thee." . . .

But always, even in his most daring undertakings, there was a goal of importance. He was never merely seeking thrills or going afield for trophies. To understand Muir and the fire that burned in him, it is necessary to realize that for him all outdoors was at once a laboratory for research and a temple for research.

Repelled by the harsh fanaticism of his father's religion, John Muir belonged to no church. He gave freely when solicited by Protestant and Catholic alike. But he affiliated himself with no formal creed. Yet he was intensely religious. The forests and the mountains formed his temple. His approach to all nature was worshipful. He saw everything evolving yet everything the direct handiwork of God. There was a spiritual and religious exaltation in his experiences with nature. And he came down from the mountains like some bearded prophet to preach of the beauty and healing he had found in this natural temple where he worshiped. He spoke with the fire of the old Covenanters. This religious fervor and spiritual intensity in Muir's response to nature contributed much to the power of his pleading for the cause of conservation. He never based his arguments on economic considerations alone. He always appealed to men on a high moral plane. I know of no other writer, with the exception of Henry Thoreau, who had so pure and lofty a vision of man's ultimate relationship to nature.

Marion Randall Parsons, the friend who helped John Muir with his last book, *Travels in Alaska,* told me that one day he said to her: "To get these glorious works of God into yourself—that's the thing; not to write about them!" Muir was fifty-six when his first book appeared. He had written only two by the time he was seventy. The remarkable thing is not that his books were so slow to appear, so long delayed, but rather that they appeared at all. He was too busy living to stop and write . . . and he died leaving notes for a dozen books that he never completed. . . .

An exactness and depth of firsthand observation characterizes all his pages. He was by turn a scientist, a poet, a mystic, a philosopher, a humorist . . . Even his records of scientific studies read like adventure stories.

There have been those who have complained, with some basis, that Muir's books tended to be "adjectivorous," that all his mountain streams "sang psalms," that he overworked such words as "glorious." . . . However, his overworking of this adjective was, in itself, a key to his character. For him, always, the world *was* glorious.

Twice Muir had prospects of making a large fortune. Both times he turned aside from the path of wealth to these glories of nature. . . .

Henry James once commented that Thoreau was not provincial, he was parochial. Muir, on the other hand, was continental and global. When he started his walk to the Gulf, he inscribed on the flyleaf of his journal: *John Muir, Earth-Planet, Uni-*

verse. . . . He needed 1000-mile walks and whole mountain ranges for his studies. . . . The impress of his work and character has been recorded on many maps.

Today Muir probably would be called an ecologist. This breadth of his interests is reflected in the varied categories in which his name appears on the lists of science. . . . Not only did Muir discover new species of plants and insects in his wanderings, he contributed in other substantial ways to the progress of science.

He was the first to discover living glaciers in the Sierra. He was the first to explore Glacier Bay in Alaska. He was the first to point out the role glaciers played in forming the Yosemite Valley. Unknown and in his early thirties when he advanced this theory, he was opposed by the distinguished and dogmatic California State Geologist, Dr. Josiah Dwight Whitney, formerly of Harvard. Whitney maintained that glaciers had nothing to do with Yosemite, that the floor of the valley had dropped down in some ancient cataclysm. Muir scoffed, "The bottom never fell out of anything God made." Whitney rejoined that the glacial hypothesis was merely the idea of a "sheepherder." So began three summers of exhausting, lone-handed field work in which Muir traced to their sources all the streams of the Tuolumne Divide. Often returning to the valley only long enough to replenish his breadsack, he followed nameless watercourses through the wild canyons in which no white man had ever set foot. Today no scientist doubts the part glaciers played in the formation of the Yosemite Valley.

Considerable as was John Muir's contribution to science, even greater was his stature in the long fight for conservation. . . . Beside a campfire at Soda Springs on the Tuolumne Meadows in 1889, he and Robert Underwood Johnson mapped the seventeen-year battle that preserved Yosemite as a national park. Beside other campfires under sequoias, while on a three-day outing with Theodore Roosevelt in 1903, he presented the case for the preservation of numerous wilderness areas with moving effect. Major credit for saving the Grand Canyon and the Petrified Forest, in Arizona, is ascribed to John Muir. He was president of the Sierra Club from the formation of that militant conservation organization in 1892, until the time of his death in 1914. His last long battle to save Hetch Hetchy, the beautiful Yosemite Park Valley flooded to form a reservoir for San Francisco water—water that could have been obtained elsewhere—ended only the year before he died. It represents one of the great heroic struggles of conservation, no less heroic because the cause was lost.

Near the end of his life Muir said to a close friend, "I have lived a bully life. I have done what I set out to do." . . . "A man in his books," he once wrote, "may be said to walk the earth long after he has gone." In his writings and in his conservation achievements, Muir seems especially present in a world that is better because he lived here. His finest monument is the wild beauty he called attention to and helped preserve—beauty, however, that is never entirely safe, beauty that needs as vigilant protection today and tomorrow as it needed yesterday.

"Give Me the Power to Serve"

Caution was the keynote of Calvin Coolidge in the building of his political career; yet when it was a question of "doing the right thing," he forgot caution. "There is no right to strike against the public safety by anybody, anywhere, any time," he declared at the outset of the Boston police strike in 1919. The country admired the way the Governor of Massachusetts risked his political popularity in the handling of this public emergency. It propelled Coolidge into national prominence.

The vice-presidency in those days was generally considered the door to oblivion; quiet, conservative Calvin Coolidge was nominated for that post on one ballot. Then death came to Warren G. Harding, and the door to oblivion became the entrance to the White House.

It seems in keeping with Calvin Coolidge's frugality and simple honesty that the oath of office was administered by his aging father in a small farmhouse room lit with a flickering kerosene lamp. Coolidge describes the scene for us in his own restrained words.

Taking the Oath of Office

BY CALVIN COOLIDGE

ON THE night of August 2, 1923, I was awakened by my father coming up the stairs, calling my name. I noticed that his voice trembled. As the only times I had ever observed that before were when death had visited our family, I knew that something of the gravest nature had occurred.

His emotion was partly due to the knowledge that a man whom he had met and liked was gone, partly to the feeling that must possess all of our citizens when the life of their President is taken from them.

But he must have been moved also by the thought of the many sacrifices he had made to place me where I was, the twenty-five mile drives in storms and in zero weather over our mountain roads to carry me to the academy, and all the tenderness and care he had lavished upon me in the thirty-eight years since the death of my mother, in the hope that I might sometime rise to a position of importance, which he now saw realized.

He had been the first to address me as President of the United States. It was the culmination of the lifelong desire of a father for the success of his son.

He placed in my hands an official report and told me that President Harding had just passed away. My wife and I at once dressed.

Before leaving the room I knelt down and, with the same prayer with which I have since approached the altar of the church, asked God to bless the American people and give me power to serve them.

My first thought was to express my sympathy for those who had been bereaved and after that was done to attempt to reassure the country with the knowledge that I proposed no sweeping displacement of the men then in office and that there were to be no violent changes in the administration of affairs. As soon as I had dispatched a telegram to Mrs. Harding, I therefore issued a short public statement declaratory of that purpose.

Meantime I had been examining the Constitution to determine what might be necessary for qualifying by taking the oath of office. It is not clear that any additional oath is required beyond what is taken by the vice president when he is sworn into office. It is the same form as that taken by the president.

Having found this form in the Constitution, I had it set up on the typewriter, and the oath was administered by my father in his capacity as a notary public, an office he had held for a great many years.

The oath was taken in what we always called the sitting room, by the light of the kerosene lamp, which was the most modern form of lighting that had then reached the neighborhood. The Bible which had belonged to my mother lay on the table at my hand. It was not officially used, as it is not the practice in Vermont or Massachusetts to use a Bible in connection with the administration of an oath.

Besides my father and myself, there were present my wife,
Senator Dale, who happened to be stopping a few miles away,
my stenographer, and my chauffeur. . . .

Where succession to the highest office in the land is by in-
heritance or appointment, no doubt there have been kings who
have participated in the induction of their sons into their office,
but in republics, where the succession comes by an election, I
do not know of any other case in history where a father has
administered to his son the qualifying oath of office which made
him the chief magistrate of a nation. It seemed a simple and
natural thing to do at the time, but I can now realize something
of the dramatic force of the event.

This room was one which was already filled with sacred
memories for me. In it my sister and my stepmother passed their
last hours. It was associated with my boyhood recollections of
my own mother, who sat and reclined there during her long
invalid years, though she passed away in an adjoining room,
where my father was to follow her within three years from this
eventful night.

Dr. Will Mayo

*One of the most famous landmarks of the Midwest is in a sense
a shrine, a living memorial to the faith and dedication of three
men. It is the Mayo Clinic at Rochester, Minnesota. Dr. William
James Mayo and Dr. Charles Horace Mayo together built this
renowned center from a small institution started by their celebrated father, Dr. William Worrell Mayo, in 1889.*

*Following their father's example, the brothers centered their
skills on the development of the whole individual; the Clinic
aims to foster happiness as well as health. Convinced of the
healing power of faith and prayer, the staff welcomes pastoral
visits to patients. Dr. Charles echoed the Roman physician
Galen: "I bound his wounds, but God healed him."*

*Adolph C. Regli, biographer of the Mayo brothers, illustrates
Dr. Will's religious philosophy by quoting his own explicit
words.*

Defender of Religion in Medicine

BY ADOLPH C. REGLI

THE Mayos were born Episcopalians and were members of the
Church but, as Dr. Will said, never "worked at it much." Despite
the fact that he had not attended the services of his church in
twenty years, he considered himself fundamentally a religious
man and was a stout defender of religion's efficacy as an aid to
medicine.

"The emotions of a man play an important part in the practice
of medicine, and religion deals with emotions," he said. "I know
there are many to whom I cannot demonstrate the existence of
God and the human soul as I can demonstrate some point in
surgery to a class. But in my own heart I know there is a God

239

and I know there is a human soul. Call it by any name you want, there is something in humanity that is above and beyond any material calculation of science.

"The world needs religion. It needs religion as distinguished from creeds born of theologians' disputes. The surgeon and physician realize quickly that they need religion to help them. I do not mean the personal religion of the surgeon and physician—I mean the personal religion of the patient. I have seen patients that were dead by all medical standards. We knew they could not live. But I have seen a minister come to the bedside of that patient and do something for that patient I could not do, although I had done everything in my professional power. But something touched some immortal spark in him and, in defiance of medical knowledge and materialistic common sense, he lived.

"Religion is the universal comforter in times of physical or spiritual distress. Let us not delude ourselves into believing that Communism or the state can take the form of spiritual belief. There is a tendency for a group of intellectuals—persons who have been educated beyond their intelligence—to underrate the value of religion as the universal comforter, but to the mass of people, religion has the same potency it has had for two thousand years. No thinking, reverent man can read the Sermon on the Mount or the life of Christ without knowing that here is truth."

Will Rogers

When an airplane crash in Alaska took the life of Will Rogers, all America mourned for one of its truly great humorists, the man who sincerely, bluntly said, "I never met a man I didn't like," and just as bluntly remarked, "All politics is Apple Sauce." Successively a cowboy, a rope-twirling vaudevillian, a radio commentator, columnist and movie star, he made his wit a national commodity. He made people laugh; but their laughter was the sort which also made them think.

He had another side. Although he cared little for the outward observances of religion, Will Rogers was a deeply spiritual man, as his wife, Betty, testifies in her biography of him: one who really lived his Christianity, with the Golden Rule the mainstay of his daily living.

A Deeply Religious Man

BY BETTY ROGERS

Aʟʟ through his career, ministers of the gospel were interested in Will and kind to him. One of his earliest weekly articles had been reprinted in several church papers. Many times he was invited to speak from the pulpit. I remember, long ago, a good-natured and amusing debate he held with a minister on the question of whether cowboys or ministers had done the most for civilization. Texts for sermons were often taken from his writings. Some two years before his death Will quoted in a weekly article his reply to a minister who had written to say that he wanted to discuss him and his philosophy in a sermon:

I was raised predominately a Methodist, [Will said] but I have traveled so much, mixed with so many people in all parts

241

of the world, I don't know now just what I am. I know I have
never been a non-believer. But I can honestly tell you that I
don't think that any one religion is *the* religion. Which way you
serve your God will never get one word of argument or condemnation out of me.

I got no "Philosophy." I don't even know what the word
means. The Fourth Reader (McGuffey's) is as far as I ever got
in schools. I am not bragging on it, I am thoroughly ashamed of
it, for I had every opportunity. Everything I have done has
been by luck, no move was premeditated. I just stumbled from
one thing to another. It might have been down. I didn't know
at the time, and I don't know yet, for I don't know what "Up"
is. I may be lower than I ever was, I don't know. I may be making the wrong use of any little talent (if any) that I accidentally
have. I don't know.

Neither Will's philosophy of life, nor his religion, were of the
formal type that can be organized into a definite creed. He had
both a religious belief and a deep-seated philosophy. But they
were a part of him, coloring his whole process of living and
thinking; not put away into a compartment of his being, from
which they might be withdrawn and explained at need.

And they served him well. Yielding to no rules and conforming
to no standards but his own, Will was very sure of himself in
many ways. He was seldom doubtful in matters of right and
wrong. Will had with him always an inner feeling of right and a
conscience free of guilt. He had this by knowing, and being confident that he did know, what was right and what was wrong,
and by always doing what he felt was right for him to do. He
tried not to offend, but Will was sure of his motives. And once
he had said a thing or done a thing, he ceased to consider the
possibility that it might have been actually wrong. I think he
never had to justify to himself a single act or word of his.

Will never said a mean thing; he refused to gossip, would have
nothing to do with such talk. When an absent person was being
raked over the coals by a group, Will invariably found something
to say in his favor. Will wouldn't pick on anyone who was down,
and he always resisted when others were doing so.

Time after time in the old vaudeville days, I saw him save acts
that were dying by going out on the stage and kidding with the
performers. Will did the same sort of thing in pictures; he spent
half his time on the movie lots thinking up new lines and bits of

business for actors whose parts were being whittled out of the script.

In after-dinner speaking, where Will was usually last on the program, it sometimes happened that an earlier speaker had been nervous and confused, or had rambled pointlessly on and on. Getting up to talk later, Will would always mention the unlucky speaker with some joke or other. The poor fellow, thinking he was in for a ribbing, would sink lower and lower in his seat. But Will would go on to say something good about him; how, after all, he had brought out one point, or had given them a new slant on this. And before Will had finished, the inept speaker would perk up and feel that maybe he hadn't been so bad at that.

Lending a helping hand or doing what he could to pick up the spirits of anyone feeling low was simply a natural reaction with Will. And because of the offhand, kidding way in which he performed them, his acts of kindness had nothing of condescension. It was of such things and the spirit that prompted them that Will's natural, living philosophy of helpfulness, honesty and tolerance was composed.

Spiritual Recovery

Dwight D. Eisenhower's prayer at his first inauguration moved millions of hearers. It also set the pattern of his devotional life in office. Simply and with little variation, he has declared in speech after speech that the United States is strong because this government and its moral values are founded on a steadfast faith; that the atheistic powers are bound to crumble; that the only durable peace must be founded on Scriptural values and principles. "Religion," his brother Arthur once remarked, was "a part of the air we breathed."

Dr. Edward L. R. Elson, the President's pastor, discusses America's "spiritual recovery," with our nation's leader emphasizing Judaeo-Christian ideals in the fulfillment of our national destiny and our worldwide responsibilities.

Dwight D. Eisenhower and the New Awakening

BY EDWARD L. R. ELSON

Early in the morning of January 20, 1953, the man who was that day to be inaugurated the nation's thirty-fourth President entered a quiet Washington church. There, surrounded by his family and joined by his Cabinet and their families, he sought strength in prayer and in the Word of God for his overwhelming new responsibilities. All of us present at that service will forever believe that the power of the Holy Spirit moved in the earnest hearts gathered in God's house on that historic day. Former presidents had gone to church with their families for private prayer on Inauguration Day, but this service was made unique by the presence of members of the Cabinet and their families.

244

The company joined with General Eisenhower in singing the familiar hymn, "Our God, Our Help in Ages Past." Among the Scripture lessons which he heard read was one containing the prayer of Solomon (for "an understanding heart") in I Kings 3:7-14. . . . Prayers were offered for the nation, for all in authority, and for world peace; then the pastor offered [a petition for Dwight D. Eisenhower]. . . . A period of silent prayer was concluded as we recited the Lord's Prayer and rose to sing the immortal words of the great hymn by Hugh T. Kerr: "God of our Life, through all the circling years, we trust in Thee." . . .

In this mood, placing the destiny of the Nation in God's hands, the company received the benediction of the Lord and lingered for a moment in silent prayer. The nation's new leader, his wife at his side, rose quietly and left the church. In the mood of this service, and in fulfillment of a long-considered desire to include his Cabinet and the nation in a very personal act of dedication, he paused for a few quiet moments in his quarters at the Statler Hotel to strike off the words which have since come to be known as "my little prayer."

In the shadow of the Capitol dome Dwight David Eisenhower placed his hand on an old family Bible and took the oath of office as President of the United States. His first two acts as President were simple acts, but filled with an enduring meaning. First, he stepped to the side of his wife and kissed her, symbolizing his personal devotion and the sacredness of the American home. Secondly, symbolizing the faith which pervades our national existence, he invited the throng before him and millions listening around the world to bow with him as he offered the prayer he had written just a little while before:

> Almighty God, as we stand here at this moment, my future associates in the executive branch of the government join me in beseeching that Thou wilt make full and complete our dedication to the service of the people in this throng and their fellow citizens everywhere. Give us, we pray, the power to discern right from wrong, and allow all our words and actions to be governed thereby and by the laws of this land. Especially, we pray that our concern shall be for all the people, regardless of station, race or calling. May co-operation be permitted and be the mutual aim of those who, under the concepts of our Constitution, hold to differing political faiths, so that all may work for the good of our beloved country and Thy glory. Amen.

This unexpected revelation of the deep spiritual quality of the new President lifted the entire ceremony to a high level and transformed all that followed thereafter. All that has transpired since then in the public life and spoken word of President Eisenhower has sprung likewise from this spiritual quality. Whatever else this President is remembered for, future generations will mark him as a President who from the highest seat in the land brought a new moral tone and spiritual virility into American life.

Before his election to the Presidency, General Eisenhower had frequently declared his concern for the recovery of America's religious foundations. Senator Frank Carlson of Kansas, his intimate friend, recalls that the President said to him at the dedication of a chapel at Kansas State College, while Eisenhower was still in the Army: "Frank, I don't believe our country will ever be the country that our forefathers had planned, and God has intended for us, unless we get back to fundamental spiritual principles."

Since his election his personal faith, grounded on the strict religious upbringing of his River Brethren parents, disciplined by Bible study and prayer, matured and modified with the passing of the years, has been evident in all he has undertaken. Twelve days after assuming office, he quietly validated his long-demonstrated Christian faith by becoming a communicant member of The National Presbyterian Church in Washington. Bearing the burdens of the heaviest office in the world, he (with Mrs. Eisenhower) regularly worships on Sunday in his own church and, when out of the city on week ends, he invariably attends some other church. . . . Being true to his own faith, Eisenhower inspires men of other faiths to greater zeal. . . .

It is not only in his habit of formal worship, but in his discipline of prayer that the President is a symbol of our contemporary religious renaissance. Several mornings after his inauguration, at a prayer-breakfast attended by Cabinet officers, members of the Congress, the Judiciary, business men and some religious leaders, President Eisenhower witnessed to the power and meaning of prayer in his life. He testified that prayer put him in touch with the Infinite and, by opening his mind and heart to God, he found Divine energies flowing through him, with which he could undertake his duties and solve his problems. He drew on several instances in his own life which confirmed his abiding faith in prayer and commended to others the way of prayer.

This Presidential leadership has come at a time in American

history when Americans are responsive to its promptings. What is important now is that this religious awakening be given every possible momentum in order that our total life may be saturated by the reality of God's presence and our nation be a citadel of spiritual strength to all mankind.

SEVEN

The Right

to Knowledge

Part of the precious heritage we hold, and hope to bequeath to our children, is the yearning Americans feel for knowledge, for education for all. The early settlers knew "the glory of the lighted mind." As soon as they made their homes secure from the elements, they turned to the teaching of their children; and the text they used was often the only book they owned—the Bible. These pioneers taught the world a powerful lesson: the only truly free man is the informed, enlightened man.

"The Little Watering Pot"

*The New England Primer has been called the most influential
school book in the history of public education in the United
States. Judged by modern standards, with our richness of readers
and texts, it seems poor and quaint—just over three inches by
five inches in size, a religious reader but eighty-eight pages thick.
Yet it was the chief school-book of the Dissenters of America
for more than a century.*

*Alice Morse Earle has made a study of the part played by this
little volume in our early history, and it is from her fine and
authoritative book,* Child Life in Colonial Days, *that the following selection has been made.*

The New England Primer

BY ALICE MORSE EARLE

THE ENGLISH philosopher, John Locke, in his *Thoughts Concerning Education*, written in 1690, says the method of teaching
children to read in England at that time was always "the ordinary road of Horn-book, Primer, Psalter, Testament, and Bible."
These, he said "engage the liking of children and tempt them
to read." The road was the same in New England, but it would
hardly be called a tempting method. . . .

A prymer or primer was specifically and ecclesiastically before
and after the Reformation in England a book of private devotions. As authorized by the Church, and written or printed par-
tially or wholly in the vernacular, it contained devotions for the
hours, the Creed, Lord's Prayer, Ten Commandments, some
psalms and certain instructions as to the elements of Christian
knowledge. These little books often opened with the criss-cross
row or alphabet arranged hornbook fashion, hence the term

251

primer naturally came to be applied to all elementary books for
children's use. . . .

The book which succeeded the hornbook in general use was
The New England Primer. It was the most universally studied
school-book that has ever been used in America; for one hundred years it was *the* school-book of America; for nearly another
hundred years it was frequently printed and much used. More
than three million copies of this *New England Primer* were
printed, so declares its historian, Paul Leicester Ford. These
were studied by many more millions of school-children. . . .
[The little book] was so religious in all its teachings and suggestions that it has been fitly called the "Little Bible of New England."

It is a poorly printed little book about five inches long and
three wide, of about eighty pages. It contains the alphabet, and
a short table of easy syllables, such as a-b ab, e-b eb, and words
up to those of six syllables. This was called a syllabarium. There
were twelve five-syllable words; of these five were *abomination,
edification, humiliation, mortification,* and *purification.* There
were a morning and evening prayer for children, and a grace
to be said before meat. Then followed a set of little rhymes
which have become known everywhere, and are frequently
quoted. Each letter of the alphabet is illustrated with a blurred
little picture. Of these, two-thirds represent Biblical incidents.
They begin:—

> "In Adam's fall
> We sinned all,"

and end with Z:—

> "Zaccheus he
> Did climb a tree
> His Lord to see."

In the early days of the Primer, all the colonies were true to
the English king, and the rhyme for the letter K reads:—

> "King Charles the Good
> No man of blood."

But by Revolutionary years the verse for K was changed to:—

> "Queens and Kings
> Are Gaudy Things."

Later verses tell the praise of George Washington. Then comes a series of Bible questions and answers; then an "alphabet of lessons for youth," consisting of verses of the Bible beginning successively with A, B, C, and so on. X was a difficult initial letter, and had to be contented with "Xhort one another daily, etc." After the Lord's Prayer and Apostle's Creed appeared sometimes a list of names for men and women, to teach children to spell their own names. The largest and most interesting picture was that of the burning at the stake of John Rogers; and after this a six-page set of pious rhymes which the martyr left at his death for his family of small children.

After the year 1750, a few very short stories were added to its pages, and were probably all the children's stories that many of the scholars of that day ever saw. It is interesting to see that the little prayer so well known to-day, [1899], beginning "Now I lay me down to sleep," is usually found in the *New England Primer* of dates later than the year 1737. The *Shorter Catechism* was, perhaps, the most important part of this primer. It was so called in contrast to the catechism in use in England, called *The Careful Father and Pious Child,* which had twelve hundred questions with answers. The *Shorter Catechism* had but a hundred and seven questions, though some of the answers were long. Usually another catechism was found in the primer, called *Spiritual Milk for Babes.* It was written by the Boston minister, John Cotton, and it had but eighty-seven questions with short answers. Sometimes a Dialogue between *Christ, Youth, and the Devil* was added.

The *Shorter Catechism* was the special delight of all New Englanders. Cotton Mather called it a "little watering pot" to shed good lessons. He begged writing masters to set sentences from it to be copied by their pupils; and he advised mothers to "continually drop something of the Catechism on their children, as Honey from the Rock." Learning the catechism was enforced by law in New England, and the deacons and ministers visited and examined families to see that the law was obeyed. Thus it may plainly be seen that this primer truly filled the requisites of what the Roxbury school trustees called "scholastical, theological, and moral discipline."

New England's First Fruits

When the General Court of Massachusetts Bay Colony voted a grant of four hundred pounds in the fall of 1636 to found a "schoole or college," it performed an historic act. This was probably the first time in history that a free people voluntarily and through their representatives had voted a sum of money for such a purpose. The sum set aside was not large enough to open the college at once, however, though the site had been chosen at New Towne (later called Cambridge, in honor of the English university where many colonists had studied).

Two years later a young Puritan minister, John Harvard, too ill for the usual pastoral duties, bequeathed to the new institution half his estate and much miscellaneous personal property, including his library of more than 400 volumes. Named in his memory, Harvard College came to life, remaining under the jurisdiction of church and state for more than two hundred years.

A tract entitled New England's First Fruits *was brought out in London several years after Harvard's establishment, publicizing the climate, products, religion, and other features of New England. The opening sentence expresses the hunger of the Puritans for education. There follows a brief description of Harvard College, its motto being "For Christ and the Church."*

The Founding of Harvard College

from *New England's First Fruits*

AFTER God had carried us safe to New England, and we had builded our houses, provided necessaries for our livelihood, reared convenient places for God's worship, and settled the Civil Government: one of the next things we longed for, and looked after was to advance *Learning* and perpetuate it to posterity; dreading to leave an illiterate Ministry to the churches, when our present ministers shall lie in the dust. And as we were thinking and consulting how to effect this great work, it pleased God to stir up the heart of one Mr. (John) Harvard (a godly gentleman, and a lover of learning, there living amongst us) to give the one half of his estate (it being in all about 1700 l.) towards the erecting of a College, and all his Library: after him another gave 300 l., others after them cast in more, and the public hand of the State added the rest: the College was, by common consent, appointed to be at Cambridge, (a place very pleasant and accommodate) and is called (according to the name of the first founder) *Harvard College.*

The Edifice is very fair and comely within and without, having in it a spacious Hall; (where they daily meet at Common Lectures) exercises, and a large Library with some books to it, the gifts of diverse of our friends. . . . And by the side of the College a fair Grammar School, for the training up of young Scholars, and fitting of them for Academical Learning, that still as they are judged ripe, they may be received into the College of this School: Master Corlet is the Mr., who hath very well approved himself for his abilities, dexterity and painfulness, in teaching and education of the youth under him.

Over the College is master Dunster placed, as President, a learned, conscionable and industrious man, who hath so trained up his Pupils in the tongues and Arts, and so seasoned them with the principles of Divinity and Christianity, that we have to our great comfort (and in truth), beyond our hopes, beheld their progress in Learning and godliness also. . . . Insomuch that we are confident, if these early blossoms may be cherished and warmed with the influence of the friends of Learning and lovers of this pious work, they will by the help of God, come to happy maturity in a short time.

Over the College are twelve Overseers chosen by the general Court, six of them are of the Magistrates, the other six of the Ministers, who are to promote the best good of it, and (having a power of influence into all persons in it) are to see that every one be diligent and proficient in his proper place.

Noah Webster

Noah Webster's fame as author of the monumental dictionary which bears his name has eclipsed his earlier accomplishments. Too few Americans realize how great was his influence as a text-book writer and an educational reformer. He perceived that eighteenth-century American education had to be freed from two restricting forces before it could fully develop: persistent European and British domination of its curriculum and methods, and the trammels of severe ecclesiastical authority.

His ideas were so well suited to the practical needs of the new nation that they seem obvious, natural, not even debatable to us. Yet it was Webster's radical innovation, for example, that the classics be read in good translations, rather than in the original. Thus time might be saved for the study of history, government, science, and our own vernacular. Stewart Holbrook, known for his writings on American subjects, here delineates the neglected aspects of Webster's life, including the background story of his "great dictionary."

Webster's Great Dictionary

BY STEWART H. HOLBROOK

Although Noah Webster's great Dictionary was published after the War of 1812, he belongs to the period between wars because it was then that he got the idea, and preached it, of making the United States less dependent intellectually on England and Europe. He was born in 1758, at West Hartford, Connecticut, of a father who apparently recognized something unusual in his son. Webster Senior mortgaged and nearly lost his fine farm in order to send the boy to Yale College; and the young man found times hard indeed, after the Revolution, for a man of intellectual bent. Young Noah studied for the law, taught school, practiced journalism, and in 1783 prepared and published his first Blue Back Spelling Book, one of the great landmarks in the history of American education.

The Blue Back Speller sold fifteen million copies within a few years. What it did to the chaotic orthography of the time can hardly be appreciated today. In eighteenth century America there were few rules as to how words, even common words, should be spelled; anyone who has read old letters, or even official documents, knows the astounding attempts at phonetic expression our forefathers made. One finds *jinerll* for *general; Pfebrewarie* is a month; *toune* was *town;* and in the matter of spelling native American place names truly stupefying efforts were made.

Young Webster, who was a pedantic and choleric fellow, wanted some order, some rules, for orthography. Moreover, he was intensely patriotic. He wanted Americans to have their own particular ways of spelling. He thought, with good reason, that an American orthography would encourage the publication of American books. More important, he said, was that "a national language is a band of national union." Let us spell in our own way, he went on, for this will "inspire us with the pride of national character." He thought that Americans, no matter how they boasted of their independence, were sheeplike and slavish in their copying English terms and spellings. He did not like his fellow Americans' "blind imitation of English manners." All of this, he said, turned their attention from their own interests and prevented them from respecting themselves.

There was little ground to go on in the business of rules, and none at all in respect to the thousands of strictly American words and expressions of which no English scholar had ever heard, much less had attempted to spell. So, Webster spelled them one and all as he thought best. He threw out most of the *-our* endings, like *honour, labour,* and substituted the simple *-or*. He lopped off the *k* from *publick* and similar words; he transposed the second *e* in *theatre* to make it *theater*. And from here he dived into the mass of Indian words and made-up frontier words and wrote them out as he thought they should be. It was a tremendous job this young Yankee set out lonehanded to do. In subsequent editions of the Speller he added new words, and in every instance also gave the proper, or what he held to be the proper, pronunciation of each word.

With publication of his first Speller, Webster faced the danger of having his work pirated without compensation; none of the newly established states had given thought to copyright law, nor had the so-called federal government, which had little authority anyway. So, Webster deliberately started on a tour to visit the thirteen capitals and in each of them to interest the legislators in a copyright law. He also wrote pamphlets recommending a stronger federal union.

His tour of the states, as far south as Charleston, gave Webster a good realization of the nation being formed. He earned his way by giving lectures on the need for an American language, with its own rules and meanings and spellings; and by teaching school and holding singing schools. He often found the way difficult, for Americans were not greatly interested in acquiring intellectual independence. Yet it is surprising that even our great men did not always appreciate Webster's efforts. "I view Webster," wrote Thomas Jefferson, in 1801, "as a mere pedagogue, of very limited understanding."

During these years Webster was giving thought to the necessity of an American dictionary. Being a man of easy irritation, he became provoked at the English dictionaries, books which coldly ignored the United States and its thousands of new and unique words; and he swore, more than once, that he would produce an American dictionary. In 1803 he gave up journalism and teaching and shut himself away from the world, and three years later his first Dictionary was published. Although this book contained more than five thousand words that had never been in any dictionary, he thought of it only as a preparation for a larger work. So it was. For the next two decades he labored prodigiously at what in 1828 was published as *An American Dictionary of the English Language*, the grandfather of all American dictionaries.

Webster's work as a lexicographer has naturally put all of his other contributions in shadow, yet there were other works of this man which affected Americans. In the medical field he wrote a sound treatise, on epidemic and pestilential diseases. He edited John Winthrop's *Journal*, a notable historical contribution. He compiled school readers that sought to indoctrinate young Americans with a love and respect for their native country, and probably were successful in doing so. The influence of Webster's readers was incalculable. He wrote pamphlets on banks, on insurance, on the decomposition of white-lead paints, on the rights of neutral nations in time of war. His monograph, *Experiments*

Respecting Dew, begun in 1790 and published in 1809, still holds an honorable place among pioneer American essays in physical science. This and other of his pamphlets doubtless hastened establishment of the United States Weather Bureau and of the Bureau of the Census. His interests were as many and as diversified as were those of Franklin and Jefferson, but for some reason, and that possibly the monumental success of his great Dictionary, they have been forgotten.

A radical only in his lexicographical life, Webster remained a confirmed Federalist conservative to the end of his days, which came in 1843; and until the last he continued to wear the tie-wig, the small clothes, the low shoes with silver buckles, that men wore in his youth. Yet, though he would have no truck with the new-fangled trousers and such, his fanaticism in respect to speech and spelling was so radical and so competent that he, perhaps more than any other one man of his time, gave Americans a feeling of being something more or less original, and not merely a copy of an Englishman.

"My Dear Patsy"

In a time and place when the education of girls was "too trivial a subject for any concern," a scholarly, landed gentleman of Virginia put aside affairs of state in order to give careful instructions to his motherless daughters, Martha and Mary Jefferson, then aged eleven and five. Thus we see that the great ideals of Thomas Jefferson were a vital, vibrant part of the loving relationships of his family life. In the following letters to his older daughter, "Patsy," he writes with solicitude for her training as a young lady, and explains his concept of what she should know.

Three Letters to Martha (Patsy) Jefferson

FROM HER FATHER
THOMAS JEFFERSON

Annapolis, Nov. 28th, 1783

My dear Patsy—After four days' journey, I arrived here without any accident, and in as good health as when I left Philadelphia. The conviction that you would be more improved in the situation I have placed you than if still with me, has solaced me on my parting with you, which my love for you has rendered a difficult thing. The acquirements which I hope you will make under the tutors I have provided for you will render you more worthy of my love; and if they cannot increase it, they will prevent its diminution. Consider the good lady who has taken you under her roof, who has undertaken to see that you perform all your exercises, and to admonish you in all those wanderings from what is right or what is clever, to which your experience would expose you: consider her, I say, as your mother, as the only person to whom, since the loss with which Heaven has pleased to afflict you, you can now look up; and that her displeasure or disapprobation, on any occasion, will be an immense misfortune, which should you be so unhappy as to incur by any unguarded act, think no concession too much to regain her goodwill. With respect to the distribution of your time, the following is what I should approve:

From 8 to 10, practice music.

From 10 to 1, dance one day and draw another.

From 1 to 2, draw on the day you dance, and write a letter next day.

From 3 to 4, read French.

From 4 to 5, exercise yourself in music.

From 5 till bedtime, read English, write, etc.

Communicate this plan to Mrs. Hopkinson, and if she approves of it, pursue it. As long as Mrs. Trist remains in Philadelphia, cultivate her affection. She has been a valuable friend to you, and her good sense and good heart make her valued by all who know her, and by nobody on earth more than me. I expect you will write me by every post. Inform me what books you read, what tunes you learn, and inclose me your best copy of every lesson in drawing. Write also one letter a week either to your Aunt Eppes, your Aunt Skipwith, your Aunt Carr, or the little lady from whom I now inclose a letter, and always put the letter you so write under cover to me. Take care that you never spell a word wrong. Always before you write a word, consider how it is spelt, and, if you do not remember it, turn to a dictionary. It produces great praise to a lady to spell well. I have placed my happiness on seeing you good and accomplished; and no distress which this world can now bring on me would equal that of your disappointing my hopes. If you love me, then strive to be good under every situation and to all living creatures, and to acquire those accomplishments which I have put in your power, and which will go far towards ensuring you the warmest love of your affectionate father,

TH. JEFFERSON.

P.S.—Keep my letters and read them at times, that you may always have present in your mind those things which will endear you to me.

Annapolis, Dec. 11th, 1783

I hope you will have good sense enough to disregard those foolish predictions that the world is to be at an end soon. The

Almighty has never made known to anybody at what time he created it; nor will he tell anybody when he will put an end to it, if he ever means to do it. As to preparations for that event, the best way is for you always to be prepared for it. The only way to be so is, never to say or do a bad thing. If ever you are about to say anything amiss, or to do anything wrong, consider before hand you will feel something within you which will tell you it is wrong, and ought not to be said or done. This is your conscience, and be sure and obey it. Our Maker has given us all this faithful internal monitor, and if you always obey it you will always be prepared for the end of the world; or for a much more certain event, which is death. This must happen to all; it puts an end to the world as to us; and the way to be ready for it is never to do a wrong act.

Annapolis, Dec. 22d, 1783

I omitted in that letter to advise you on the subject of dress, which I know you are a little apt to neglect. I do not wish you to be gayly clothed at this time of life, but that your wear should be fine of its kind. But above all things and at all times let your clothes be neat, whole, and properly put on. Do not fancy you must wear them till the dirt is visible to the eye. You will be the last one who is sensible of this. Some ladies think they may, under the privileges of the *déshabillé*, be loose and negligent of their dress in the morning. But be you, from the moment you rise till you go to bed, as cleanly and properly dressed as at the hours of dinner or tea. A lady who has been seen as a sloven or a slut in the morning, will never efface the impression she has made, with all the dress and pageantry she can afterwards involve herself in. Nothing is so disgusting to our sex as a want of cleanliness and delicacy in yours. I hope, therefore, the moment you rise from bed, your first work will be to dress yourself in such style, as that you may be seen by any gentleman without his being able to discover a pin amiss, or any other circumstance of neatness wanting.

Classes in the Kitchen

The early colonists brought over with them from England an institution known as the "petty" or "dame" school. A group of very young children would gather in the kitchen or living room of the home of a housewife (frequently a "reduced" gentlewoman) who had acquired the rudiments of an education. For a few pennies a week she taught them such reading and spelling as she knew, thereby earning a pittance with which to eke out her slender resources.

The English poet, George Crabbe, described such a dame school:

> . . . a deaf, poor, patient widow sits
> And awes some thirty infants as she knits:
> Infants of humble, busy wives who pay
> Some trifling price for freedom through the day.
> At this good matron's hut the children meet,
> Who thus becomes the mother of the street.
> Her room is small, they cannot widely stray.
> Her threshold high, they cannot run away.
> With band of yarn she keeps offenders in,
> And to her gown the sturdiest rogue can pin.

In her delightful biography, Grandma Brown's Hundred Years, Harriet Connor Brown has drawn a charming picture of one of these little schools which flourished during the early settlement of Ohio. Under the direction of Grandma Brown's remarkable Grandma Foster, education included manners and morals, as well as reading and spelling. And it was here that the lively little girl who later became Grandma Brown gained her early appreciation of beauty, and began to know her Bible.

Grandma Foster's School

BY HARRIET CONNOR BROWN

Prominent in Maria's family background stood out her two grandmothers. Each of them made a deep impression on her youthful mind. "Were the two good friends?" I asked. "Oh, yes," she laughed, "both were good Presbyterians.

"Grandma Foster was a tiny little body, always immaculately dressed. She taught school for many years in the house which my father built for her in 1822. Many important persons in Ohio history sat before her in their infancy. Boys and girls were in her classes, her own grandchildren and great-grandchildren among the number.

"I remember well the first time I went to school. I was about two years old. One of Aunt Betsy's children took me as a visitor. There was a new long clock in the corner of the schoolroom which I hadn't seen before. Its little feet were black. I pointed to it and cried, 'Oh, what pretty little feet!' 'You mustn't talk out loud, Maria,' Grandma Foster told me firmly, and I was awed.

"At Grandma Foster's school, little girls learned not only to read and write, but to sew and knit also. When the boys got so they could read well in the Testament, they were graduated.

"When I was six years old, I had pieced a patchwork quilt. Sister Libbie had made two. There were nine pieces in each patch. We sewed the pieces together with tiny over and over stitches after Grandma had cut them out and basted them for us. If we took our stitches too deep, we had to pick them out. We were taught to turn a hem and to do it nicely. Sometimes Ma would send a kerchief to be hemmed or an apron to be made. There never was a more useful school.

"We learned knitting, too. First we knit our garters, afterwards our stockings. I knit eight pairs of socks for soldiers in the World War, but I didn't follow the instructions of the Red Cross; I shaped the feet the way Grandma Foster had taught me nearly ninety years before.

"When we were little girls and went some place, we always took our knitting along. We had to knit so many times around before we could play. Children must learn to be useful, they thought in those days. My cousin, Lucinda Gillmore, came to play one day. 'My children have done their task,' said Ma. 'Just give me your knitting and I'll do yours.' We went running down to the orchard to the swing while our mother did Cindy's knitting. It made a great impression on me—Ma's doing Cindy's stint for her.

"After sewing and knitting came spelling and reading. We used *Webster's Elementary Spelling Book,* beginning with the a—b-; e—b; and so on. Then came short sentences of just one line. Like this: 'Brass is made of zinc and copper.' Then another line telling something else that would be useful to know. Every line different, all important. We had the *New England Primer,* too. Then Grandma taught us the Roman numerals, so that we could open the Bible and know what chapter it was.

"We were taught good manners, too, at Grandma Foster's school. At recess, the little girls used to play under the apple tree, while the boys would romp in the street. I remember that one day, when I had been laughing boisterously, Grandma called me to her and said mildly,—she always corrected us very quietly, —'My child, if something amuses you, laugh, but not so loud.' When school was dismissed, it wasn't just open the door and go out, but first the girls filed past Grandma making a deep obeisance, and then the little boys marched by, cap in hand.

"I never remember Grandma Foster having a rod, never in my time. I do remember the dunce block. It used to stand over in the corner by the fireplace. I can just see the smooth piece of black walnut. Oh, that kind of punishment didn't hurt us; but it *was* humiliating.

"Grandma Foster taught until four days before she died at the age of eighty-one. Every night she used to pray the Lord: 'I beg that I may not outlive my usefulness.' One day she dismissed her school, saying that she did not feel very well. Four days later, she calmly breathed her last. When they went to pay for her coffin they found that she had paid for it herself, several years before.

"She had eight children, and taught school at least thirty-five years after her husband died," said Grandmother Brown. "That's what I call a full life."

Horace Mann

In the same year that Mary Lyon opened her Mount Holyoke Seminary for Women, Horace Mann was appointed secretary of the newly instituted Massachusetts Board of Education. Though himself president of the State Senate, he had to cope with a legislature coldly disposed toward expenditures for education. In an uphill fight, he covered the entire state visiting schools, studying teaching methods, addressing audiences for his great cause: bridging, in short, the educational voids of local training systems.

Horace Mann supported other humanitarian causes—the establishment of state hospitals for the insane, special instruction of the handicapped, and the restriction of slavery and the liquor traffic. But his greatest contribution to his time and ours was the understanding he brought to the public of the need for school betterment. From the writings of Emerson and the Scotch philosopher-phrenologist George Combes, but primarily from his own Christianity, Mann derived a profound faith in the power of education to improve the human race.

Among the numerous books and articles on this famous educational reformer, Louise Tharp's remarkable biography, Until Victory, stands out. Here presented is a brief, poetic selection from that volume, followed by a longer biographical account excerpted and condensed from the Life of Horace Mann, written by his devoted and brilliant wife, Mary Peabody Mann.

Until Victory

BY LOUISE HALL THARP

CHILDREN troop down city streets or they gather at country crossroads waiting for the school bus—all over these United States. Large or small, famous or unknown—it is still a *Horace Mann School* which thousands attend. Or if a school has not this magic name graven in granite over the door, then somewhere a vivid face smiles down upon the children from a photograph on the wall—or a plaque with a fine profile bears the words: *Be ashamed to die until you have won some victory for humanity.*

Not in the United States alone, but in many lands, children in free schools are Horace Mann's living memorial. Mann's words have been translated into many languages and devoted teachers have taught rising generations "to obey their own laws" or "be held in bondage to the law of tyrants." It is a hard lesson, not always understood, but those who teach and those who listen are winning their victory for humanity. They are the living proof that Horace Mann's whole life was victory.

The Life of Horace Mann*

BY MARY PEABODY MANN

IN JULY, 1837, a gaunt, overworked lawyer of forty-one locked up the office in Boston where he had been practising and living for three disconsolate years. Jubilantly he wrote a friend: "My law-books are for sale. My office is 'to let.' I have abandoned jurisprudence, and betaken myself to the larger sphere of mind and morals. Having found the present generation composed of

* A condensation

materials most unmalleable, I am about transferring my efforts to the next. Men are cast iron, but children are wax."

Horace Mann, known everywhere as the founder of America's modern public school system, had just accepted the secretaryship of Massachusetts' newly created board of education. "Henceforth," he noted in his journal, "I devote myself to the supremest welfare of mankind upon earth. Faith is the only sustainer. I have faith in the improvability of the race. Love is a universal solvent. Here is a clew given by God to lead us through the labyrinth of the world."

In pursuance of his duty, the great champion and apostle of free education for all children set out on a circuit through Massachusetts "to collect information of the actual condition and efficiency of the common schools and other means of popular education, and to diffuse as widely as possible, throughout every part of the Commonwealth, information of the most approved and successful modes of instruction."

Horace Mann was uniquely suited to the work of reform. In a childhood made unhappy by excessive poverty and the rugged nursing of Toil on his father's farm, he had suffered a hunger for knowledge that nothing could satisfy. When incorporated in 1785, the little town where Mann was born eleven years later, was named after Dr. Benjamin Franklin. In acknowledgment of the compliment, the great American offered them a bell for their church; but afterwards, saying that he thought they would prefer sense to sound, he changed the gift into a small library. From the pages of these old histories and theologies, miserably adapted to the needs of children, the boy gained the rudiments of an education. In addition, his parents intensified his love of learning. They taught him to take care of a few schoolbooks, earned by braiding straw, as though there was something sacred about them. They spoke of learning and learned men with reverence. Until he was fifteen Horace Mann had never attended school more than eight or ten weeks in a year, and there he was subjected to poor teaching and severe discipline.

More than by labor and privation, the inward joy of his youth was blighted by the hyper-Calvinist Dr. Emmons, a pure intellectualist, who ruled his people more than half a century, preaching unflinchingly the extremity of hell torments. Often the sensitive boy, envisioning the doom of judgment day, wept until he fell asleep from exhaustion. One of his childhood sorrows was the death by drowning of his charming twelve year old brother. When the clergyman gave a funeral address on the tortures of dying unconverted, Horace saw in his mother's tender face a despair beyond the grief of losing a beloved son. His whole being rose up in revolt against such a cruel Creator, and in an agony of suffering he broke the spell that had bound him and began to construct a theory of Christian ethics and doctrine, of time and eternity, given by a loving God and His providence, out of which life flowed.

At length a fine, but erratic classical teacher crossed the young man's path, and after six months' study he entered the sophomore class of Brown University in September, 1816. There he met the lovely, fragile Charlotte Messer, daughter of the college president, whom he married many years later.

Horace Mann took the first place in his class at graduation. The subject of his valedictory oration was "The Progressive Character of the Human Race," always his favorite theme, the basis of his actions in both education and politics. After tutoring in the classics at Brown, Mann entered the Law School at Litchfield, and through exhaustive study he was soon admitted to the Norfolk bar.

Early in his legal career, he was elected to the Massachusetts legislature, where his first speech, in defence of religious liberty, was a consummate success. Another followed in favor of railroads. His whole advance in that period was marked by devotion to the interests of public charities, education, civil, political, and religious freedom, care of the handicapped, temperance, and morals of every description.

Mr. Mann married Charlotte Messer after he had attained some eminence in his profession and in community welfare. But first he paid the debts incurred for his education and acquired a small competence. All this he might have secured a decade earlier, had he yielded to the temptation to defend the wrong or to accept a case in which he did not wholly believe.

After less than two years of married happiness, the links of the family circle were broken. His wife, always delicate in health, died suddenly at night, while he was watching at her side, with no one within call. The terrors of that vigil revisited him with fearful power every anniversary as long as he lived. Then in swift succession he lost the others whom he most loved: his best friend, his honored father-in-law, his gentle mother whose every expression was full of beauty for him, and last his brother, whose debts and expenses he had assumed, paying them off through years of painful deprivation.

When Mr. Mann returned to the world from his solitary period of mourning, he was ready to do all he could to supply its needs. Without a family he felt the call of all humanity touching him. His dedication to reforms, combined with unusual ability as a lawyer and public speaker, was recognized by his many friends, such souls as William Ellery Channing, Reverend E. Taylor, Dr. George Combe, Charles Sumner, Dr. Samuel Gridley Howe. They pushed him forward as a candidate for political honors. He was sent to the legislature, first to the House, then to the Senate, where he became the presiding officer. There he supported all the good causes that were in need of resolute friends. Following in the footsteps of Franklin, Washington, and Jefferson, he pleaded for free, unbiased education, the only sound foundation for temporal and spiritual progress in a republic. Believing it to be the duty of the state to train all its children for good citizenship, he demanded this as a right, and he fought for it until victory.

It was time. In Massachusetts, once renowned for its schools, the free system had sadly degenerated from the original views of the Pilgrim Fathers. As citizens accumulated wealth, private schools and academies sprang up everywhere, while the common schools were allowed to deteriorate into neglected schools for the poor only. Mr. Mann wished to make them so good that rich and poor alike could once more be educated together in these nurseries of democracy. To this end he and his friends battled with strength and ingenuity for the establishment of a Board of Education whose members were to serve without salary. The sum of fifteen hundred dollars was to be paid to the secretary, the post to which Horace Mann was unanimously appointed. Out of this he reserved five hundred dollars for personal use, allocating the rest to his work where the need was greatest.

Many questioned the advisability of his acceptance, but explaining it to his sister, he wrote:

If I can be the means of ascertaining what is the best construction of schoolhouses, what are the best books, what is the best arrangement of studies, what are the best modes of instruction; if I can discover by what appliance of means, a non-thinking, non-reflecting, non-speaking child can most surely be trained into a noble citizen, ready to contend for the right and to die for the right; if I can only obtain and diffuse throughout the State a few good ideas on these and similar subjects, may I not flatter myself that my ministry has not been wholly in vain?

Again he noted: "The common school is the institution that can receive and train up children in the elements of all good knowledge and of virtue before they are subjected to the alienating competitions of life. This institution is the greatest discovery ever made by man; we repeat it—*the common school is the greatest discovery ever made by man.*"

Post riding from county to county like a gospel preacher, he found in two thirds of the schools wholly unqualified teachers, men whose annual salary was $185, women who worked for $65. Textbooks of every variety were in use. About one hundred towns depended upon any volumes available. Often the entire term lasted only two or three months; often a third of the children were absent during the winter. Most of the buildings were dirty and dilapidated. Horace Mann sprang into action. He held conventions, delivered lectures at churches and lycaeums, set up meetings for parents, and in Boston organized weekly discussion groups and lectures with emphasis on moral training. Fears of his own inadequacy threw over his progress a pall of apprehension, though to others it seemed like a triumphal procession.

But resistance to the Board of Education and its aims was widespread and bitter. Thousands viewed with actual hostility the fundamental principles of American government, which promised equal opportunities for all, and prominent citizens formed a movement to abolish the Board itself. Many were dull and apathetic. Many thought public instruction needed no improvement; they wanted common schools kept for common people, and they were already good enough for that. Some said that Horace Mann was a hopeless visionary, that the higher classes would not mix with the lower. Others accused him of "exclusion of the religion of the Bible from the schools," when actually he was fighting denominationalism, exposing and deploring the absence of moral and religious instruction. Constantly he sought books of a non-sectarian nature which contained the ideals of piety and virtue shared by all sects of Christians. But bigots, disappointed book-makers, the hidebound religious press, the straitlaced clergy, cranks, demagogues, and political madmen could not unclinch Horace Mann from his labors for mankind.

In the midst of his troubles he received a proposition to go to Missouri as president of a college on "a salary of three thousand dollars a year, a splendid house, gardens, etc." He declined, for he said, "I would rather remain here, and work for mere bread, than go there for the wealth of the great valley of the Mississippi." He sought no reward save success. The highest welfare of free education was his only ambition, and he was determined to achieve it.

He fathered grade, high, and normal schools, teachers' institutes and training academies. He scattered well-chosen libraries everywhere, as the sower sows his wheatfield. He established the *Common School Journal* to aid teachers and instruct citizens. When public funds were denied him, he persuaded wealthy friends to donate large sums, provided the state would match them. When opposition endangered the first normal school in America and the project was to be abandoned, he sold his own law library to fit up the new building. On his tiny income he prepared several nieces and nephews for study there and paid their bills in addition. When he learned that a schoolhouse in West Newton could be purchased for fifteen hundred dollars, he rushed to the office of Hon. Josiah Quincy and promised him the highest seat in heaven for that amount, which was gladly given.

For twelve years, 1836-1848, Horace Mann presented annually to the Board a detailed and eloquent report of his own doings and the condition and progress of the common schools. In all of them he emphasized the needs of education and its relationship to the progress of civilization. These papers are among the memorials of his great achievements.

In May, 1843, apparently on the brink of physical collapse, Horace Mann married Mary Peabody, and they sailed for Europe on a double honeymoon with Dr. Samuel Gridley Howe and his bride, Julia Ward Howe. Mann gave his exhausted energies no rest, but spent the entire time studying British and European schools, especially those of Germany, and exchanging ideas with eminent foreign authorities on education. His Seventh Report, 1844, showing the inferiority of the Massachusetts schools to the best abroad, stirred up the bitterest controversy of his career and became international news, activating reform everywhere, especially in France, South America, and even Asia.

Then once again his devotion to mankind sent him back to the halls of legislation. Suddenly, owing to the death of John Quincy Adams, came the demand for his services as representative to the National Congress. It was a time of crisis for liberty, and when Mann saw that the new office had bearings on the Great Cause, he allowed himself to be persuaded. In Washington he was a strong addition to the antislavery leaders and an indefatigable worker in defence of lofty principles.

In September, 1852, Mr. Mann was nominated for governor of Massachusetts. On the same day, he was chosen President of coeducational Antioch College at Yellow Springs, Ohio. He accepted the latter office and soon journeyed to that barren, unsettled part of the country, to begin his duties, even before the college buildings were completed.

Horace Mann had foreseen serious difficulties, but the burdens thrust upon him exceeded all expectations, and his health failed rapidly, impaired by overwork and worry. The poverty of the institution, the mismanagement of its finances, limited facilities, and lack of official cooperation placed too heavy a load upon his shoulders. He had further to cope with the crowding of students, many of them poor, rough, and ignorant, but all desirous of an education under the president's inspiring personality. In June, 1859, victorious over every difficulty, he succeeded in selling the college to an independent body of men, a close corporation largely made up of his eastern friends, including Josiah Quincy. With the whole care of the graduating class left in his hands, he hastily prepared the Baccalaureate, without time to read it over before delivery. The festivities lasted more than twelve hours, followed by the college dinner and the president's levee.

The next day Mr. Mann was almost speechless with fatigue. A fever raged in his veins, while the hot weather turned the soil to burning sand and dried up the brackish wells. Several weeks passed, and the outcome became clear. Toward the end, Horace Mann spoke earnestly to all about him, to his sorrowing students, to the saintly Reverend Fay, whom he had trained as his successor, to his friends and family. Again and again he uttered the words, "Man, duty, God!" conveying clearly how he wished them to live. He sent messages to those who were absent, expressed his love for all humanity. To his children he said, "When you wish to know what to do, ask yourselves what Christ would have done in the same circumstances."

At last God mercifully gave him rest, and he spoke no more. But in the last words he uttered in public, he gave to the world his own immortal rule of life: "Be ashamed to die until you have won some victory for humanity."

A Self-Educated Society

The story of Iowa, from early pioneer days to the last years of the nineteenth century, was the story told lovingly and in immense detail by Herbert Quick in a series of novels published after the First World War. Quick came to literature from the law and politics; he worked his way to national prominence as a writer and editor after a childhood dogged by poverty and a crippling attack of polio. Quick's autobiography, One Man's Life, *is a treasury of Americana; and from it, we have this excerpt about early American educational methods.*

"The Children Taught One Another"

BY HERBERT QUICK

NONE of my teachers, with one exception, had any literary attainments. Of course they could read, write, cipher, and tell whether or not we had memorized the simple texts of our schoolbooks. Our schools were created by the society they served. Our teachers were our own boys and girls. Teachers we must have, and, as the supply of educated ones was not sufficient for even the villages and towns, we taught ourselves through the use of such members of society as were thought competent. I have in years not long past had letters from elderly men and women who held certificates as teachers in the schools when I was young. They were the letters of persons just above the plane of illiteracy. Yet, they did a most important work in education.

Self-educated persons are not seldom met; but who has sung the praises of a self-educated society? What a marvelous thing it was for a great, primitive, newly gathered, democratic, independent, self-reliant, uncultured people like that of the Middle West in America, to grapple with the task of educating itself;

275

and, sublimely ignorant of its incapacity, go blunderingly on to such success as it has achieved! . . .

A hundred years ago both this country and Great Britain were aroused to a deep interest in the Lancastrian system of education, in which most of the teaching was done by monitors, or pupil teachers. The children taught one another. Well, though we were quite unaware of it, our whole system in Iowa was a sort of Lancastrian system. We instructed one another. A whole society was taught by those who, figuratively, and often literally, studied at night the lessons they taught next day, and did their whole duty by keeping one lesson ahead of their pupils. There has never been anything like it in the history of any country but this. The weaknesses of the system are obvious. Its merits in uplifting the whole community by making education a thing to be mastered, to be paid for by self-levied taxes, in making the welfare of the schools an obligation of every citizen instead of a ruling class or person, have not often been recognized. Those illiterate teachers were the rudimentary organs, formed by the society out of its own flesh and blood, which have developed into colleges and universities with troops of professors and doctors. Poor and inefficient as they were, I speak of them with reverence.

The McGuffey Readers

In the years between 1836 and 1910, an estimated one hundred and twenty-two million *copies of McGuffey Readers were sold. What were these books, called by Herbert Quick "the most influential volumes ever published in America," and "the most popular reading books for generations?"*

They were, above all, the first textbooks ever designed to "fit the child's education to the child's world." Though completely non-sectarian, they nevertheless emphasized moral and religious attitudes with simple stories of family life and familiar animals. And significantly, all of the selections contained in the McGuffey Readers came from the classics.

William Holmes McGuffey compiled the first of these historic books. As a farmboy, he had astonished his neighbors with prodigious feats of memory; he often recited whole chapters of the Bible while walking behind the plow. He went on to become a professor of philology and philosophy, then a college president. The first four volumes in his famed series appeared in 1836 and 1837. The last two were compiled by his brother Alexander in 1844 and 1854.

These books represented, Herbert Quick says, the "spirit of America at its best." And then in his autobiography, One Man's Life, *he continues:*

And no wonder. The father of the McGuffey brothers was a pioneer in western Pennsylvania. He was a scout in the Indian wars during and succeeding the Revolution, and was selected for scouting service because he was the fastest runner, the best rifleman and the wisest warrior in the forces. William McGuffey's mother was praying aloud in her garden one day, when a man passed who was connected with an academy. Prayer was heard in that case, by the passer-by anyhow. He heard this pioneer mother praying for an education for her son. He saw to it that William had his chance to attend the academy where his tuition cost the sum of three dollars a year, and his board seventy-five cents a week. This was in the Old Stone Academy at Darlington, Pennsylvania, and the man who heard Mrs. McGuffey's prayer was the head and the owner of it, the Reverend Thomas Hughes. . . .

Sons of such a mother, of such a father, and of the log cabin, filled with their sublime faith—sublime even if a little naif and mistaken—in education as a redemptive force, not only for the individual but for society, with family traditions steeped in the sufferings, the pleasures and the conflicts of the old frontier, they could not fail after they had become possessed of a rather comprehensive and liberal scholarship, to instill into their textbooks a soul very much *en rapport* with the aspirations of a boy like myself.

Phyllis McGinley, widely known for her light verse, continues this account of the McGuffey Readers with her spirited article, "Lessons for Today."

Lessons for Today: From McGuffey's Readers*

BY PHYLLIS McGINLEY

In times of public crisis there is a temptation, on the part of public men, to look back with longing on the Good Old Days. Blurred by the mists of history, softened and gently tinted, the virtues of the past seem magnified, the faults reduced to molehills. Some lament that mankind has lost its nobility; or, with former President Truman, they make regretful comparisons between the educational ideas of this century and those at work in the Age of McGuffey's Readers. White House visitors have often heard the [former] President's reflections that modern textbooks have forgotten the McGuffey aims of teaching—educating for ethics as well as intellect, building character along with vocabulary—and that as a result American education has suffered a tremendous blow.

The famous "Eclectic Readers" that for generations fed the minds of millions of school children are curiosities now, like

* Condensed from *The New York Times Magazine*.

flintlocks and covered wagons. Yet, though the old Readers may be dated, their secret of teaching is still valid.

When, in 1836, Professor McGuffey compiled for a firm of publishers in Cincinnati his First Reader, he was initiating something rather daring. Here were schoolbooks enormously different from the spellers, the religious tracts and primers which had been the basic fare of helpless young Americans. McGuffey gave the children three ambitious gifts: reading material planned for the age level of the child, selections of real literary worth, and moral teaching wrapped in an acceptable package.

None of us is quite free of McGuffey. If today even non-poetry readers have, stored away in the attics of their minds, such familiar fragments as "Oft in the stilly night" or "Break, break, break, on thy cold gray stones, O Sea!" or "Backward, turn backward, O Time, in your flight," or " 'Make way for Liberty,' he cried," or "The melancholy days are come," it is because Professor McGuffey was one of the greatest anthologists who ever lived. And his choices remained static in many school readers long after his own book had vanished from the curriculum.

McGuffey himself would never have been so behind the times. When he included in his Readers such items as "Speech of Logan, Chief of the Mingoes" or stirred the hearts of sixth-graders with "At midnight, in his guarded tent," he was being modern. The authors of his choice—Longfellow and Whittier and Lowell and Dickens and Hawthorne—were contemporaries who spoke the contemporary idiom. How many fifth- and sixth-grade reading lists today are rich with selections from Shaw and Sinclair Lewis and Faulkner and Robert Frost and Ogden Nash? Don't lift an eyebrow. Every one of those authors has written something which might be enjoyed by a literate child.

How many children are storing away in their memories quotable bits of contemporary literature? It is against the rules to insist on memorizing as an exercise. Still, dull as it must have seemed back in the nineteenth century to have to learn by rote "When Freedom from her mountain height unfurled her standard to the air," those lines became part of the child's later heritage. We teach children—or used to—to put their nickels in the bank against a rainy day. Perhaps we should go back to persuading them to store up a quotation or two against the famine of middle age.

Glancing through McGuffey is like taking a guided tour of nineteenth-century writing. But how familiar the landscape looks!

Here is that sweetly sentimental little opus, "The Blue and the Gray." (And how contemporary *that* was in 1867!) Here is "Out of the North the wild news came," with its—then—heart-lifting last stanza:

> *"Who dares"—this was the patriot's cry,*
> *As striding from the desk he came—*
> *"Come out with me, in Freedom's name,*
> *For her to live, for her to die?"*
> *A hundred hands flung up reply,*
> *A hundred voices answered, "I!"*

And here are the extravagant puns of Hood's "Faithless Nelly Gray," which begins:

> *Ben Battle was a soldier bold*
> *And used to war's alarms.*
> *But a cannonball took off his legs,*
> *So he laid down his arms!*

They misjudge the Professor who believe he was all grimness, morality and sentiment. It was one of the greatest of his innovations that he brought lightness and warmth to textbooks. If a sixth-grader's tears were summoned by "The Death of Little Nell," they could be gently fanned away by the gaiety of "The Barefoot Boy" or Whittier's "The Fish I Didn't Catch."

Even the primary Readers were not so dispiriting as their traducers would have us believe. The little lessons, carefully planned for children's burgeoning vocabularies, are rather charming.

"One cold night, after old Mr. Post had gone to bed, he heard a noise at the door. So he got up, and went out. And what do you think he found?" (It was a baby, of course; not a chipmunk or a rabbit, as it would be today.) So Mr. Post "held it to the fire until it was warm, and then took it in his arms, and went to bed." (And when little Mary grew up she was, as you may suppose and the children certainly expected, a great comfort to old Mr. Post. Which is more than the chipmunk would have been.)

As one browses through the old favorites, the McGuffey aim and its successful accomplishment seem startlingly appealing. Here are selections from "the best literature" with a clear but not oppressive emphasis on ethical conduct, on loving one's neighbor, on loving one's country, on behaving not only as a gentleman (or a lady) but also as a man (or a woman). The pragmatic ideal is not absent—virtue is presented as not only its own reward but as a thing that pays off.

The little chimney sweep notices a gold watch and refrains from stealing it in spite of terrible temptation. So the lady who owns the watch "let him stay, and live in her house. For many years she sent him to a school." Charles, another honest boy, receives a whole hatful of oranges for his honesty, while Jack Pilfer receives a mighty kick.

I do not think it ever hurt any child to learn early that to "Waste not" is to "want not," that "If at first you don't succeed, try, try again." Children are not subtle. Perhaps it takes a moral, blunt and obvious, to penetrate the hard heart and insulated conscience of a child. Perhaps we have too much sugar-coated the lessons we wish to teach today. Or perhaps the lessons themselves are not vigorous enough.

I have been browsing through dozens of textbooks wheedled from the public school of my county—a county famous for its advanced educational methods. They seem tame fare after the Eclectic Readers. The children in them do such ordinary things! They saw and they hammer, they go to birthday parties, they shop in the stores. They learn about fire departments; they talk to mailmen and grocers. But there is never any melodrama. No babies left on doorsteps. No naughty boys destroyed by avalanches because they disobeyed their papas. And only one moral taught over and over: Understand your neighbor.

Now that is an excellent precept and vitally necessary to One World or many. But it is not the only one. Our children will know a great deal about running a tractor. They will comprehend that one is expected to cooperate in a clay-modeling project. But will they be grounded, steeped, wrapped around in the assurance that honesty is the best policy, thrift is a virtue, hard work pays off, and that America, for all its faults, is a great and exciting experiment?

No doubt these little textbooks, so scientifically arranged, so measured on yardsticks by whole committees of Ph.D.s, will not only illuminate ignorance but build up a better civic conscience. But one lack they will always have—the personality behind the famous series. Great books are seldom written in committee.

It could be that what we need is not McGuffey but the McGuffey secret—the mind of a great teacher, and a great preacher as well, operating on the millions of young minds all over the nation. Perhaps minds so molded would not conceive it admirable to influence Congressmen for gain or to betray the secrets of one's country to another power.

No, we cannot go back to McGuffey. We live in a different climate with different literary tastes and different necessities for survival. But his aspirations are still valid.

My child and yours might find it rewarding, even now, to go to sleep at night with the words of the ballad marching through his head:

> *And how can man die better*
> *Than facing fearful odds*
> *For the ashes of his Fathers*
> *And the Temples of his Gods?*

Or, if that speech of Horatius seems too martial for the times, or if it is not tactful to teach them to cry with Patrick Henry, "Is life so dear, or peace so sweet, as to be purchased at the price of chains and slavery?" then let them repeat with Southey and the open-minded McGuffey these shrewdly pacific lines:

> *"And everybody praised the Duke*
> *Who this great fight did win."*
> *"But what good came of it at last?"*
> *Quoth little Peterkin.*
> *"Why, that I cannot tell," said he,*
> *"But 'twas a famous victory."*

Booker T. Washington Supervises
an Indian Class

*"What do we live for, except to do the impossible in the strength
of God?" This question, from the lips of General Samuel C.
Armstrong, principal of Hampton Institute, directed to fame the
steps of at least one youth who heard it.*

*Booker T. Washington was the boy, the son of a white father
and a slave mother, born into a life of squalor and hardship.
He did the impossible in the strength of God: he became an
educator, the companion and adviser of Presidents, the leading
spokesman of his race, and the founder of America's major institution for Negro education, Alabama's Tuskegee Institute.*

*As a young student at Hampton, Booker Washington was
given the opportunity to supervise the education of a group of
seventy-five American Indians. To that task he brought sympathy, compassion and respect—the brotherhood one member of
a depressed group should feel for another in like circumstances.
Here is Booker Washington's story of that experiment, as it appears in his classic autobiography,* Up From Slavery.

Black Race and Red Race

BY BOOKER T. WASHINGTON

About this time the experiment was being tried for the first
time, by General Armstrong, of educating Indians at Hampton.
Few people then had any confidence in the ability of the Indians to receive education and to profit by it. General Armstrong was anxious to try the experiment systematically on a
large scale. He secured from the reservations in the Western
states over one hundred wild and for the most part perfectly

ignorant Indians, the greater proportion of whom were young men. The special work which the General desired me to do was to be a sort of "house father" to the Indian young men—that is, I was to live in the building with them and have the charge of their discipline, clothing, rooms, and so on. This was a very tempting offer, but I had become so much absorbed in my work in West Virginia that I dreaded to give it up. However, I tore myself away from it. I did not know how to refuse to perform any service that General Armstrong desired of me.

On going to Hampton, I took up my residence in a building with about seventy-five Indian youths. I was the only person in the building who was not a member of their race. At first I had a good deal of doubt about my ability to succeed. I knew that the average Indian felt himself above the white man, and, of course, he felt himself far above the Negro, largely on account of the fact of the Negro having submitted to slavery—a thing which the Indian would never do. The Indians, in the Indian Territory, owned a large number of slaves during the days of slavery. Aside from this, there was a general feeling that the attempt to educate and civilize the red men at Hampton would be a failure. All this made me proceed very cautiously, for I felt keenly the great responsibility. But I was determined to succeed. It was not long before I had the complete confidence of the Indians, and not only this, but I think I am safe in saying that I had their love and respect. I found that they were about like any other human beings; that they responded to kind treatment and resented ill-treatment. They were continually planning to do something that would add to my happiness and comfort. The things that they disliked most, I think, were to have their long hair cut, to give up wearing their blankets, and to cease smoking; but no white American ever thinks that any other race is wholly civilized until he wears the white man's clothes, eats the white man's food, speaks the white man's language, and professes the white man's religion.

When the difficulty of learning the English language was subtracted, I found that in the matter of learning trades and in mastering academic studies there was little difference between the coloured and Indian students. It was a constant delight to me to note the interest which the coloured students took in trying to help the Indians in every way possible. There were a few of the coloured students who felt that the Indians ought not to be admitted to Hampton, but these were in the minority. Whenever they were asked to do so, the Negro students gladly took the Indians as room-mates, in order that they might teach them to speak English and to acquire civilized habits.

I have often wondered if there was a white institution in this country whose students would have welcomed the incoming of more than a hundred companions of another race in the cordial way that these black students at Hampton welcomed the red ones. How often I have wanted to say to white students that they lift themselves up in proportion as they help to lift others, and the more unfortunate the race, and the lower in the scale of civilization, the more does one raise one's self by giving the assistance.

This reminds me of a conversation which I once had with the Hon. Frederick Douglass. At one time Mr. Douglass was travelling in the state of Pennsylvania, and was forced, on account of his colour, to ride in the baggage-car, in spite of the fact that he had paid the same price for his passage that the other passengers had paid. When some of the white passengers went into the baggage-car to console Mr. Douglass, and one of them said to him: "I am sorry, Mr. Douglass, that you have been degraded in this manner," Mr. Douglass straightened himself up on the box upon which he was sitting, and replied: "They cannot degrade Frederick Douglass. The soul that is within me no man can degrade. I am not the one that is being degraded on account of this treatment, but those who are inflicting it upon me."

Summer Assembly on the Lake

The "Chautauqua Movement" for family education has been linked to two earlier institutions of American life—the Lyceum, and the camp meetings where circuit-riding ministers served frontier families who came together annually to attend prolonged and dramatic preaching services.

It was because of their desire to improve Sunday school teacher-training that Dr. John H. Vincent and Lewis Miller founded a "Summer Assembly" on Lake Chautauqua in 1874. The project flourished from the start, far surpassing expectations. Soon a wide variety of the best secular courses available in the arts, sciences, and humanities was added to the basic curriculum.

Although many communities initiated similar programs, none quite caught the spirit of the original Chautauqua, which continues to be a force in American intellectual life even today. For many years its magnificent auditorium has provided a forum for notable figures in every sphere of life.

Ida Tarbell, author, editor, lecturer, and reformer, spent many summers at Chautauqua. From her memories she sketches the simple but picturesque beginnings of the famous institution which Theodore Roosevelt once called "The most American thing in America."

The Chautauqua Movement

BY IDA M. TARBELL

THE Chautauqua Movement had grown out of a Methodist camp meeting held annually at Fair Point on the pleasant lake which in my childhood had been the terminus of our most ambitious all-day excursions. The president of this Association by 1870 was a man justly respected in all that part of the world for his good deeds, as well as his business acumen—Lewis Miller, a manufacturer of Akron, Ohio. Mr. Miller was to be known nationally as the father-in-law of Thomas Edison, but old-time Chautauquans put it the other way: "Edison is Lewis Miller's son-in-law." That was enough recommendation for Edison in their minds.

Lewis Miller's interest in Chautauqua went beyond the annual camp meeting. He saw the opportunity to build up there a summer home where parents could give their children healthy out-of-door amusement, protection from the evil ways of the unregenerate, and sound modern instruction in the Bible. Sympathy with this program induced a half-dozen families in the Titusville Methodist Church to join in the purchase of a lot on the outskirts of the grounds and start a Titusville settlement— a cottage with a mess hall and a few rooms—tents serving as sleeping quarters for extras. Father joined the colony soon after we moved to Titusville. We had a tent and a flat-bottomed boat.

Through the years I have been recalling, the years in high school, college, as Preceptress of Poland Union Seminary, part of all my summers had been spent at Chautauqua. Lewis Miller's laudable attempt to furnish attractive instruction in the Bible meant little or nothing to me at first; the flat-bottomed boat meant a great deal. But in 1874 something happened that dragged me away from the water. Lewis Miller had persuaded the most eminent advocate of the Sunday school in America, Dr. (afterwards Bishop) John H. Vincent, to select Fair Point as the home of a National Interdenominational Sunday School Institute which he and those who saw with him had been for some time planning. The first session of this new organization was held in 1874 under the name of the Chautauqua Assembly. It was recognized at once as a revolution upsetting the old order.

The most spectacular feature of the revolution was the Chautauqua platform, making as it did stirring, challenging contacts with current intellectual life. There one heard the great speakers of the day on all sorts of subjects. There fine concerts were given. . . .

There were many of these undertakings. Dr. Vincent saw to that. A man better fitted by experience, conviction, and personality to persuade a half-asleep, wholly satisfied community to accept a new order could not have been found in the America of the eighties. John Vincent was forty-two years old when he came to Chautauqua—handsome, confident, alert, energetic, radiating well-being. And he was an orator, and orating at Chautauqua made men tolerant even of heresy. He went about his business of organizing the work of the Assembly with a skill which commanded the admiration of everybody, even those hostile to the secularization of their beloved camp meeting. As a platform manager I never have known his equal. He had magnetism, but he knew when and how to turn it on; he was shrewd, cunning, pungent. He pricked bubbles, disciplined his audience. The Chautauqua audience came to be one of the best behaved out-of-door audiences in the country. The fact that we were out of doors had persuaded us that we were free to leave meetings if we were bored or suddenly remembered that we had left bread in the oven, or that the baby must have wakened. When the performance had been stopped once or twice to "give that lady a chance to go out without further disturbing the speaker" we learned to stay at home or to sit out the lecture.

There is only one word to describe what Lewis Miller and Dr. Vincent now did to Chautauqua, and that is "electrification."

. . . Dr. Vincent kept the place on its toes not only by the steady improvement of its platform, its amusements, in the quality of the people who came to teach and preach, but by a steady flow of new undertakings. He planned incessantly to stir not only our souls but our minds. We came to expect new ideas at each successive session and were never disappointed if sometimes a little bewildered. Behind all these various undertakings was the steadying hand of Lewis Miller, the silent partner, who had begun by spying out the land, establishing a community, laying the foundations for the Institution as it exists today—a center of democratic, Christian culture.

Dr. Vincent's masterpiece, as I always thought, came in 1878 when he laid before his Chautauquans a plan which had been long simmering in his never quiet mind. He did this in the finest of what we call inspirational talks that I ever heard—at least it stirred me so deeply that I have never forgotten the face of the orator nor, more important, the upturned faces of his hearers. He announced a scheme for a four-year course of home reading under the direction of the Chautauqua management adapted to men and women who had missed a college education, but who felt a deep desire for knowledge and were willing to adopt any practical plan which would give them a college outlook. It was to be called the Chautauqua Literary and Scientific Circle.

Now this does not sound exciting; but as a matter of fact it was deeply exciting, for the speaker was pouring out his heart. He had never had a college education; he had never ceased to feel the lack of what he believed it would have given him. He had struggled to make up for his loss by persistent, systematic daily reading and study. Establishing the habit as a boy, he had never abandoned it. It had given him deep satisfaction; it supplied, he thought, the college outlook. He believed there were thousands of men and women in the United States, scores, possibly hundreds, in his audience, who had been forced, as he had been, to sacrifice their early ambitions for education. They had hidden the hunger in their hearts where at times it still gnawed. He was offering them the same help he had found, and confidently, glowingly, he outlined the course of home reading which Dr. John H. Finley has so aptly named the American Adult Education Pioneer.

The uplifted faces all about me told the story, particularly the faces of the women of thirty or more. Women of that generation had had their natural desire for knowledge intensified by the Woman's Rights movement, in which the strongest plank had been a demand for the opportunity for higher education. These women were now beyond the day when they could go to college, but here was something which they saw intuitively was practical. . . .

Well, it was a great emotional experience with large and immediate practical results, for, before the summer session was over, eight thousand people had joined the Chautauqua Literary and Scientific Circle.

Doers of the Word

*The names of Dwight L. Moody and Ira L. Sankey are synony-
mous with religious revival in America. But their influence was
felt in other ways as well. With the huge royalties amassed
from their collections of gospel hymns, Moody founded a group
of educational institutions, schools based on his own ideals and
planned for those "in the humbler walks of life, who never would
get a Christian education but for a school like this."*

*And in the annual "Northfield Summer Conferences of Chris-
tian Workers," Dwight Moody and Ira Sankey have another of
their great memorials. These gatherings, attracting church leaders,
reformers, and philanthropists from many corners of the world,
have been of incalculable influence.*

*Janet Mabie, who grew up in Northfield at the turn of the cen-
tury, wrote a book about the impact of these summer conferences.
Called* Heaven on Earth, *it reflects all she felt about these stirring events of her childhood. In the following selection, she describes one such portentous evening, "when the whole town
crowded the Auditorium."*

Round Top and Auditorium

BY JANET MABIE

The times when my parents let me go to the Auditorium in the
evening were few and far between. They explained, if I pouted
about being left behind, that I wouldn't understand the address,
which was true enough (Mr. F. B. Meyer, on "The Inspiration
of the Bible") and would only grow sleepy and disturb the
grown-ups by fidgeting. Also neither of my parents cared for a
growing child to be sleeping across their laps while they listened
to someone preach.

However, every evening during the Conferences—unless it rained and it was moved indoors, at gloomy Stone Hall—there was a service on Round Top at six-thirty. Like everything else that went on in Northfield, this was for grown-ups; but people did tell incidents at Round Top which a child would understand, a little, anyhow. And the service was at the prettiest time of day. The lemon light of afterglow would be lying in long wedges along the whole length of the drowsing valley. Somewhere a phoebe would be singing. The evening star would be hanging like a small silver lantern in the dooryard of the blue crystal sky.

My parents were willing for me to go to Round Top providing someone would take me home afterward, seeing that I went straight to bed. Round Top was different from the Auditorium—with the lights, and huge moth millers wheeling about over people's heads, and the tingle your feet got from the floor when the organist used the full organ, and the biggest pedal stops, the bourdon and the open diapason, for the last verse of "In the cross of Christ I glory, Tow'ring o'er the wrecks of time." But Round Top was better than always just staying home and going to bed.

The most important preachers never appeared at Round Top. The platform of the Auditorium was their place, and you only saw them there. (In the summer of 1950 a New York theatrical producer, Richard Aldrich, owner of the ranking New England summer theater, said something about this; looking back on many summers spent at Northfield when he was growing up, he said, "The platform of the Auditorium was a stage; there was better acting on it than most summer theaters ever see.")

Once, when there wasn't any Round Top, I got to go to the Auditorium in the evening anyway. Father said he thought any growing child ought to see the President of the United States, if the opportunity offered.

Mr. Theodore Roosevelt was traveling through New England, making speeches to get people to think about electing him. He took a side trip down from Brattleboro to Mt. Hermon. Senator Henry Cabot Lodge, a neat man with stick-up hair and a pointed beard, met Mr. Roosevelt, with some other men, and they visited Mr. Moody's school for the boys. Then he came across the river in a carriage drawn by four borrowed white horses, and had dinner at the hotel and rested, before going to the Auditorium to make a speech. So many people crowded around the hotel, cheering, and calling out, "Mr. Roosevelt! Mr. Roosevelt! Yeh!" that, before he could take his rest he had to come out on the porch. The setting sun made his glasses and his big teeth glitter. He stood in the circular part of the porch and waved at everybody, calling out, "How are you? Glad to see you."

Having decided that the whole household should go to see the President, Father hardly let us finish our supper. "We'll get no seats unless we hurry!" he kept saying, and finally left half his raisin rice pudding to rush off and get ready.

Mother got her best cashmere shawl and a pair of new white gloves. It was a warm Indian summer evening, but she said it would be cold when we came home and I was to wear a warm coat.

The horse was in one of her foolish moods, giving little jumps and tossing her head while Father tried to hitch her up. "Whoa, you hammerhead!" he shouted, and you could see he was very excited by the President being in Northfield, because he was fond of the horse and it wasn't like him to call her such a name.

"Come along! Come along!" he kept crying out to us, although we couldn't very well start till the horse was harnessed. . . .

The Auditorium was packed to the roof and sounded like a beehive as big as all of Hog's Back Mountain. Everybody looked lively, gay. Ladies had extra handkerchiefs, big ones, and called out to their friends, "For the Chautauqua salute, you know!"

Father didn't like waiting for things to begin. He looked around, pulled on his beard, took out his handkerchief and blew his nose, tapped his feet. A few seats away he noticed Dr. A. T. Pierson. He jumped up. "Mother," he said, "don't let anyone take my seat. I'll just step over and have a few words with Pierson."

Dr. Pierson was a nice man, very friendly with children. He had bright, happy eyes, a long, fluffy white beard and looked to me a little like pictures of the prophet Elijah, only thinner.

The Piersons lived about a mile from us, over on the other road. He was a walker. Even if you offered him a ride part way home from the Auditorium he wouldn't accept. After morning service, if it was a hot day, he would shade himself with a very large black cotton umbrella. If we passed him on the road at night he would be carrying a tin lantern and turn out to let us pass, calling a few words of greeting in a jaunty voice.

All of a sudden there was shouting outside the Auditorium. And a noise of people running. *"Hurrah! Hooray! Hey, Teddy! —Yeh—Hooray—Hooray—"*

Mr. Roosevelt came bounding through a little door under the

end of the platform, and up the stairs. He had on a claw-hammer coat and wide-striped trousers, and a gold ring just under the knot in his necktie. With his head thrown way back, he showed his teeth and waved at the audience. A lot of men clustered around him.

Father leaned across me and said in an important tone to Mother, "Some of those men are the Secret Service; they go everywhere a President goes, to protect him from harm."

"Who would harm him?" I asked my father. Nobody harmed anybody in Northfield. You never even locked up the house. No one would ever bother anything.

"A President is very important," he tossed at me, "they can't be too careful about him."

The air was full of handkerchiefs, snapping back and forth in the Chautauqua salute. Everybody stamped their feet and yelled, even people who hardly ever seemed to find anything in Northfield to smile about.

Mother's cheeks were pink with excitement. She waved her lace handkerchief demurely, though she couldn't make up her mind to make any sound.

Father stood on tiptoe, gazing eagerly over the heads and clapping his hands approvingly. He wouldn't yell "Hooray! Hooray!" either but he looked as though he were having a fine time just the same. Gazing around, his eye happened to fall on me. "Well, Ducky," he said, in a very good mood, "there's the President of our country. I am very glad for you to have the opportunity to see him right here in Northfield."

Someone on the platform stepped forward to quiet things. Mr. Roosevelt sat down with a plunk, hoisting one leg over the other and peering at the audience in a very interested way.

Dr. Pentacost was asked to offer prayer. He had on his white linen suit and bright-red necktie, and a red rambler rosebud in his buttonhole. He put out his chest and began praying, "O Lord God Almight—" in that big rich voice, curling the edges of his *r*'s and making the words sound very fine.

A few people traveling with the President were called on and they jumped up and spoke. No one listened to what they said because everyone was waiting to hear the President.

Then Senator Lodge said, "Ladies and gentlemen, the President of the United States," and Mr. Roosevelt leaped out of his chair.

First he pulled a small Testament out of the pocket in his coattails and read a passage from the Bible.

"Be ye doers of the word, not hearers only. . . . Not slothful in business, fervent in spirit, serving the Lord. . . ." No one expected the President of the United States to read the Bible in the Auditorium, it seemed to me, and everyone looked surprised, and pleased too.

Then, after saying he was glad to be in Northfield, he said, in quite a high, scratchy voice, "I am glad to see these schools founded by Dwight L. Moody to teach boys and girls to be good citizens. It is good to learn to work with hands as well as heads. A person is no good unless he knows how to do both."

George Washington Carver

"Stolen in infancy," George Washington Carver's biography reads. "Bought from his captors for a race horse valued at $300 . . ." At the end of the Civil War food was scarce and living precarious in the border states—this was Missouri—but his new mother lovingly nursed the infant George Washington Carver back to life. Later, Sue Carver taught him her own unusual skills in the home. It remained, however, for him to teach himself to read, and this he did with the aid of the Bible and a blue-backed speller.

Though the family treated him kindly, he was early to feel the ban on his race, for he had to leave home at the age of ten, and travel far to find a school which would admit a Negro boy. He took any kind of work he could get in the years that followed, anything which would help pay for further education. He received sound training in art; he took courses in agriculture; he obtained advanced degrees.

When Booker T. Washington called him to Tuskegee Institute, Carver found there no laboratory and not a penny for equipment. But he put his brown hands to the dry brown soil and brought forth miracles: paints from clays, hundreds of products from the peanut and the sweet potato. His many contributions to our science and agriculture won him recognition both here and in Great Britain, and an honored place in our national history. With tenderness and sympathy Mary Jenness highlights Carver's constant sense of the closeness of God, a gift which he passed on to his students as his most precious possession.

The Man Who Asked God Questions

BY MARY JENNESS

IT WAS the first time that test tubes had been ranged alongside
the president's Bible in that college chapel. The baccalaureate
speaker had brought them to Simpson College in 1941 to interpret his address. He was a distinguished graduate who wore the
gown of a Doctor of Science, bestowed by his alma mater thirteen years before. His face was as black as his hair was white,
but his manner was so winning that the students promptly forgot the striking combination. He talked to them as informally as
to his famous Bible class at Tuskegee Institute. And he told
them that he had made all his scientific discoveries by walking
and talking with God before dawn. He dramatized such a conversation for them:

"Mr. Creator," I asked him, "I want to know all about the
peanut."

"Little man, your mind is too small to take it in. Ask something more your size."

"But, Mr. Creator, why did you make the peanut?"

"Behold, . . . I have given every green herb for food." [That
verse of Scripture, which indeed Professor Carver had chosen
for the text of his baccalaureate sermon, had called for more
research in 1910. In that year of disaster Southern farmers had
found no market for peanuts as food.] Professor Carver went on
with a question that was likewise a prayer for enlightenment.

"But, Mr. Creator, what is in the peanut?" That query drove
much closer to the chemical heart of the problem.

"I have given you some brains. ('But He didn't say how
many,' was Dr. Carver's comment.) I will give you a handful of
peanuts. Take them into your laboratory and take them apart."

"So I found out what peanuts are made of." Professor Carver
reeled off a string of long names with an impish glee that con-
vulsed the students. "I still didn't know what to do with the
parts. I looked at the Creator, and He looked at me."

"Put them together again," said the Creator, "using my laws of compatibility, temperature, and pressure."

Whereupon Dr. Carver pulled out a sack of peanuts from under his scholar's gown. Then he reached for the test tubes that held the products of the peanut, discovered after his "walk and talk with God."

"This is what you must do," he told the students in closing. "Put together in new ways the things that you have learned, and there is no limit to what you can do to benefit mankind."

"I will lift up mine eyes unto the hills," was another of Dr. Carver's favorite texts. He used to say: "God doesn't mean just looking at the hills without seeing anything. God wants us to *search* with everything we know, with chemistry and physics and botany."

He himself could search with the knowledge of an artist who mixed his own pigments. Once his trained eye saw blue in a red claybank. He worked over that clay with an unheard-of process that he described as "chemical gymnastics" until he drew out an intense and striking blue. Artists seized upon it with joy but asked doubtfully, "Will it last?"

"God put that color into the hills of Alabama," he replied, "and it has stayed there, unchanged, for centuries. Why should it fade when I use it to paint a flower?"

Though Professor Carver had given up art in order to serve his people, he still painted for recreation and for his friends. One of his paintings, after passing out of his hands, was sold for $4,000. Another, "Three Peaches," painted with pigments drawn from Alabama clays, was asked for by the Luxembourg Galleries in Paris. Professor Carver refused to sell it. It is now on display at the George Washington Carver Foundation at Tuskegee, along with his "Yucca Gloriosa" and fifty-nine of his other paintings.

It was no wonder that students at the Institute begged Professor Carver to start a Bible class. He did so, for boys only, while the Institute was still a high school. Bible history was a required subject, but the students did not rush to those classes as they did to Professor Carver's. His group soon was crowding the largest assembly hall. It met every Sunday evening between supper and vespers, to the regret of those who had to go to choir practice.

"We had to bring our Bibles," said a student of the mid-twenties, "because he always asked one of us to read the passage that he had selected. One evening it was 'Behold, . . . I have given every green herb for food.' (See *Genesis* 1:28-30.) His favorite story was the story of creation, and he always used it to show that science does not conflict with religion. Once he had asked a student in agriculture to bring in wild vegetables from his father's farm. Professor Carver held them up and asked what they were, but most of the boys thought they were just weeds. I remember the wild onion and the pepper grass. Only the botany students knew both the common name and the book name.

" 'God created these plants for man's use,' said Professor Carver, 'but without science you don't even know what they are. Now I will tell you what they are good for.' He told us that nobody ever needed to starve if he could recognize such wild vegetables as these and use them for food.

"I remember best the story of the twelve spies who went up into the Promised Land to look it over. After the reading, Professor Carver always asked, 'What does this mean to you?' It didn't mean much to me before, but I'll never forget what he told us. The most important man in the story, he said, was the man from the smallest tribe with the least influence. The other eleven men said that Canaan was a land flowing with milk and honey. Now that was true, but the 'beehives' were in the rocks, and the milk was in the udders of the goats. They thought there was too much work to do [a sly thrust of Professor Carver's at those students who had come to school in order to get away from farm labor]. Besides, the eleven spies reported there were giants in the way, and nobody could get past them. But first Caleb and then Joshua, they said, 'There's nothing to be afraid of if God is with us.'

"Professor Carver said that the rest tabled the minority report, just as it's done now. But Caleb and Joshua were the ones who turned out to be right about it."

Professor Carver knew all about the giants that stand in the path of a colored boy's education. He knew how many of the students in that very class had been working hard all day through the week and going to their high school classes at night. In summer most of them scattered off to work on the railroads or up in the tobacco fields of Connecticut. In the early twenties the churches had only just begun to have a care for such migrant laborers. These boys were willing to live like animals—some of them had to—if only they could get back to school in September.

"So he put heart into us," said his former student at Tuskegee, "for everybody knew that he had had to get his education the hard way, just like us. 'If God is with you, do not be afraid.'"

The Stronghold of Freedom

It has not always been easy to buy or borrow a book. This was the fact which prompted James Hulme Canfield to become a "library pioneer."

Dorothy Canfield Fisher, his daughter, reveals how high were the hopes which James Canfield had for a free library system. As president of the Universities of Nebraska and Ohio State, and later as Librarian of Columbia University, he implemented his ideals with tangible achievements. Mrs. Fisher has herself carried on the same spirit—the author of many valuable textbooks and articles in the educational field, she is also a distinguished novelist and translator.

Public Libraries in a Democracy

BY DOROTHY CANFIELD FISHER

THE one true library pioneer whom I knew intimately was my father. He was an educator who preached a crusade for universal free public education long before that principle was taken for granted. When the movement was well started and would obviously go forward of its own impetus, he began another crusade —for universal free public libraries. These he saw as the needed rung in the educational ladder before the American citizenry could step off into that permanent intellectual maturity without which the hopes of the country's founders would come to nothing. What was the use of teaching Americans to read intelligently if they did not find around them an adequate supply of intelligently selected books to read?

My father and other generous-spirited library pioneers of his generation never doubted that with books and readers brought together the trick was done. But there have been times when I

300

have been glad that they were in their graves and not with me as I have looked, shocked, at the echoing emptiness of certain well-stocked but neglected libraries. My father's wholehearted drive towards providing books might have lost some of the power of his ardor and courage had he guessed what nobody then knew—that there are mysterious, shut doors inside human heads which must be opened before the right books are taken from those open shelves and read. How could the pioneers of the library movement dream of the invisible barrier which rears itself inexplicably between the busy, happy reading-public of childhood, clustering in well-conducted children's rooms reading children's classics with delight, and those children grown up to be the general public, who read no classics, none, nothing but an occasional best seller, and the magazines? . . .

They took for granted—that an educated citizenry . . . would spontaneously and eagerly throng into the public library in knowledge-hungry crowds, if the doors could be opened to them, using books as tools to advance themselves steadily year by year in good taste, cultivation, good judgment, sound information. There is no doubt that they would be aghast to see that this is not exactly what happens—to put it mildly. They would be horrified by the statistics showing the large percentage of our population which cannot read with ease, and will not of its own accord read any book beyond the comprehension of an eighth grade child (or is it a sixth grade one?). They would be staggered by the small proportion of the population of any community which uses the books so freely offered by the public libraries. . . . Yes, I think the forefathers of the free public library would have turned rather pale at some of the things we know, and they did not, about the relationship between books and human beings.

But, remembering their ardor, their willingness to give their lives to the cause, I do not for a moment believe that they would be disheartened. I am sure that after they had had time just to catch their breath they would have turned from their crusade for a wider public recognition of the vital need for books in a democracy, to an impassioned attack on the mystery of why a democracy doesn't use its books as it should. They were determined . . . to open to their countrymen those doors to knowledge, understanding and joy called books. . . .

Rising with a strong wingbeat of the imagination, they may catch a glimpse of libraries of the future circulating not only those sheets of paper marked with printed symbols of words which so large a part of our race translate with difficulty into ideas, but paintings, music (why not?), records of poems read by the poets themselves, motion-picture films of far places, of mechanical processes hard to put into these word symbols, of the stars in their courses, of instruction in sports and dancing, in hygiene, in homemaking, in the care of children, in gardening, in all the arts.

Yet there is an aspect of the library movement now, in our troubled times, rising melodramatically into view, undreamed of, I think, by its founders, with all their greatness of vision. They took for granted some forms of freedom, assumed that liberty to think was as pervasive in modern life as the air we breathe. And we have been tragically taught that this freedom is the first object of attack whenever democracy is threatened. Highly as the founders valued the institution of public libraries . . . it did not occur to them, I think, that public libraries play a vital part in preserving that intellectual freedom without which any form of government is a blighting tyranny. It was only in the lurid light from the book-burning autos-da-fé in Germany, that the library took on its true shape of protecting fortress, that we saw it as the very stronghold of freedom.

Each One Teach One

With a faith strong enough to move mountains, and a gift for fusing the ideal with the real, Dr. Frank Laubach, missionary extraordinary, has made his own dreams of an awakened mankind come true. It was among the headhunters of Mindanao that he began his life work of bringing enlightenment and Christian comfort to backward peoples. Since then he has moved through a swift panorama of colorful countries, peoples, and events. Everywhere his name is synonymous with his slogan, "Each one teach one."

In this crusade, Frank Laubach has freed more than sixty million people from ignorance and illiteracy. Almost invariably, a series of practical reforms, the natural by-product of thinking and reading, has followed in these areas. Biographer Dana Thomas takes the reader directly into the thrilling drama of Laubach's world mission, where his understanding of basic human needs has imparted new meaning to brotherhood and aspiration among all nations and races of men.

Frank Laubach

BY DANA THOMAS

ONE afternoon on the Island of Mindanao in the southern Philippines, a bald-headed, broad-shouldered American missionary stood up in a former saloon and faced as ferocious looking a group of Filipinos as had ever congregated under a white man's roof. They were the dreaded Moros, warriors who in times past had given the United States Army some of the roughest fighting in its history. For twenty-five years no civilized man had dared to walk among them without a gun. But times had changed. On this particular afternoon, close to a hundred of the savages were sitting as meekly as nursery children at the feet of a gentle-man-nered missionary, listening enthralled to what he had to say.

The American pointed to a large wall chart covered with bold-printed letters and brightly colored pictures. "Now, repeat after me, 'Ma, mi, mo, mu!'"

And each Moro obediently opened his mouth and recited, "Ma, mi, mo, mu."

From time to time natives put down the books they were hold-ing, leaped to their feet with shining eyes and shouted, "Teacher, I can spell the words! I can really read. Listen to me!"

When the class was dismissed, a savage old fellow came up to the missionary and indicating that he wished to speak to him privately, beckoned him into a corner. This Moro was one of the most feared outlaws in Lanao.

"You are doing a great thing for me, Teacher. You are the very best friend I have in this world. Is there anybody in Lanao you want assassinated? I shall do the job free of charge for you!"

"No, thank you, brother. Go home and teach others what you have learned here. That will make me happy."

Frank Laubach, the teacher who "loves these natives into learn-ing," has taught the ABC's not only to Filipino Moros, but to Solomon Island head hunters, Haitian medicine men, New Guinea cannibals, Australian bushmen, and numerous other primitive peoples from pole to pole. He has been at this profession for twenty-five years now, and he won't be satisfied until a good proportion of the twelve hundred million people who are still un-able to sign their names or read a newspaper are given the tools of literacy.

Laubach stumbled on his unique vocation as the result of a personal crisis. Born in Benton, Pennsylvania, a doctor of phi-losophy from Columbia University and an authority on slum set-tlement work, he arrived in the Philippines in 1915, and spent thirteen years as a Presbyterian missionary in Cayagan and Ma-nila. Then in 1928 he received an assignment to go among the Moros of Mindanao. Upon arriving, he was confronted with a baffling situation; the Moros were unapproachable. He spent months in Lanao without gaining a hearing with them.

Day after day he climbed a hill in back of his cottage and prayed. Then one afternoon—as Frank Laubach tells it—"My lips began to move, and it seemed to me that God was speaking. 'My child . . . you have failed because you do not really love these Moros. You feel superior to them because you are white. If you can forget you are an American and think only how you can love them, they will respond.' "

That was Frank Laubach's sudden insight into things. "In that terrible, wonderful hour, I became colorblind!"

"If you want the Moros to be fair to your religion," he told himself, "be fair to theirs. Study their Koran with them."

He immediately sought out two Moslem priests (the Moros are a Moslem people) and told them through an interpreter that he wanted to study the Koran. He would, in return, teach them the Christian Bible. "We will share what we have," he said. The next day several priests came to his cottage with Korans under their arms. Laubach studied with them the teachings of Mohammed and in turn translated several Old Testament stories and the Gospel of St. Luke into Arabic.

And since he wanted to reach the common people as well as the priests, he applied himself to the study of the popular language, Maranaw. The task was by no means easy. Maranaw was a spoken language only; it had never been written down. Laubach listened to each word, and when he had discovered what it meant, he wrote it down phonetically. His teacher was an old Moro named Pambaya, who had been sentenced to twenty years in prison for murder but had managed to "beat the rap."

In learning Maranaw in this fashion, Laubach became the only man in the world to reduce it to a form in which it could be written and read. And he was inspired with an idea. Why not teach the Moros to read and write their language exactly as he was learning to do?

He immediately set about developing a system for teaching them. He reduced the language to its basic phonetic sounds, then presented it in a modified Roman alphabet. Each key syllable was accompanied by a key picture, an object familiar to the people. Laubach knew that most illiterates have a highly developed sense of observation. The name of each object selected was the same as the sound of the syllable; very often the identity was established by the use of a pun.

Laubach developed three charts incorporating every syllable of the language. Converting a saloon on the United States Army post at Lanao into a classroom, he selected a group of illiterates for a test, and was amazed at the results. Several of the people actually began to read their language after no more than an hour of instruction. Others were able to pick out the words haltingly, slowly, but accurately, within a day. After thorough testing, Laubach discovered that the average illiterate learned the essentials of reading and writing in four or five days.

The reaction of these backward people, when the implications of what Laubach was doing for them became fully understood, was tremendously heartwarming. He won their confidence to a degree that amazed the other white inhabitants of the Philippines. Whole villages of Moros flocked to his classroom. Men and women emerged from their lesson, their faces wreathed in smiles, murmuring, "It is very easy. He was surprised at my bright mind." A chieftain brought six wives from his harem to be educated. One village Romeo lured a bevy of young ladies to class by writing a love letter to a young woman who had recently acquired her ABC's, informing her that her learning had turned her into positively the loveliest lady in Lanao. The girl showed the letter to all her female friends. And the rush for an education was on. One enthusiastic native used his newly gained education to write a long letter to the President of the United States, and he hounded Laubach until he translated it and mailed it to the White House.

The Moros were spectacular in their gratitude. When Laubach decided to purchase land on which to build a school for Moro girls, the native owner of the property paid him a visit and offered it to him free of charge. . . .

Since Laubach could not personally teach the thousands who desired to learn, he instructed each of his pupils to pass on his knowledge to another. "Each one teach one" became his slogan for mass literacy.

He was profoundly moved by episodes he witnessed. "At the church in Cavite, I taught one girl to read, and the next day she taught the chart beautifully to another girl in front of some thirty people. . . . The teacher was so overcome with joy that she wiped away the tears from her eyes with her red handkerchief as she taught. The women who watched her wept, and the men turned their backs and blew their noses." Chiefs came from distant towns, took lessons from Laubach, and departed with a colorfully decorated chart under one arm, a diploma under the other, and a broad smile on their faces, to instruct their people back home.

A magazine put out by the United States Government awarded prizes to Moro communities in which the greatest number of inhabitants had learned to read and write within a specified period.

One month the editor announced that the prize had been won by the Davao Penal Colony. "The prisons are becoming universities," he declared.

Before Laubach appeared with his charts, only four per cent of the Moros were literate, mostly priests and members of upper classes, who were educated in Arabic. Two years after Laubach began his classes, twenty per cent were able to read and write, and literacy was increasing at the rate of twelve per cent a year. Today, three out of four Moros are literate. They have one of the highest voting records of any group in the Philippine Islands.

Laubach prepared special literature for his new readers. He edited a newspaper containing articles on Christianity, summaries of world news, simple discussions of agriculture, sanitation, and other local problems. He published books graded to the reading skill of his audience. He opened folk schools in Mindanao. One of his star pupils translated a hundred pages of the Old Testament and prepared a booklet on the care of babies.

The degree to which Frank Laubach and his fellow Americans gained the affection of the Moros was impressively demonstrated during World War II, when thousands of natives signed a pledge to resist the attempts of the Japanese Army to overthrow the United States Government on Mindanao.

Frank Laubach's literacy campaign did not end with the Moros. He had, in fact, developed techniques to abolish illiteracy all over the world. Educational and missionary circles, and even governments, were quick to grasp the implications. Three out of every five members of the human race were disqualified from entering the market of skilled labor because they were unable to read simple directions for using a tool. Nine-tenths of the people in Asia were incapable of obtaining informed knowledge about political, economic, and social problems through the printed word. In India, which in 1947 had the responsibility of freedom suddenly thrust upon it, more than three hundred million people were unable even to read a candidate's name on a voting ballot.

"The most bruised people on this planet," Laubach declared, "the naked, the hungry, the fallen among thieves, the sick, the imprisoned in mind and soul, are the twelve hundred million illiterates."

Laubach's first invitation to apply his educational techniques outside Mindanao came from missionaries in India who for thirty years had "beaten their heads against the stone wall" of illiteracy.

They asked him to come with his phonetic charts and, at the same time, warned him to expect "a task about equal to shoveling the Himalayas into the Indian Ocean."

When Laubach left Lanao on this new assignment, his Moro friends saw him off in a highly emotional manner. Five big truckloads of natives followed his automobile down to the seaport twenty-five miles away. "They swarmed onto the ship and spilled over the wharf. Every high *dato* (Moslem priest) in Lanao wanted to make a speech on how they were sending me to bring light to mankind and how this was to be the beginning of the emancipation of the human race. At ten that night, the captain blew his whistle to warn that he was about to cast off, but the Moros laughed and went on talking. The captain subsided for fear they would cut his head off."

Upon arriving in India, the missionary paid a visit to Mohandas Gandhi. The two sat down cross-legged on the floor, and Laubach unrolled a sample picture-syllable chart to explain his educational methods. He could hardly believe his ears when the sardonic old Mahatma declared, "I doubt whether India ought to become literate."

"You are the first one I've ever heard say that. What do you mean?"

Gandhi shrugged. "The literature you publish in the West is not fit for India to read. Look at what you are selling us on every railroad stand."

"You are right," Laubach admitted. "But on the other hand, millions of us admire you and have read your books with great blessing. If you had not written these books and if we had not learned to read, we should never have heard of you."

The thrust went home.

Since the languages spoken in India are more complex than Maranaw, Laubach had greater difficulty in constructing charts for the Indians than for the Moros. However, after exhaustive tests, he succeeded in developing an effective syllable-picture system, and the people responded to it with zeal.

Following his trip to India, Laubach was besieged with invitations to visit other countries. Practically overnight he became the world's foremost traveling salesman of the alphabet. To date, as a special representative of the Committee on World Literacy and Christian Literature, he has carried suitcases crammed with primers and sample reading charts to more than sixty different nations, teaching millions of illiterates to read and write in more than two hundred different languages. An artist accompanies him on his trips; for to unlock the mind of a Fiji Islander or a Chaco Indian, the painter's brush is as mighty as the pen. Laubach enters a language area, has a discussion with local educators to pick out the key words in their tongues, prepares his astonishingly effective word-picture charts for native teachers to employ in the "Each One Teach One" crusade, and then departs for another region.

He has brought his pedagogic wizardry as far as Dhamatri on the edge of the Indian jungle, where tigers have crossed the path of his auto and peered into the headlights at night. He has drilled phonetics into the heads of Egyptian "fellahin" within sight of the ancient pyramid of Cheops, "where the air seemed full of the spirits of millions of those slaves who had toiled in that sand five thousand years ago." In the marketplace of Zanzibar he has taught descendants of native African slave traders to write their names in Swahili.

Everywhere he has gone he has been welcomed with enthusiasm. In New Guinea, drum and bush signals telegraphed his arrival among the tribes. Two rival cannibal villages almost went to war over which should be taught by him first. African Zulus hiked hundreds of miles to get the new "injection against ignorance." At Baroda, Laubach was met by Hindus attired smartly in Scotch kilts who, after serenading him with bag-pipes, escorted him in a parade to a large public square where four thousand children from thirty-five schools lustily sang a song he had prepared as a means of teaching phonetics, the words of which were painted on a large building behind them.

> *"Everybody's singing, ka, ke, ki, ko, ku*
> *All the boys are singing, ka, ke, ki, ko, ku*
> *All the girls are singing, ka, ke, ki, ko, ku*
> *All Baroda's singing, ka, ke, ki, ko, ku."*

Today, Laubach, in association with the Mutual Security Administration through the United States' Point Four Program, is working overtime to provide people with the essential education they require for minimum economic security. Frank Laubach has always been a *doer*. He knows that the people of Asia and Africa will never be won to our way of life by sermons alone.

"When we come to them and say, 'Listen to the story of Jesus,' they do not hear the story; they are interested in . . . *us*. The

Bible they read in *our* faces. . . . If they fail to see Christ in us, they have no interest in our Book. Our kind words . . . do not convince unless they *cost something*. . . . This is a terrifying responsibility.

"Millions have accustomed themselves to living compartmentalized lives until they have developed into well-meaning, sincere, self-deceived hypocrites. . . . The greatest hindrance to Christ in non-Christian lands is that so many of us talk like Christians and act like heathens in our social and business relationships."

Laubach asserts that what the world needs today is not more good books, but good men and women who will live daringly and adventurously, "who will share the sufferings of the . . . South African gold miners, or the slums of Kobe." What the world needs is a "tremendous cooperative resolve to turn its back upon *self* and go with Christ to meet human need." An army so mobilized "would rock the world."

EIGHT

One World

In its early days, America turned from oppression in Europe; abstained from entangling alliances; tried to stay aloof from foreign conflict. Yet even then, individual Americans traveled to other countries, dedicated to working toward the brotherhood of man. Now, on a planet grown small, a pitiful cry for freedom in Europe or Asia is sharply heard in the smallest American town. Now, as a nation, we strive and pray for the time when all the citizens and countries of this one world will cherish justice, the dignity of man, and will live in the love of God.

Adoniram Judson

The American republic had been in existence for less than three decades when, in 1814, a young Baptist minister landed on the "Golden Shore" of Burma. Many impulses and ambitions had combined to carry Adoniram Judson from Andover, Massachusetts, to Rangoon; but the greatest of these was his sense of Christian responsibility to peoples of other nations. Judson, the first American missionary to carry the Gospel to the East, endured severe and countless hardships; his achievements, however, were extraordinary, and included the first translation of the Bible into Burmese, as well as the preparation of the first English-Burmese dictionary.

The way that was opened by Adoniram Judson has been followed by both ministers of God and of government. Courtney Anderson, writer and producer of documentary films, has written a vivid, exciting biography of Judson titled To the Golden Shore; *and in these excerpts from it, he makes us humbly aware of the mighty force which was fashioned by a scattering of students at Andover.*

America's First Foreign Missionary

Everything in his life had prepared Adoniram Judson for the idea. A career as the first American foreign missionary curiously combined his many conflicting ambitions. Fame, eminence, humility, self-sacrifice, obscurity, adventure, uniqueness, the service of God—it had all of these.

No work in the ministry could be more useful. Dark souls by the million were waiting to learn about the Gospel, the only key to salvation. Did not Jeremiah say, "O earth, earth, earth, hear the word of the Lord"? And Matthew, "Go ye therefore, and teach all nations, baptizing them in the name of the Father, and

of the Son and of the Holy Ghost"? Had not Hopkins, spiritual
mentor of Adoniram's father, written of the time when "Christianity shall spread over the whole world . . . forming men to
a high degree of universal benevolence and disinterested affection . . . uniting all mankind into one happy family, teaching
them to love each other as brethren, each seeking and rejoicing
in the public good and in the happiness of individuals"?

And did not all foreign missionaries have to be translators?
How could the natives read the Gospel unless it were put into
their own tongue? And who had more aptitude for languages
than Adoniram Judson?

. . . "For some days," Adoniram wrote years later, "I was
unable to attend to the studies of my class, and spent my time
in wondering at my past stupidity, depicting the most romantic
scenes in missionary life, and roving about the college rooms
declaiming on the subject of missions." He even talked rather
wildly about offering himself to the London Missionary Society
at once, since there was no American organization able to send
him.

His enthusiasm kindled no answering flame whatever in the
other students. His ideas were "condemned by all and not in-
frequently ridiculed and reproached." Under this deluge of cold
water he began keeping his thoughts a little more to himself.
Meanwhile, he "devoured with great greediness every scrap of
information concerning Eastern countries." In this pursuit he
presently came across a book entitled *An Account of an Embassy
to the Kingdom of Ava*. It had been written by Michael Symes,
a British army officer who had been sent in 1795 by the Governor General of India to the mysterious empire of Burma. It
began provocatively, "There are no countries on the habitable
globe, where the arts of civilized life are understood, of which
we have so limited a knowledge, as those that lie between the
British possessions in India and the empire of Burma."

Much of the book was given over to long accounts of past
wars and Symes's fruitless negotiations with the Burman court.
But through this dull matter one could glimpse bright reflections
of a strange, colorful, feudal empire, populous and rich, which
had no counterpart on the globe.

Its people were civilized. They could read and write, and had
an extensive literature along with so overweening a national
pride that "Like the Sovereign of China, his Majesty of Ava
acknowledges no equal; indeed it is the fixed principle of all

nations eastward of Bengal, to consider foreign ministers as suppliants come to solicit protection, not as representatives who may demand redress; rather as vassals to render homage, than as persons vested with authority to treat on equal terms". . . .

The country contained incalculable riches—not only great forests of teak, so much desired by the English for building ships, but mines of gold and silver, rubies and sapphires, amethysts, garnets, chrysolite, jasper, and amber. It even had wells of a natural oil, earth oil, sometimes called "petroleum" by scientists, a nauseous liquid which was collected in barrels and used in lamps all over the kingdom. Symes, however, was scarcely interested enough in this useless substance to visit the wells himself.

The people were utterly pagan, wrote Symes. They worshiped Buddha and believed each person went through many cycles of existence, sometimes as a human, sometimes as an animal—a dog, a cat, even an insect. Yet—read Adoniram with special interest—His Majesty granted toleration to all sects. There was even one missionary, a Catholic, an Italian named Sangermano, whose "congregation consisted of the descendants of former Portuguese colonists, who, though numerous, are in general very poor."

What a prospect for a missionary! thought Adoniram as he turned the pages of Symes's book. Surely a people like this needed nothing but the true Word of God. Once it was brought to them, literate and civilized as they were, they would certainly seize on it. What other place on earth offered promise of such a harvest of souls? And no missionaries except Sangermano, who, since he was both a Catholic and a minister to Europeans rather than Burmans, hardly counted. . . .

He debated the problems with himself all through that fall of 1809. Christmas passed, and the New Year came. The snow lay thick on the ground. Then one day in February, coldest month of the year, a message came to him while he was walking in the grove. One can imagine him slowly pacing the snowy ground between the bare, spectral trees, his breath pluming in the frost, his mittened hands stuffed in his coat pockets. It may have been late in the afternoon with the pale sun low in the west and the first lights gleaming from under the eaves of Phillips Hall. He never recorded the day or the time of day. We know only that "It was during a solitary walk in the woods behind the college, while meditating and praying on the subject, and feeling half inclined to give it up, that the command of Christ, 'Go into all the world and preach the Gospel to every creature' was presented to my mind with such clearness and power, that I came to a full decision, and though great difficulties appeared in my way, resolved to obey the command at all events."

Every urge, every experience from the beginning of his life, had brought its influence to this one focus.

From this time on, he never doubted his destiny.

*   *   *

Unknown to Adoniram, at least four other students in the seminary had considered foreign missions even earlier than he had. They had heard Adoniram "declaiming on the subject of missions," but they had kept their own counsel for various reasons: reluctance to take the final plunge—uncertainty whether to go abroad or to the American West—or, possibly, a doubt of Adoniram's sincerity and determination.

One of the four was Samuel Newell, who had begun to think of becoming a missionary while still an undergraduate at Harvard. Another was Samuel Nott, who had arrived in Andover the previous November. . . . He had come to the conclusion that his future lay in missions about the time Adoniram had entered the seminary in 1808. And it was Samuel Nott who approached Adoniram first that spring. Although he had felt for more than a year that it was his duty to become a missionary, he had hesitated to commit himself. Now his doubts melted quickly under Adoniram's enthusiasm. Samuel Newell joined these two next. If either Nott or Newell had cherished any idea of missions on the American continent, Adoniram soon persuaded them that Asia was the best field. He had fixed his own eye on Burma, but there was room in Asia for an army of missionaries. The important thing was to translate intentions into action. All three were seniors. There was no time to waste if they hoped to set out for their stations as soon as possible after graduation.

The third and fourth missionary-minded students had dedicated themselves as long ago as 1806. . . . Their names were James Richards and Samuel J. Mills. . . .

[*Editor's Note:* Joined by others, the young students discussed ways and means to attain their dream, consulting their professors and gradually winning their support. Eventually Adoniram was granted permission to submit his proposal before the General Association, moderated by the venerable Manasseh Cutler.]

A hush fell as Adoniram stepped forward in front of the pulpit, coolly surveyed the delegates, guests and audience, a paper in his hand, and then with complete self-possession, began reading in a calm, clear, powerful voice. As soon as he opened his mouth the other three must have rejoiced inwardly that they had selected Adoniram to present the memorial, for it was instantly apparent that he had that rarest of attributes, a commanding stage presence.

"The undersigned," he read, "members of the Divinity College, respectfully request the attention of their reverend fathers, convened in the General Association at Bradford, to the following statement and inquiries. . . ."

To John Keep, who had been at the meeting at Professor Stuart's house, the memory of that scene was still vivid five decades later. Knowing what was to come, he recalled, "some of us held our breath."

"They beg leave to state," went on Adoniram, "that their minds have long been impressed with the duty and importance of personally attempting a mission to the heathen; that the impressions on their minds have induced a serious, and, they trust, a prayerful consideration of the subject in its various attitudes, particularly in relation to the probable success and the difficulties attending such an attempt; and that, after examining all the information which they can obtain, they consider themselves as devoted to this work for life, whenever God, in His providence, shall open the way."

A gasp, a barely perceptible indrawing of breath, came from the audience in the gallery. The rumors were true, then, that the young men were offering themselves as foreign missionaries!

"They now offer the following inquiries," continued Adoniram, "on which they solicit the opinion and advice of this Association: Whether, with their present views and feelings, they ought to renounce the object of missions, as either visionary or impracticable; if not, whether they ought to direct their attention to the Eastern or Western world; whether they may expect patronage and support from a missionary society in this country, or must commit themselves to the direction of a European society; and what preparatory measures they ought to take previous to actual engagement.

"The undersigned, feeling their youth and inexperience, look up to their fathers in the Church, and respectfully solicit their advice, direction, and prayers."

Adoniram paused for a moment, then slowly read the four names signed to the memorial: "Adoniram Judson, Jr.; Samuel Nott, Jr.; Samuel J. Mills; Samuel Newell." Without further words, he laid the paper on the baize-covered table in front of Moderator Cutler and resumed his seat. Not three minutes had elapsed between the time he had risen with the paper in his hand and the time he laid it on the table.

Now, one by one, each of the four rose, made a short personal statement telling why and how he had come to the conclusion that he must be a foreign missionary, and answered questions from the delegates. At this point the hush—by now a hush almost of awe—dissolved, as tears began to roll down the cheeks of the people in the audience, while some covered their faces with their hands and sobbed. The delegates themselves must have had difficulty maintaining their composure.

The Association took no action that session. A committee of three was appointed to consider and report its recommendation the next day. Since two of the members were Samuel Spring and Samuel Worcester, who had the plan of a missionary organization already clear in their minds, and since the third—Mr. Hale, secretary of the meeting—could be expected to follow their lead, a favorable report was a foregone conclusion. By four the session was over and the convention adjourned for public worship.

Theodore Roosevelt's Message to America

"Fear God, and take your own part!" cried Theodore Roosevelt to a nation which in 1915 and 1916 seemed to be groping for a security that did not exist. The religious impulse was strong in Roosevelt; it fitted no conventional pattern, but he knew that just as the most important thing for him was to "keep his honor clean," so, too, the vital thing for his country was that it preserve its soul, retain and hold high its ultimate values. Peace at the price of these values was unthinkable to him; freedom to choose was the prerequisite for the soul's integrity.

In many writings, Hermann Hagedorn, his friend, admirer and interpreter, has projected Roosevelt's unique personality and noble philosophy. He tells how the Colonel, heartbroken at the death of his son Quentin, wrote an article entitled "The Great Adventure." There Theodore Roosevelt voiced his love of country and glorified the torchbearers of liberty. This was his eloquent message to America: only by self-denial, service, and sacrifice, by laying down life itself if need be, can we make our country and a world shrunk by the tragedy of war, a better place for our children.

"The Great Adventure"

BY HERMANN HAGEDORN

Into a brief article, which Theodore Roosevelt called "The Great Adventure," a heartbreaking tribute to his dead son and his son's mother and to all mothers who might be called upon to experience bereavement like hers, in prose chastened by sorrow and filled with somber yet heroic music, he poured all that sixty years of wholehearted living had taught him of birth and death,

and motherhood and fatherhood and grief and aspiration and
love of country.

Only those are fit to live who do not fear to die; and none are
fit to die who have shrunk from the joy of life and the duty of
life. Both life and death are part of the same Great Adventure.
Never yet was worthy adventure worthily carried through by
the man who put his personal safety first. Never yet was a country worth living in unless its sons and daughters were of that
stern stuff which bade them die for it at need; and never yet
was a country worth dying for unless its sons and daughters
thought of life not as something concerned with the selfish
evanescence of the individual, but as a link in the great chain
of creation and causation, so that each person is seen in his true
relations as an essential part of the whole, whose life must be
made to serve the larger and continuing life of the world. . . .
Alone of human beings the good and wise mother stands on
a plane of equal honor with the bravest soldier; for she has
gladly gone down to the brink of the chasm of darkness to bring
back the children in whose hands rests the future of the years.
. . . In America today all our people are summoned to service
and sacrifice. Pride is the portion only of those who know bitter
sorrow or the foreboding of bitter sorrow. But all of us who give
service, and stand ready for sacrifice, are the torchbearers. We
run with the torches until we fall, content if we can then pass
them to the hands of other runners. The torches whose flame is
brightest are borne by the gallant men at the front, and by the
gallant women whose husbands and lovers, whose sons and
brothers are at the front. These men are high of soul as they
face their fate on the shell-shattered earth or in the skies above
or in the waters beneath; and no less high of soul are the women
with torn hearts and shining eyes; the girls whose boy-lovers
have been struck down in their golden morning, and the mothers
and wives to whom word has been brought that henceforth they
must walk in the shadow.

These are the torch-bearers; these are they who have dared
the Great Adventure.

. . . The Colonel knew, as no other statesman of his time, that
he who would save his life will lose it, and he who loses his life
for the sake of eternal values will save it. At a time when self-
interest seemed to many to have almost divine sanction, he
understood the shattering paradox, and lived it, "spending and
being spent," his last years, to make his fellow countrymen understand and live it, too. It was at the basis of his conception of in-

ternational order: There could be no peace until some great people proved willing to pay the price of peace, no world community
until some strong nation, promising nothing which it could not
fulfill, proved willing to disregard its own immediate interests and
offer blood and treasure to save a nation which was weak and
oppressed.

Self-interest seemed to him as misleading a guide in national
as in personal affairs. As in personal life, so in national, there is
no self-fulfillment, except in self-denial; no love, no achievement,
no peace, and in the end, no security, except in self-forgetful
daring, the giving of everything that makes life sweet for the
sake of the one thing that gives life meaning.

And that is what the Colonel is saying to America today.

A Trip to Latin America

Herbert Hoover, a respected mining engineer, happened to be in Belgium on business when Germany ignited World War I. This is the coincidence which led to his later appointment as Food Administrator by President Wilson, and, ultimately, to his own election as President. In Europe he set up relief organizations; at home, as Food Administrator, he devised a plan for sending concentrated food to our fighting men and to our hungry allies.

Before his inauguration, the President-elect made a special trip to Latin America. While serving as Secretary of Commerce he had become convinced that the fomenting of good will between ourselves and our southern neighbors was long overdue. His conviction was borne out in his tour among the Latin Americans, as the following description of his findings clearly shows. In this trip —and in the lasting results it produced—Herbert Hoover laid the cornerstone of the "Good Neighbor" policy which dominates inter-American relations today.

Good Neighbors

BY HERBERT HOOVER

During the four months between election and inauguration, I undertook three major tasks.

Mrs. Hoover and I made a journey of about six weeks to the Latin-American countries.

I assembled my administrative staff.

I formulated, so far as I could see ahead, our major policies for the next few years.

As Secretary of Commerce I had developed an increasing dissatisfaction with our policies toward Latin America. I was convinced that unless we displayed an entirely different attitude we should never dispel the suspicions and fears of the "Colossus of the North" nor win the respect of those nations. An interpretation of the Monroe Doctrine to the effect that we had the right to maintain order in those states by military force, in order not to give excuse for European intervention, created antagonisms and suspicions which dominated the politics of much of the Latin area. The German-, Italian-, and British-subsidized South American press constantly encouraged this antagonism as part of their trade propaganda. Moreover, our "dollar diplomacy," by threats and intimidation on behalf of our speculative citizens when their investments went wrong, added fuel to the fire. The policy of military intervention practiced by the Wilson Administration had been continued by Harding and Coolidge. At this time, we had troops in Haiti and Nicaragua. The United States, to put it mildly, was not popular in the rest of the Hemisphere.

I regarded an improvement in these relations as especially vital, for it seemed to me that in the future outlook of the world, we in the Western Hemisphere not only shared mutual interests, but common threats to those interests.

I asked Mr. Coolidge for a battleship on which to make the journey. He suggested that I take a cruiser—"it would not cost so much." However, since battleships as well as cruisers always must keep steam up and their crews aboard, that did not worry me much. I wanted room enough to take Mrs. Hoover, whose California upbringing enabled her to speak considerable Spanish. Also I wanted a diplomatic staff and representatives of the press, so as not only to evidence great interest in these countries but to educate the American people a little on our neighbors to the south. Finally Mr. Coolidge put the battleship *Maryland* at my disposal going south; and the battleship *Utah* met us at Montevideo and brought us home.

We were accompanied by Henry P. Fletcher, former Under Secretary of State, and John Mott, a leading California lawyer, as a special interpreter, and some of our best press correspondents —about twenty of them, including my old friends Mark Sullivan and Will Irwin.

We visited Honduras, Salvador, Nicaragua, Costa Rica, Ecuador, Peru, Chile, Argentina, Uruguay, and Brazil. I met with the President of Bolivia and I had intended to visit Mexico and Cuba later on.

We had a real welcome accompanied by parades, banquets, receptions, and speeches. Our Latin neighbors have an exquisite

politeness and hospitality. Their leaders are usually understanding and eloquent men.

Some incidents added interest to the journey. In Nicaragua
Mr. Coolidge had indirectly imposed a presidential election to
stop a civil war, and had it conducted by our Marines. When
the Marines registered the voters, they required each registrant
to dip a finger in a chemical solution which stained it yellow. At
election a few days later only the yellow fingers might vote, and
as they left the polls on election day voters were required to dip
another finger in a red solution. Thus repeaters were eliminated.
I asked the Marine officer in charge where he got that idea. He
replied, "I lived once in Tammany New York and proposed it as
a cure for one of Tammany's bad habits, but everybody said it
would be insulting."

As a result of the election the incumbent President had been
defeated. Our diplomatic representatives informed me that he
was not going to give up his office peaceably. Therefore, I invited
the President-elect and the outgoing President to lunch on the
Maryland. Neither President wanted to refuse the invitation, but
as one of the naval officers observed in mixed metaphor, "They
stepped around like fighting cocks making dog-eyes at each
other." I found they were both delightful and intellectual men. I
did not assume any friction, but we talked at length upon the
problems of their country and the need of a reputation for orderly
government. I announced that we were going to withdraw our
troops and invited them both to visit the United States. In any
event, there was no further revolution, for a while.

President Gonzalez Viquez of Costa Rica possessed a fine sense
of humor. We were reviewing a parade of the military and civic
bodies when he pointed to the 150 soldiers and a military band
of 150 pieces and remarked: "That is our total armed force except for another military band. You will observe the variety and
expressiveness of the uniforms. But we have 1,800 schoolteachers.
They are much more important in maintaining public order."

Arriving by train at Buenos Aires from Santiago, we were met
by President Irigoyen. To prevent Communist outbreaks and to
hold back the large crowd of civilians, three lines of protection
had been provided along the station platform—police, soldiers,
and firemen, one behind another, apparently under separate command. After we had alighted and shaken hands with the President and important officials something went wrong, for the whole

platform turned into a seething jam with civilians crowding among the guards. President Irigoyen was pushed about, and his coat ripped up the back, at which he became properly excited. Our naval aides kept Mrs. Hoover and me from being crushed. When we arrived at the American Embassy one of our Secret Service men complained to the Buenos Aires Chief of Police that he had been robbed of his pocketbook in the melee. The Chief replied, "Well, they got my wrist watch."

The formal banquet tendered us by President Irigoyen developed protocol trouble. He informed us that he did not make speeches and would ask the Argentine Secretary of State to speak for him. The American Ambassador replied that this was perfectly agreeable, and that Mr. Fletcher would reply for me. Whereupon the President decided to make a speech after all, and the Ambassador replied that, in that case, I would reply personally to this special honor. Nevertheless, the program was changed two or three times, so Mr. Fletcher and I went to the banquet each with a speech, waiting to see who was the lead-off for Argentina. President Irigoyen spoke, and spoke well. He afterwards remarked to me that he did not find it as terrible as he had anticipated.

I made fourteen short addresses during the journey and emphasized several different themes. These were later published in English, Spanish, and Portuguese. Some paragraphs from addresses at the different capitals indicate the nature of those addresses:

I come to pay a call of friendship. In a sense I represent on this occasion the people of the United States extending a friendly greeting to our fellow democracies on the American continent. I would wish to symbolize the friendly visit of one *good neighbor* to another. In our daily life, good neighbors call upon each other as the evidence of solicitude for the common welfare and to learn of the circumstances and point of view of each, so that there may come both understanding and respect which are the cementing forces of all enduring society. This should be equally true amongst nations. We have a desire to maintain not only the cordial relations of governments with each other but the relations of *good neighbors*.

I have come on a visit as a neighbor. I have thought that perhaps I might symbolize the good-will which I know my country holds toward your own. My hope and my purpose and my

aspiration are that better acquaintance, larger knowledge of our
sister republics of Latin America, and the personal contact of
government may enable me to better execute the task which lies
before me. And a large part of that task is the cooperation with
other nations for the common upbuilding of prosperity and of
progress throughout the world. . . .

. . . Democracy is more than a form of political organization;
it is a human faith. True democracy is not and cannot be im-
perialistic. The brotherhood of this faith is the guarantee of
good-will.

We who are public servants can do but little in our time. Our
minute part of a few years is soon forgotten. But if we can contribute to diminish destructive forces, if we can strengthen the
forces of material and spiritual progress, if we can upbuild the
institutions of government which assure liberty and freedom we
shall have served our part.

. . . There is abundant reason why friendship and understanding between us should be deeply rooted in the hearts of the people of both our nations. We have on both sides a history of
common labor, of building in the new world a new form of
government founded upon a new conception of human rights;
the supreme experience of rebellion from the political and social
systems of the Old World; the subjugation of the wilderness;
of developments of economic life through the application of the
great discoveries of science; the effort to lift the moral and cultural levels of our countries.

Generally the theme stressed a "good neighbor." I suggested
immediate measures for development of our relations—one of
them was a better organization of intellectual exchanges such
as students and professors.

The other theme, more materialistic, was the development of
inter-American aviation and determination of the basis of aviation rights. In each country I discussed this question with the
President and officials. Having learned in each country the basis
upon which common airways could be established, I was able
upon my return home to advance the matter rapidly.

One result of the journey was the settlement of the long-stand-
ing Tacna-Arica dispute between Peru and Bolivia. The United
States had some time before been asked by the two countries
to arbitrate the matter. The attempts hitherto had failed. By

cautious inquiry I learned from the officials of the two governments the approximate limits of concession that both sides would make. Putting these together upon my return to Washington, I was able to offer a compromise which settled the controversy.

A Bill of Rights for Humanity

Britain's fate—and with it, the fate of the Free World—was still hanging in the balance when the two great wartime leaders, Roosevelt and Churchill, arranged to meet in Newfoundland in the late summer of 1941. There they were destined to hammer out a document which would mean to the world what the Magna Carta had once meant to a nation. The "Four Freedoms" which Roosevelt had earlier expounded in one of his Fireside Chats took on substance in the "Atlantic Charter," or "Great Charter," as it has come to be called.

In his colorful and straightforward biography of Franklin D. Roosevelt, Alden Hatch describes this first meeting of two great men, and the touching moment of prayer that brought tears to the eyes of both.

The Great Charter

BY ALDEN HATCH

THE Japanese were a sideshow. In Roosevelt's mind the really serious danger lay in the Nazi surge toward world domination. In the last days of 1940, the peril was growing graver. England, the last fortress of democracy in Europe, was being mercilessly battered. Her cities were blazing infernos; her shipping was being decimated; and she was rapidly approaching bankruptcy. The day that she could no longer pay for food and munitions from us would see the end of freedom in Europe, and the beginning of the end of democracy in all the world. Roosevelt saw that he must lead the American people one step farther. On December 29, in a Fireside Chat, he painted the picture in all its somber terror, and called on America to be "the great arsenal of democracy."

But merely to be against something was not enough. America must have a positive program. In the Fireside Chat the President had described the world the Nazis desired; a week later in his annual address to Congress he pictured the world that America could look forward to, "founded on four essential human freedoms:

"The first is freedom of speech and expression—everywhere in the world.

"The second is freedom of every person to worship God in his own way—everywhere in the world.

"The third is freedom from want . . . everywhere in the world.

"The fourth is freedom from fear . . . everywhere in the world."

That speech showed truly great leadership, for it crystallized the aspirations of free men—everywhere in the world.

England needed support in two things—material and morale. If America was to be the arsenal of democracy, a way must be found to make her products available to England and her allies, who could no longer pay for them. There were two obvious methods, outright gift or huge loans of money. Roosevelt knew that Congress and public opinion would not sanction the first. In his constant preoccupation to avoid the mistakes of the last war and, particularly of the peace, he rejected the second. There should be no residuum of enormous unpayable debts to confound the effort to build a happier world on the ruins of the old one.

Roosevelt ever took the greatest delight in his political dexterity; and his subtle brain never devised a more ingenious formula than Lend-Lease. We would lend not money but the things themselves. Those that were used against the common enemy should be regarded as having been expended in our service; those that remained should revert to us. Lend-Lease exactly fitted the particular mood of the majority of Americans. It enabled us to support the Allies generously without feeling that we were suckers. Congress passed the bill, which the President's love of historical echoes caused to be numbered HR1776, by comfortable majorities.

Meanwhile, Roosevelt felt the need for closer association with Winston Churchill to assure complete cooperation. Early in January he sent Harry Hopkins to England. Hopkins had lived at the White House ever since the day Hitler attacked the Low

Countries. He was as close to being Franklin's other self as a
twin brother. Their minds exactly matched and there was never
a substantial disagreement between them. Franklin knew that
Harry's estimate of a man or a situation would be the same as
his own. To have him living intimately with Churchill was the
next best thing to being there himself.

The English liked Hopkins' sloppy clothes, his casual manner,
and his quick, sympathetic understanding of their problems.
Then Roosevelt got an unexpected opportunity to give English
morale a further boost. Wendell Willkie telephoned that he
would like to go to England to study conditions there and gain
further ammunition for his campaign for Aid to Britain.

"Come and see me," the President said.

Big and tough and tousled, Willkie sat facing the President
across the crowded desk in the Executive Office, as he had sat
once before when he came to fight for Commonwealth & Southern and those other forgotten men, the small investors. As he
slouched in the mahogany armchair that seemed too small to
support his great frame, he had the relaxed alertness of a boxer.
His vivid blue eyes were direct and challenging.

"Wendell," said the President, "I think this is a good idea of
yours."

"I'm glad to hear that, Mr. President," Willkie said. "I am
very anxious to go."

"You not only shall go," said Franklin, "but I want you to
represent me there, in a sense."

Willkie absorbed the shock of surprise with hardly a perceptible reaction, but his eyes grew wary.

"Surely you are well represented there," he said, "with Winant
and Hopkins."

"Yes, I am," Roosevelt agreed. "But the Republican Party is
not. The British think of the United States as disunited—the
isolationists are fewer in numbers but noisier than ever. I want
to counteract that impression. You are the head of the Republican Party, the leader of His Majesty's opposition, so to speak;
if you are acting for me, it will convince the British that America
is united in her support."

"I see," said Willkie. He leaned back in his chair and looked
up at the ceiling. "You know," he added, "that going on a mission for you isn't going to do me any good with the Republican
Party?"

The President's eyes glinted quizzically and his cigarette holder shot up to the perpendicular.

"It's awfully bad politics," he agreed, "but a great public service. Will you accept, Wendell?"

Willkie slammed his feet down on the floor. "Of course I will," he said, "provided there are no restrictions on what I say and do!"

"No strings at all," Roosevelt agreed. "You see I trust you."

"Thank you, Mr. President," Willkie said sardonically. Then both men laughed.

"Now that's settled," Franklin said, "we've got to figure out a way of making your visit semi-official. I think I'll have you carry a letter from me to Churchill."

"Am I to know what's in it?" Willkie asked.

"All the world shall know," the President said.

He pulled a piece of writing paper toward him and wrote rapidly. Then he handed it across the desk. "Read it aloud," he said.

Mr. Willkie began to read. Then he lowered the letter and continued from memory. His harsh voice filled the room with the power of his emotion:

> Thou, too, sail on, O Ship of State!
> Sail on, O Union, strong and great!
> Humanity with all its fears,
> With all the hopes of future years,
> Is hanging breathless on thy fate!

As he finished he looked directly at the President. Their eyes met, for once not as enemies, but as fellow-Americans joined in a common purpose.

When Willkie reached England he found that Churchill was rather mistrustful of Roosevelt. The Prime Minister was a convinced conservative, and the President's liberalism frightened him. Willkie found himself in the odd position of defending his great opponent. But so well did he do it, and so touched was Churchill by Roosevelt's letter, that then and there the Prime Minister began to change his opinion about the American President.

Late in July, Roosevelt announced that he needed a longer rest, a fishing trip. The *Potomac* was made ready, and on August

3, he sailed in her from New London. Not even Eleanor knew
where he was going. But it did seem an odd time for the President to go fishing.

The President sat in an easy chair under an awning on the
forward turret of the U.S.S. *Augusta,* lying at anchor in Placentia
Bay, Newfoundland. It was a misty August morning. Other war-
ships were anchored in a double line, standing out sharply from
the pale water in their battle paint of black-gray. There was the
Tuscaloosa, and the old battleship *Arkansas,* with her single
trellis mast, like an elongated scrap basket, rising from her fore-
deck. Light cruisers and destroyers completed the picture.

The sky was busy overhead. Fighter planes circled ceaselessly
above the ships; seaplanes of the Atlantic Patrol swept over from
beyond the low barren hills. Roosevelt knew that these went out
armed with bombs and often returned without them. That was
by his orders, and by his orders, too, American destroyers
guarded the long, slow convoys that bore the Lend-Lease goods
to England. As Franklin reckoned it, the American people had
approved Lend-Lease—and so expressed the intention that the
materials should get to England. The President was determined
to deliver the goods even though we had to sink every U-boat
and shoot down every German plane that threatened them. To
guard the convoys' flanks, American Marines had occupied
Greenland and Iceland, by his orders. It was a shooting war all
right, only in the curious modern fashion it was not called war.

Nor were the issues clearly defined. The President had a passionate faith in the justice of the cause for which on his lonely
responsibility he had ordered the boys up there in those planes
to fight, perhaps to die. But so far there was no declaration of
principle or of objectives. He had attempted it in his Four Freedoms speech. But the trouble with that was it was unilateral.
It had the weakness of Wilson's Fourteen Points; it bound us
but not our allies. What the President wanted was a joint statement of American and British aims and aspirations; a declaration to the world of the high purpose for which we fought.

The President strained his eyes toward the low headland that
curved out toward the mouth of the Bay. There was still no sign,
and he turned to chat with his staff who stood waiting behind
him. Sumner Welles was the only one not in uniform. Admiral
Stark was there and Admiral Ernest J. King, Commander-in-
Chief of the Atlantic Fleet. General H. H. Arnold, of the Air

Force, and General George C. Marshall, Chief of Staff, were talking genially with Pa Watson. George was a good man, the President thought. He had selected Marshall, not only for his fine military record, but because he had a warm humaneness, rare among professional soldiers, that made him seem the right sort of man to command a citizen army. Elliott Roosevelt, in his new uniform of a captain in the Air Force, was acting as aide to his father.

"Ship ahoy!" shouted a rating from the bow.

Franklin saw the sharp black bow of a destroyer pass the point. It was followed by five more destroyers, some of them flying the Stars and Stripes and others the Canadian Ensign. Then came a more ponderous shape, a massive battleship in the zig-zag motley of camouflage. At her stern the White Ensign of England was a bright oriflamme.

"Give me the binoculars, Elliott," the President said.

He trained the glasses on the bridge of H.M.S. *Prince of Wales*. Almost at once he picked out a familiar bulky figure that could be no one but Winston Churchill and, standing beside him, the frail form of Harry Hopkins.

The British battleship steamed slowly through the American squadron. On the *Augusta*'s quarterdeck the bandmaster raised his baton.

"Help me up," the President commanded.

Elliott lifted him to his feet while McIntire bent to lock his braces. The President took off his hat and stood at salute as the *Prince of Wales* swept by. He could see Churchill plainly, saluting from the bridge of the British battleship. The *Augusta*'s band was playing "God Save the King," and an answering echo of "The Star-Spangled Banner" came down the wind. Then the Britisher was past, turning toward a flag-marked buoy. She reached it, and the thunder of her anchor chains rolled over the quiet water.

Promptly at eleven o'clock the Admiral's barge pulled away from the *Prince of Wales*. The President stood waiting at the *Augusta*'s gangway. The barge came aboard, and Churchill in the vaguely naval uniform of Trinity House mounted the ladder to the squealing of pipes and the clash of arms as the Marine Guard presented arms.

The Prime Minister was square and bluff and powerful, the spirit of England incarnate. He halted and ceremoniously saluted

the quarterdeck. Then beaming like a cherub he came forward
with outstretched hand.

"At long last, Mr. President!"

"Glad to see you aboard, Mr. Churchill," Roosevelt replied.

Their hands met in a strong clasp that transmitted a high
voltage current of emotion. To both of them the meeting was
symbolic of the thing that they had hoped for, striven for, and
carried through. In their persons England and America joined
hands.

The conferences began at once; there was so much to say
that time seemed very short. Sir Alexander Cadogan, the British
Permanent Under-Secretary for Foreign Affairs, and Sumner
Welles went into a huddle on the *Tuscaloosa;* the British and
American army, air, and naval people got together on grand
strategy, while Churchill, Roosevelt, and Harry Hopkins retired
to the President's cabin to take the world apart and put it together again.

That day the discussion was gravely concerned with Japan
and her menacing advance toward the Indies and the Malay.
Churchill and Roosevelt agreed that the Japanese must go no
farther south than the Cam Ranh Bay in French Indo-China,
but that everything possible should be done to delay the outbreak of war.

"How long would you say we've got?" asked Churchill.

"I think I can baby the Japs along for another three months,"
Roosevelt replied. Then Churchill pressed strongly for an immediate American declaration of war against Germany. Roosevelt did not think the people were ready.

The next day, Sunday, there was another great symbolic ceremony, a church parade for British and Americans aboard the
Prince of Wales. The President went over in the American destroyer *McDougal.* Sitting in the sunshine on the quarterdeck
of the British battleship, he found his mind busy with the vast
implications of the scene—this mingling of two great seafaring
peoples; this comradeship in worship and in arms of those who
shared a faith in God and in the right of human freedom.

"Stablish our hearts, O God, in the day of battle," prayed the
Chaplain, "and strengthen our resolve, that we fight not in enmity
against men, but against the powers of darkness enslaving the
souls of men, 'til all the enmity and oppression be done away
and the peoples of the world be set free from fear to serve one
another as the children of our Father,"

"Amen," said President Roosevelt, and beside him a deeper voice echoed, "Amen."

Then the mingled voices of thousands of young men rose in the sailors' hymn, that Franklin himself had chosen for this day:

> *Eternal Father, strong to save,*
> *Whose arm hath bound the restless wave,*
> *Who bidd'st the mighty ocean deep*
> *Its own appointed limits keep*
> *Oh hear us when we cry to Thee*
> *For those in peril on the sea.*

The President's heart was full as he fought to hold back the tears that stung his eyes. Instinctively he shot an embarrassed glance at his companion. The Defender of Britain was furtively wiping his eyes.

Harry Hopkins brought good news from Russia. Stalin had opened his books of mystery and shown the secret figures of tanks and guns and planes and men. They were far greater than anyone had guessed. Stalin had categorically stated: "The Germans won't get Moscow this year."

"I believe him," Harry said.

The staff talks continued. Welles and Cadogan were still incommunicado. Roosevelt and Churchill had endless discussions, one in particular most secret.

"Have you people done anything about nuclear fission?" Roosevelt asked, when he was alone with Churchill and Harry Hopkins.

"Quite a lot," said Churchill. "Send for Cherwell."

Lord Cherwell described the research that British scientists were conducting under the direction of Sir John Anderson. The results coincided closely with those obtained by American scientists. In some ways the British were ahead of us.

"This can be terrific," Roosevelt pointed out. "We'd better get together and beat the Nazis to it."

"Most certainly," Churchill said, and an agreement was immediately reached for pooling all information.

On the last day, August 12, they wrote the Atlantic Charter, in the big square cabin on the *Augusta* with its plain white bulkheads and portholes veiled by an Atlantic fog. Present, besides Churchill and Roosevelt, were Welles and Cadogan, who had worked up a rough draft, Henry Hopkins, and Lord Beaver-brook, who had just arrived by air from England.

The President read slowly in his beautiful clear voice: "Joint declaration of the President of the United States of America and the Prime Minister, Mr. Churchill, representing his Majesty's Government, who deem it right . . ."

"Mr. President," Churchill interrupted, "shouldn't we say, 'being met together deem it right'?"

"Winston, I love it," Roosevelt exclaimed. "The right phrase. . . . Who being met together deem it right to make known certain common principles of their respective countries on which they base their hopes for a better future for the world."

So they wrote it, phrase by phrase, sometimes agreeing, some-times arguing fiercely, shaping, as a sculptor painfully hews a monument from rugged granite, the great document that be-came the Magna Carta of the free world. Its essence was the guaranty of the Four Freedoms to all the peoples of the world.

When they had done, and it was copied plain, they did not sign it; the spoken word was enough between these two. They simply gave it to the world.

Meanwhile the ships were waiting with steam up—there was desperate haste. The President was urgently needed in Wash-ington, the Prime Minister even more anxiously awaited in Lon-don, and in between, now that the meeting was known, the Nazis would be waiting.

On the deck of the *Augusta*, Winston Churchill warmly shook his new friend's hand, and hurried down the ladder to his barge. Mixed with his elation was a pang that he was always afterward to feel when they parted. For beyond admiration, a deep, spon-taneous affection had sprung up between the two great leaders. The Prime Minister stood in the stern of the speeding barge, looking backward. He made the V sign to the President, who stood at the *Augusta's* rail, laughing and waving.

Churchill felt immense relief, a sense of burdens shared. That gay and gallant figure, diminishing in the distance, was a sign that the free world would survive. The Englishman recalled the jokes and nonsense they had talked in moments of relaxation; the quick comprehension, the earnest thought, the warm com-passion, and the wide range of vision that the President had shown at the council table. He strained his eyes for one last glimpse of that calm, classic face, which, for all its gaiety, was being etched by acid care with the deep lines of greatness. What incredible good fortune—no, not fortune but the evidence of God's abiding care, that at this perilous moment such a man is President of the United States.

Future World Security

A few short months after the Four Freedoms were given to the world in the Atlantic Charter, the "Declaration of the United Nations" was signed by twenty-six nations. It pledged full support against the Axis powers; but, more important, it looked to the development of plans for the care of liberated countries and for future world security. This was the first vital step in establishing the world organization which has done so much to bring sanity and justice into international disputes. Its first agency, appropriately enough, was distinctively humanitarian in character —the United Nations Relief and Rehabilitation Administration.

In spite of frequent crises, misunderstandings, criticism, and innumerable other obstacles, the United Nations has survived and served. Here Gertrude Hartman narrates this contemporary story, beginning with the moment when the group came into being and started "a great movement for an organized and peaceful world."

The United Nations

BY GERTRUDE HARTMAN

On April 25, 1945, delegates of the United Nations met in San Francisco. There were representatives of fifty nations, men and women of different races, different creeds, different customs, and different languages. All were meeting with a common purpose: to make a plan for an international organization to bring lasting peace and security to the people of the world. With the Dumbarton Oaks proposals and the Yalta agreements as their guide, they began the work of making a charter for such an organization.

Edward R. Stettinius, Secretary of State, was chairman of the conference and directed its work. There were many large meetings of all the delegates which were addressed by people from various nations. Numerous committees were formed to deal with special problems. Every nation had a part in making the charter, and the interests of every nation were considered. There often were differences of opinion among the delegates, but ways of meeting problems were found which were acceptable to all the representatives.

As the members of the delegations spoke different languages, the work of translating the speeches and discussions was a tremendous job. There were five official languages—Russian, Chinese, French, Spanish, and English. One hundred and thirty-five translators worked day and night throughout the conference, and typists using special machines mimeographed over a million words a day. By the latter part of June, after nine weeks of discussions and conferences, the work of drafting the charter had come to an end. Every part of it had been carefully studied and approved.

The charter of the United Nations opens with the following preamble:

We, the peoples of the United Nations, determined to save succeeding generations from the scourge of war, which twice in our lifetime has brought untold sorrow to mankind, and

To reaffirm faith in fundamental human rights, in the dignity and worth of the human person, in the equal rights of men and women and of nations large and small, and

To establish conditions under which justice and respect for law and the pledged word can be maintained, and

To promote social progress and better standards of life in larger freedom, and for these ends

To practice tolerance and live together in peace with one another as good neighbors, and

To unite our strength to maintain international peace and security, and to ensure, by the acceptance of principles and the institution of methods, that armed force shall not be used, save in the common interest, and

To employ international machinery for the promotion of the economic and social advancement of all peoples, have resolved to combine our efforts to accomplish these aims.

Accordingly, our respective governments, through representatives assembled in the City of San Francisco, who have exhibited their full powers found to be in good and due form, have agreed to the present Charter of the United Nations and do hereby establish an international organization to be known as the United Nations.

The world organization set up by the charter provides for a General Assembly composed of all member nations. Each nation may have as many as five representatives in the Assembly, but each nation, whether large or small, may have only one vote. The Assembly will consider general world problems and will lay down the general policies to be followed to maintain world peace. It will meet at least once a year.

The Security Council is to have the responsibility of preventing wars. This council will investigate any disputes between nations which might lead to war. It will try to settle differences between nations peacefully. If its efforts fail it may take whatever action is necessary to prevent war. The council will consist of eleven members. The five most powerful nations—China, France, Great Britain, Russia, and the United States—will be permanent members; the other six members will be elected by the General Assembly for a term of two years each.

The statesmen at San Francisco recognized that we live in an age in which economic problems are often the cause of war. They planned for a Social and Economic Council to bring about economic improvements in various parts of the world. This council will work for higher standards of living and to promote human rights to the fundamental freedoms which are named in the Atlantic Charter.

The charter of the United Nations also provides for an International Court of Justice to decide points of law and to help in adjusting disputes between nations.

A number of special agencies are included to deal with important problems such as labor, health, nutrition, international trade, communications, and industrial developments. There will be an international office of education to promote education and cultural cooperation among the nations of the world.

The final session of the conference was addressed by President Truman, who closed with an appeal not only to the delegates but to the world to make the charter a success.

By this charter you have realized the objectives of many men of vision in your own countries who have devoted their lives to the cause of world organization for peace.

Upon all of us, in all our countries, is now laid the duty of transforming into action these words which you have written. Upon our decisive action rests the hope of those who have fallen, those now living, those yet unborn—the hope for a world of free countries—with decent standards of living—which will work and co-operate in a friendly civilized community of nations.

Let us not fail to grasp this supreme chance to establish a world-wide rule of reason—to create an enduring peace under the guidance of God.

The San Francisco charter does not by itself guarantee world peace. No charter could do that. The charter provides the machinery to prevent war, to secure justice, and to promote the welfare and human rights of people all over the world. Those who made it earnestly believed it to be a guide making possible the progress of the world in peaceful ways. The future of the world will depend, however, upon what use is made of the charter.

President Truman made this clear in his address to the delegates: "You have created a great instrument for peace and security and human progress in the world. The world must now use it."

The Faith That Is America

He came into the national spotlight like a meteor, this great hulk of a man with hands like hams, and a lock of hair that seemed to have a mind of its own.

"I ride on nobody's coattails," he said.

His name was Wendell Willkie; and he coined a phrase that has become part of our national vocabulary, that will always be associated in the hearts and minds of the American people with his name. One World.

On August 26, 1942, a Liberator bomber, converted for transport service, took off from Mitchell Field with Wendell Willkie aboard. His idea was to circle the globe and visit the battle-fronts in the interest of world unity and peace. He went as an unofficial ambassador, with President Roosevelt's blessing. On his return he reported to the nation in a broadcast, and then followed it, some months later, with one of the noblest books ever written by a great public figure, One World. *In words ringing with truth and sincerity, his message is as significant today as it was in 1942.*

One World

BY WENDELL L. WILLKIE

WHEN the United Nations pact was announced, hundreds of millions of men and women in South America, in Africa, in Russia, in China, in the British Commonwealth, in the United States, in the conquered countries of Europe, perhaps even deep in Germany and Italy, thought they saw a vision of the nations signatory to that pact joining as partners in a common struggle to work together to free mankind. They thought that those nations would, during the war, sit in common council of strategy,

342

of economic warfare, of planning for the future. For they knew that thus the war would be brought to a speedier end. They also knew that to learn to work together now would be the best insurance that the nations would learn to live together in the future. . . .

Today the United Nations is a great symbol and a treaty of alliance. But we must face the fact that if hopeful billions of human beings are not to be disappointed, if the world of which we dream is to be achieved, even in part, then today, not tomorrow, the United Nations must become a common council, not only for the winning of the war but for the future welfare of mankind.

At the end of the last war, not a single plane had flown across the Atlantic. Today that ocean is a mere ribbon, with airplanes making regular scheduled flights. The Pacific is only a slightly wider ribbon in the ocean of the air, and Europe and Asia are at our very doorstep.

America must choose one of three courses after this war: narrow nationalism, which inevitably means the ultimate loss of our own liberty; international imperialism, which means the sacrifice of some other nation's liberty; or the creation of a world in which there shall be an equality of opportunity for every race and every nation. I am convinced the American people will choose, by overwhelming majority, the last of these courses. To make this choice effective, we must win not only the war, but also the peace, and we must start winning it now.

To win this peace three things seem to me necessary—first, we must plan now for peace on a world basis; second, the world must be free, politically and economically, for nations and for men, that peace may exist for it; third, America must play an active, constructive part in freeing it and keeping its peace.

When I say that peace must be planned on a world basis, I mean quite literally that it must embrace the earth. Continents and oceans are plainly only parts of a whole, seen, as I have seen them from the air. England and America are parts. Russia and China, Egypt, Syria and Turkey, Iraq and Iran are also parts. And it is inescapable that there can be no peace for any part of the world unless the foundations of peace are made secure throughout all parts of the world.

The End of a War

Seldom in the history of the United States has the event of war so inflamed our passions as in the case of the Japanese attack on Pearl Harbor, for never before had the nation been caught wholly unaware and unsuspecting. What sort of revenge would we exact from this enemy? How would we deal with the war lords and their countless partisans in the Japanese Empire?

Dean Acheson, distinguished former Secretary of State, presided at San Francisco over the meeting of Allies who witnessed the signing of the peace treaty. The spirit of the treaty was not revenge, but rather moderation and understanding. In here describing what lay behind that treaty, Dean Acheson at the same time gives utterance to the spiritual strength of America.

The Spirit of the Japanese Peace Treaty

BY DEAN G. ACHESON

WE WERE able to accomplish here what we have accomplished [the signing of the Japanese peace treaty] because all of us, in the words of Benjamin Franklin, doubted something of our infallibility, and all of us worked together, giving up much that was close to our hearts, much that was close to our economic interests, for the purpose of bringing about this peace of reconciliation.

And we were able to do that because we were doing something which lifted our spirits, something of which we were proud. There was nothing mean. There was nothing sordid which lurked in any corner of this treaty. There was nothing hidden, nothing that could not bear the broad great light of day. And we were able to join in that sort of effort, and we were able to sink our differences because we were going forward in a great effort, making a great new step in history, and hoping from this day forward a new chapter is opening in the history of the world.

. . . We signed this great treaty this morning, but we must live this treaty from this day on. And it depends upon each nation represented here, each individual represented here, each individual of each nation, to make this treaty *be* what it is in words.

. . . And may I close this conference with words which, in many languages, in many forms, in many religions have brought comfort and strength. "May the peace of God, which passeth all understanding, be amongst us and remain with us always."

General Douglas MacArthur

It is almost a tradition in our history that our greatest military leaders have also been among our greatest fighters for peace. In our own time one such leader has been made chief executive of the land. Another, General Douglas MacArthur, after achieving the accolades of a grateful nation for heroic war service, won further honor as a peacemaker and as the architect of a new Japan.

The real and lasting victories are not those of war, but of peace. Here Ambassador George Kenney gives us a moving description of that great tenet in action—when General Douglas MacArthur extended his country's offer of help to a nation prostrated by the scourge of war.

Pledging Help to Korea

BY GEORGE CHURCHILL KENNEY

On September 28, MacArthur sent word to me that he wanted me to meet him at Kimpo Airdrome, about twelve miles west of Seoul, the following morning at 9:30. That was the day set for the ceremony at the Capitol in Seoul during which the General was to turn over the government of the Republic of Korea to President Syngman Rhee.

I met him the next morning at Kimpo. He put his arm around my shoulder and said:

"It's good to see you here, George. I had you with me that day in Manila and on the deck of the *Missouri*, and I wanted you at this ceremony too."

The cavalcade of generals, admirals, Korean officials, and guards formed, and we drove to the Capitol. Fires were still

346

burning from the fighting inside the city during the previous day or two, and the dive-bombers were working on a hill a couple of miles north of Seoul, which was still held by the Reds.

I took the place assigned me in the front row of seats in the legislative chamber directly in front of the rostrum. On my right were two Korean cabinet members. General Walker, the 8th Army Commander, and General Stratemeyer, the Air Force Commander, were on my left. About three hundred Americans and Koreans, military and civilians, with a full complement of newspapermen and photographers, filled the room.

General MacArthur began his speech. "By the grace of a merciful Providence . . ." You are impressed when you hear MacArthur mention God. He is deeply religious and his sincerity is so evident that you realize at once that here is no pose. The reference is not there as a matter of form. It is there because Douglas MacArthur believes it.

He then spoke about the poor Koreans and how they had been treated. He said we were not in their country to build bases for ourselves but simply to liberate them from slavery to a despotic creed of despair.

I looked at Syngman Rhee and saw the tears in his eyes. Madame Rhee, next to him, was weeping. As I glanced around the room I saw practically all the Koreans in tears. I wondered then how many Americans could make a Korean audience weep. I knew I couldn't and I didn't know anyone else who could except Douglas MacArthur.

As he warmed up to his subject, MacArthur caught the fire of his own emotion. Tears stood in his eyes as they had that day at the Malacanan Palace in Manila when he turned the government of the Philippines over to President Osmena. His voice dropped a little lower, the words came with a little more difficulty. I couldn't help thinking of the dramatic but tragic occasion at Milwaukee back in 1912. His father, General Arthur MacArthur, against doctor's orders, had attended the fiftieth annual reunion of the Wisconsin regiment in which he had served from 1861 to 1865 and finally had commanded. He had enlisted when he was seventeen years old. Four years later he was a colonel, had been wounded four times and awarded the highest decoration of his country—the Congressional Medal of Honor. After a brilliant career he had retired in 1909. He was an inspiring speaker and his adoring comrades leaned forward in their seats as he began to deliver what he had said was to be his farewell tribute to his old comrades. His was an emotional speech, too, and General Arthur MacArthur also became carried away by his own emotion. As he reached the fiery climax, he suddenly swayed and fell to the floor—dead. As his old adjutant, with tears streaming down his cheeks, draped the old regimental colors over the body, he too swayed and fell, mortally stricken, beside his old commander.

I couldn't help a little feeling that I didn't like—not exactly apprehension but something disturbing. I was listening to every word he said, but I wanted the speech to end.

"And now," he concluded, "I ask that all present rise and join me in reciting the Lord's Prayer."

I have never heard anything more in keeping with the occasion or more impressive.

> *"Our father which art in heaven,*
> *Hallowed be thy name.*
> *Thy kingdom come. Thy will be done*
> *On earth as it is in Heaven."*

There it was again. The acknowledgment of the Deity who had blessed our efforts.

> *"Give us this day—our daily bread."*

The way that he stressed *"our daily bread"* reminded every soul in that hall that this was what it was all about. Food—life itself—was back of all the stirring and upheavals in Asia today.

> *"And forgive us our debts,*
> *As we forgive our debtors.*
> *And lead us not into temptation,*
> *But deliver us from evil:"*

He had told them that we were going to help them. We were pledging our full effort toward their relief. He hadn't said they had to pay for that relief. We were not in Korea to set up an empire for ourselves and we must not entertain such ideas.

> *"For thine is the kingdom,*
> *And the power, and the glory,*
> *For ever,*
> *Amen."*

Finally, a fitting salute to the Great Giver and a further acknowledgment of the sovereignty of the Supreme Being. I heard an officer in back of me whisper to another seated beside him, "That's the first time I've ever really heard the Lord's Prayer."

MacArthur sat down. Syngman Rhee rose and walked to the rostrum, wiped his eyes, and read his speech. He speaks excellent English, but it was difficult to understand him. Emotion had gripped him, too. His voice was broken and at times hardly audible. He finished and presented a scroll to General MacArthur, which was the award of the Order of Merit of the Republic of Korea, their highest decoration. You found yourself sorry for Rhee when he apologized for not having the medal itself or even a ribbon to give MacArthur. It was understandable, of course. After all, Seoul had been captured and cleared of the enemy just long enough to hold this ceremony, only a day or two ago. But the scene had pathos in it just the same.

Ministering to a Wounded World

". . . and him to whom much is given, of him shall much be required."

This biblical injunction refers, of course, to talents of mind and body as well as material goods. America has taken it to heart, and has shared and shared again with nations less fortunate, and with peoples suffering from elemental want through war and its aftermath.

The most vitalizing offer of such assistance took place with the advent of the Marshall Plan, sometimes called "The Truman Doctrine." This program helped bridge vast chasms of suffering and want in Europe, saving whole nations from that twentieth-century slough of despair, Communism. Former President Truman describes how the Plan came alive and restored men's faith in the democratic ideals of justice, of hope, and of truth.

The "Marshall Plan"

BY HARRY S. TRUMAN

WE HAD sent food to Europe, but millions there still did not have enough to eat. We had made loans to the countries of Europe, but the war had so disrupted the patterns of trade and industry there that the amounts we loaned were far less effective than we had hoped. I was disturbed because the loan to Britain had failed to accomplish what we thought it would.

Detailed reports came to my office daily from our government agencies about conditions abroad. A steady stream of appeals poured in from representative leaders of many foreign nations, virtually all of whom expressed the gravest concern over the economic situation and over the gains which Communism might score if there were no improvement. On April 26, when Secretary

Marshall returned from the Moscow conference of Foreign Ministers, he arrived in a pessimistic mood. He had gone to Moscow with the hope that he could persuade the Russians that the United States was working for peace. The Russians, however, were interested only in their own plans and were coldly determined to exploit the helpless condition of Europe to further Communism rather than cooperate with the rest of the world.

Marshall's report confirmed my conviction that there was no time to lose in finding a method for the revival of Europe. General Marshall is one of the most astute and profound men I have ever known. Whenever any problem was brought before him, he seemed to be able to put his finger at once on the very basic approach that later would usually be proposed by the staff as the best solution. He talked very little but listened carefully to everything that was said. Sometimes he would sit for an hour with little or no expression on his face, but when he had heard enough, he would come up with a statement of his own that invariably cut to the very bone of the matter under discussion.

As Secretary of State, Marshall had to listen to more staff talk than when he was Chief of Staff. He would listen for a long time without comment, but when the debates between members of his staff seemed destined to go on interminably and he could stand it no longer, he would say, "Gentlemen, don't fight the problem; decide it." Dean Acheson told me a characteristic story about Marshall when he first took over as Secretary of State. Marshall had asked Dean Acheson to stay on as Under Secretary and said, "I want the most complete and blunt truths from you, particularly about myself." Dean Acheson replied, "Do you, General?" "Yes," Marshall said. "I have no feelings except a few which I reserve for Mrs. Marshall."

What Marshall perceived in the plans which his State Department staff laid before him was the importance of the economic unity of Europe. If the nations of Europe could be induced to develop their own solution of Europe's economic problems, viewed as a whole and tackled co-operatively rather than as separate national problems, United States aid would be more effective and the strength of a recovered Europe would be better sustained.

This was precisely the approach I had in mind. Marshall and I were in perfect agreement. It was my feeling that, beyond economic considerations, the idea of co-operation would stimulate new hope and confidence among the nations of Europe and

thus provide a realistic argument against the Communists' counsel of despair.

This idea, as an approach to the European problem, was first
expressed in public at Cleveland, Mississippi, on May 8, 1947,
when Under Secretary of State Dean Acheson delivered what
might be called the prologue to the Marshall Plan. Originally,
it had been planned for me to speak at this meeting, but I had
other commitments and asked Dean Acheson to fill the engagement. The Acheson speech contained the basic elements of the
proposal which was given full development and expression a
month later by Marshall.

The key point of the Acheson speech was his emphasis that
the reconstruction of Europe would have to be dealt with as *one*
problem. He stressed the interrelation of food and freedom. "The
war," he said, "will not be over until the people of the world
can again feed and clothe themselves and face the future with
some degree of confidence." He then went on to offer a balance
sheet of our past relief efforts and pointed out that further, more
comprehensive financing would be necessary. Such use of our
economic and financial resources would help preserve our own
freedoms and democratic institutions because it would contribute to the security of our nation to widen the economic margins
on which human dignity and free institutions abroad were
struggling to survive.

Acheson's speech did not receive the attention it deserved at
the time, although it contained the beginning of the proposal
later made at Harvard by Secretary Marshall. On June 5, 1947,
the Secretary of State outlined to a commencement audience a
course of action for the United States in dealing with the European crisis.

This was a speech that was typical of the man. It was matter-
of-fact and without oratorical flourishes, compact and to the
point, and the Secretary began it with a brief review of the
economic condition of Europe.

Then he went on to set out a course of action: "It is logical,"
he said, "that the United States should do whatever it is able
to do to assist in the return of normal economic health in the
world, without which there can be no political stability and no
assured peace. Our policy is directed not against any country
or doctrine but against hunger, poverty, desperation and chaos.
Its purpose should be the revival of a working economy in the
world so as to permit the emergence of political and social con-

ditions in which free institutions can exist. Such assistance must not be on a piecemeal basis as various crises develop. Any assistance that this government may render in the future should provide a cure rather than a mere palliative. Any government that is willing to assist in the task of recovery will find full co-operation . . . on the part of the United States Government. Any government which maneuvers to block the recovery of other countries cannot expect help from us. Furthermore, governments, political parties or groups which seek to perpetuate human misery in order to profit therefrom politically or otherwise will encounter the opposition of the United States."

Then came the key section of the plan: "It is already evident that, before the United States Government can proceed much further in its efforts to alleviate the situation and help start the European world on its way to recovery, there must be some agreement among the countries of Europe as to the requirement of the situation and the part those countries themselves will take in order to give proper effect to whatever action might be undertaken by the government. It would be neither fitting nor efficacious for this government to undertake to draw up unilaterally a program designed to place Europe on its feet economically. This is the business of the Europeans. The initiative, I think, must come from Europe. The role of this country should consist of friendly aid in the drafting of a European program and of later support of such a program so far as it may be practical for us to do so."

This was our proposal, that the countries of Europe agree on a co-operative plan in order to utilize the full productive resources of the continent, supported by whatever material assistance we could render to make the plan successful.

I had referred to the idea as the "Marshall Plan" when it was discussed in staff meetings, because I wanted General Marshall to get full credit for his brilliant contributions to the measure which he helped formulate. And it was Marshall who had envisioned the full scope of this approach. He had perceived the inspirational as well as the economic value of the proposal. History, rightly, will always associate his name with this program, which helped save Europe from economic disaster and lifted it from the shadow of enslavement by Russian Communism. Almost immediately following his enunciation of the idea in his Harvard speech, the term "Marshall Plan" became commonplace in the press and radio of the United States and other countries around the world, and I was glad to see his name identified with the plan. I believe the fact that a man of Marshall's world standing made the proposal of this policy helped greatly in its eventual adoption. He was one of the very few men in the government who had stayed in intimate contact with the day-by-day developments of this country's wartime operations in both hemispheres. Both as military strategist and diplomat, he was known and respected abroad as few men have been in the history of the United States. And at home he enjoyed the confidence and esteem of the average citizen regardless of political preferences, as well as the admiration of congressional leaders. Marshall's entire personality inspired confidence. I recall the worried months of early 1944, just before the Normandy invasion. There were many men in the Congress who harbored doubts and misgivings about the cross-Channel attack that was then generally expected, but General Marshall came to Capitol Hill and spoke to about four hundred and fifty of us members of Congress, and his quiet, determined manner, his complete command of all the facts of the situation quieted whatever fears anyone may have had. Most notably, too, everyone present respected the secrecy which the general asked us to observe. This was typical of the manner in which the man affected those who knew him. It is not surprising that all his recent detractors are men who never knew the measure of responsibility that was Marshall's, nor the manner in which he discharged that responsibility.

His many years in wartime Washington had endowed Marshall with a thorough knowledge and appreciation of the role of Congress. As head of the vast Army of World War II, he had dealt with administrative problems of unprecedented magnitude. These experiences proved invaluable when he addressed himself to the practical implementation of the plan which his Harvard University speech had set in motion.

Ambassador to India

*He played his role as Ambassador in the only way he knew—
simply by being himself. He mingled with the local populace,
sent his children to native schools, and used a bicycle instead
of a Rolls Royce to get about. Therefore Chester Bowles found
it something of a shock to discover that his approach to diplomatic matters and his activities as Ambassador to India merited
long columns in the daily newspapers of that country as well
as in his own United States.*

*Just by being himself, Ambassador Bowles brought a new di-
mension into daily diplomacy. His was an approach in which humanity and friendship took high precedence over protocol. In the
understanding that he engendered between America and India in
the crucial post-war years, Chester Bowles not only made a lasting contribution to his country, but also became a recognized
world statesman.*

In his noteworthy book, Ambassador's Report, *Mr. Bowles
gives us a fascinating account of his life in India.*

The Friendly America

BY CHESTER BOWLES

. . . Not all of our early impressions were happy ones. From
our first conversations after our arrival and the first Indian newspapers that appeared on our breakfast table (excellent English-
language papers such as the *Times of India, Hindustan Times,
Statesman and India Express*), we had realized the extent of mis-
understanding about America. The irresponsible statements of
some American military men had been fanned by Communist
propaganda until a large section of Indian public opinion believed America to be actually seeking war. . . .

I decided that it would be helpful to hold a press conference. I prepared a three-thousand-word statement and announced that I would attempt to answer any questions about America and American policies. Knowing the intensity of anti-Americanism at that time among part of the Indian press, and being accustomed to more indirect diplomatic ways of doing things, a few of the Embassy staff for whom I had great respect strongly opposed the move, and I approached it with some nervousness.

My statement stressed things about America that we take for granted, but which I discovered were almost totally misunderstood in India. "We believe in freedom of religion," I said. "We believe in the family as the basis of all civilized life. We believe in the right of all peoples to live under a government of their own choosing. And with the most intense feeling, we dislike and deplore the conflict which is now threatening the peace of the world."

I stressed the areas of agreement between India and America, and particularly our mutual desire for peace, disarmament and the rapid economic development of the new free nations of Asia and Africa.

"But," I added, "we Americans believe that disarmament cannot be a one-way street. We believe disarmament must cover all weapons and not simply those in which we are strong and others are weak. We believe that disarmament must include full inspection in all countries to make sure that the conditions are carefully and fully met."

As I later discovered is almost invariably the case in any Asian press conference or forum, the number one question was, "What about America's treatment of the Negro?" This is a situation in which my own feelings run deep, and I answered fully and honestly, frankly describing the problem as I saw it, and reporting with precise examples and statistics the progress which is now being made. I then suggested that, more than any other people, Indians should understand the very real obstacles to rapid progress in America, since they face a somewhat similar problem in dealing with the situation of their own untouchables.

When a persistent Indian reporter asked if America's real hope was not to make India lean toward the Western democracies, I replied: "Certainly. At least we hope you won't lean the other way. But really how you lean is your own business. We only want to see you strong enough and free and independent enough so that you can choose which way you want to lean, and we have no doubt of your answer. What we want in India above all therefore is to see Indian democracy succeed."

The next day all Indian papers printed several columns, covering the press conferences in detail. At least a dozen papers printed my three-thousand-word statement in full. Some say that this was the first time a balanced answer to the racial question was ever printed in the Indian press. I felt immensely encouraged, for now it was clear that literate Indian people could be reached with a frank and straightforward talk. . . .

India and Asia do not expect to find American diplomacy British-bound in stuffy precedents. Prestige in terms of big houses and shiny limousines is out of place in a land of mud huts and awakening villagers.

When Cornwallis surrendered to Washington at Yorktown the band played "The World Turned Upside Down" and that is the music that the people of Asia expect from us today. In many ways this is 1776 in the colonial world. This is Asia's democratic revolution.

Since our purpose in India was to understand the Asian revolution and to find the right role for America, in these first steps we felt that we were only crossing the threshold to our real task. But we were reassured that we were going in the right direction when Radio Moscow found it appropriate to launch a series of violent personal attacks on me in which among other things they called me "the scheming agent of the Wall Street monopolists."

We were even more reassured when Ashadevi Aryanayakam, a beautiful disciple of Gandhi from his mud hut village of Sevagram, told a friend of ours that she felt as much at home staying with us as with anyone in Delhi. We had been a little embarrassed that whenever she stopped with us she had to double up with Sally.

"It is the friendly America, the family America, that India wants to see," Ashadevi said. If this was anything more than a kind compliment, it was only because we, too, were feeling at home.

"Hope—Shared by All"

In the first year of his administration President Dwight D. Eisenhower spoke before the United Nations in New York City, setting forth a policy by which "the minds of men, the hopes of men, the souls of men everywhere, can move forward toward peace and happiness and well being." In his speech about the future of atomic energy, he firmly delineated his country's idealism when he said, "It is with the book of history, and not with isolated pages, that the United States will ever wish to be identified. . . . It wants itself to live in freedom, and in the confidence that the people of every other nation enjoy equally the right of choosing their own way of life."

This expressed desire to work with other peoples and other nations for peace has guided the President's foreign policy since he first assumed office. His "atoms for peace" address, as it has come to be known, is a speech which knows no limitations of time or place in this atomic age. It marks the first time a nation has said to the world: "Here are materials which were developed for destruction. Join with us, share them with us, so that they may be used for peace, health and well being."

Atomic Power for Peace

BY PRESIDENT DWIGHT D. EISENHOWER

NEVER before in history has so much hope for so many people been gathered together in a single organization. Your deliberations and decisions during these somber years have already realized part of those hopes.

But the great tests and the great accomplishments still lie ahead. And in the confident expectation of those accomplishments, I would use the office which, for the time being, I hold, to assure

358

you that the Government of the United States will remain steadfast in its support of this body. This we shall do in the conviction that you will provide a great share of the wisdom, the courage, and the faith which can bring to this world lasting peace for all nations, and happiness and well being for all men. . . .

I know that the American people share my deep belief that if a danger exists in the world, it is a danger shared by all—and equally, that if hope exists in the mind of one nation, that hope should be shared by all.

Finally, if there is to be advanced any proposal designed to ease even by the smallest measure the tensions of today's world, what more appropriate audience could there be than the members of the General Assembly of the United Nations?

I feel impelled to speak today in a language that in a sense is new—one which I, who have spent so much of my life in the military profession, would have preferred never to use.

That new language is the language of atomic warfare.

The atomic age has moved forward at such a pace that every citizen of the world should have some comprehension, at least in comparative terms, of the extent of this development, of the utmost significance to every one of us. Clearly, if the peoples of the world are to conduct an intelligent search for peace, they must be armed with the significant facts of today's existence. . . .

Atomic bombs today are more than twenty-five times as powerful as the weapons with which the atomic age dawned, while hydrogen weapons are in the ranges of millions of tons of TNT equivalent. . . .

If at one time the United States possessed what might have been called a monopoly of atomic power, that monopoly ceased to exist several years ago. Therefore, although our earlier start has permitted us to accumulate what is today a great quantitative advantage, the atomic realities of today comprehend two facts of even greater significance.

First, the knowledge now possessed by several nations will eventually be shared by others—possibly all others.

Second, even a vast superiority in numbers of weapons, and a consequent capability of devastating retaliation, is no preventive, of itself, against the fearful material damage and toll of human lives that would be inflicted by surprise aggression.

The free world, at least dimly aware of these facts, has naturally embarked on a large program of warning and defense systems. That program will be accelerated and expanded.

But let no one think that the expenditure of vast sums for weapons and systems of defense can guarantee absolute safety for the cities and citizens of any nation. The awful arithmetic of the atomic bomb does not permit of any such easy solution. Even against the most powerful defense, an aggressor in possession of the effective minimum number of atomic bombs for a surprise attack could probably place a sufficient number of his bombs on the chosen targets to cause hideous damage. . . .

To pause there would be to confirm the hopeless finality of a belief that two atomic colossi are doomed malevolently to eye each other indefinitely across a trembling world. To stop there would be to accept helplessly the probability of civilization destroyed—the annihilation of the irreplaceable heritage of mankind handed down to us generation from generation—and the condemnation of mankind to begin all over again the age-old struggle upward from savagery toward decency, and right, and justice.

Surely no sane member of the human race could discover victory in such desolation. Could anyone wish his name to be coupled by history with such human degradation and destruction?

Occasional pages of history do record the faces of the "Great Destroyers" but the whole book of history reveals mankind's never-ending quest for peace, and mankind's God-given capacity to build.

It is with the book of history, and not with isolated pages, that the United States will ever wish to be identified. My country wants to be constructive, not destructive. It wants agreements, not wars, among nations. It wants itself to live in freedom, and in the confidence that the people of every other nation enjoy equally the right of choosing their own way of life.

So my country's purpose is to help us move out of the dark chamber of horrors into the light, to find a way by which the minds of men, the hopes of men, the souls of men everywhere, can move forward toward peace and happiness and well being.

In this quest, I know that we must not lack patience.

I know that in a world divided, such as ours today, salvation cannot be attained by one dramatic act.

I know that many steps will have to be taken over many months before the world can look at itself one day and truly realize that a new climate of mutually peaceful confidence is abroad in the world.

But I know, above all else, that we must start to take these steps
—NOW. . . .

We seek a harmonious family of free European nations, with
none a threat to the other, and least of all a threat to the peoples
of Russia.

Beyond the turmoil and strife and misery of Asia, we seek
peaceful opportunity for these peoples to develop their natural
resources and to elevate their lives.

These are not idle words or shallow visions. Behind them lies
a story of nations lately come to independence, not as a result
of war, but through free grant or peaceful negotiation. There is
a record, already written, of assistance gladly given by nations
of the West to needy peoples, and to those suffering the temporary
effects of famine, drought, and natural disaster.

These are deeds of peace. They speak more loudly than
promises or protestations of peaceful intent.

But I do not wish to rest either upon the reiteration of past
proposals or the restatement of past deeds. The gravity of the
time is such that every new avenue of peace, no matter how dimly
discernible, should be explored.

There is at least one new avenue of peace which has not yet
been well explored—an avenue now laid out by the General Assembly of the United Nations.

The United States, heeding the suggestion of the General Assembly of the United Nations, is instantly prepared to meet
privately with such other countries as may be "principally involved," to seek "an aceptable solution" to the atomic armaments
race which overshadows not only the peace, but the very life of
the world.

We shall carry into these private or diplomatic talks a new conception.

The United States would seek more than the mere reduction
or elimination of atomic materials for military purposes.

It is not enough to take this weapon out of the hands of the
soldiers. It must be put into the hands of those who will know how
to strip its military casing and adapt it to the arts of peace.

The United States knows that if the fearful trend of atomic
military buildup can be reversed, this greatest of destructive
forces can be developed into a great boon, for the benefit of all
mankind.

The United States know that peaceful power from atomic

energy is no dream of the future. That capability, already proved, is here—now—today. Who can doubt, if the entire body of the world's scientists and engineers had adequate amounts of fissionable material with which to test and develop their ideas, that this capacity would rapidly be transformed into universal, efficient, and economic usage?

To hasten the day when fear of the atom will begin to disappear from the minds of people, and the governments of the East and West, there are certain steps that can be taken now.

I therefore make the following proposals:

The Governments principally involved, to the extent permitted by elementary prudence, to begin now and continue to make joint contributions from their stockpiles of normal uranium and fissionable materials to an International Atomic Energy Agency. We would expect that such an agency would be set up under the aegis of the United Nations. . . .

The more important responsibility of this Atomic Energy Agency would be to devise methods whereby this fissionable material would be allocated to serve the peaceful pursuits of mankind. Experts would be mobilized to apply atomic energy to the needs of agriculture, medicine, and other peaceful activities. A special purpose would be to provide abundant electrical energy in the power-starved areas of the world. Thus the contributing powers would be dedicating some of their strength to serve the needs rather than the fears of mankind.

The United States would be more than willing—it would be proud to take up with others "principally involved" the development of plans whereby such peaceful use of atomic energy would be expedited. . . .

Against the dark background of the atomic bomb, the United States does not wish merely to present strength, but also the desire and the hope for peace. . . . The United States pledges before you—and therefore before the world—its determination to help solve the fearful atomic dilemma—to devote its entire heart and mind to find the way by which the miraculous inventiveness of man shall not be dedicated to his death, but consecrated to his life.